raúlrsalinas and the Jail Machine

HISTORY, CULTURE, AND SOCIETY SERIES
Center for Mexican American Studies (CMAS)
University of Texas at Austin

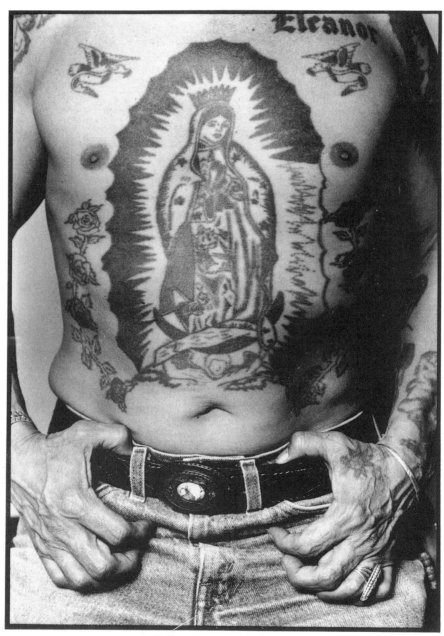

Salinas's tattooed chest.

raúlrsalinas and the Jail Machine

■ ■ ■ ■ ■ ■ ▼ ■ ■ ■ ■ ■

My Weapon Is My Pen

Selected writings by Raúl Salinas

Edited and with an introduction by Louis G. Mendoza

University of Texas Press ✛ Austin

Library of Congress Cataloging-in-Publication Data

raúlrsalinas, 1934–
    raúlrsalinas and the jail machine : my weapon is my pen : selected writings / by Raúl Salinas ; edited and with an introduction by Louis G. Mendoza. — 1st ed.
        p.   cm. — (History, culture, and society series)
    Includes bibliographical references.
    ISBN-13: 978-0-292-71284-3 ((cl.) : alk. paper)
    ISBN-10: 0-292-71284-7
    ISBN-13: 978-0-292-71328-4 ((pbk.) : alk. paper)
    ISBN-10: 0-292-71328-2
    1. Prisoners' writings, American.   2. raúlrsalinas, 1934—Imprisonment.
3. Prisoners as authors—United Sates.   4. Prisoners—Literary collections.
5. Prisons—Literary collections.   I. Mendoza, Louis Gerard, 1960–   II. Title.
III. Series.
    PS3568.A82R38   2006
    818'.5408—dc22
                                                            2006002204

This book is dedicated to those who continue to struggle against the injustices of the jail machine from the inside and the so-called free world. May we triumph against those cages of iron and those cages of the mind that prohibit the full realization of our humanity.

Contents

. . . somewhere beyond
        Majestic Mount Ranier
in dungeons built by evil men
        are brothers/sisters (prisoners)
            who are still not free
As I am still not free . . .
        though I walk [the city] streets.

            —raúlrsalinas, adapted from "Crash Landing,"
            Un Trip through the Mind Jail y Otras Excursions

Acknowledgments

THIS PROJECT was many years in the making and involved many collaborators and the help of many good people along the way. The staff at Stanford University's Green Library who oversee Special Collections were instrumental in helping us identify, retrieve, and duplicate materials. These include Margaret J. Kimball, Polly Armstrong, and Tim Noules, among others. Mr. Roberto Trujillo's diligence in ensuring that Raúl Salinas' archives will remain preserved for the benefit of future generations is of utmost importance.

Financial assistance and resources were also provided by various people along the way, including funds from the College of Liberal and Fine Arts Faculty Development Leave and the Dean's Circle Award at the University of Texas at San Antonio. Research funds from the College of Liberal Arts at the University of Minnesota were also important in helping to finish this project on a timely basis. Barbara Harlow and Bill Mullen were strong advocates for the completion of this project. Melissa Bueno provided some intense and dedicated labor in the initial transcription of a significant portion of the handwritten letters in Salinas' archive included here. Faculty in the English departments at the University of Texas at Austin and the University of Houston as well as the Department of Chicano Studies at the University of Minnesota provided constructive criticism on excerpts of this project presented to them. Omar Vásquez Barbosa and Patricia Trujillo also assisted in the transcription and proofreading of letters in the early stage of this project. Alondra Espejel at the University of Minnesota worked diligently on acquiring the permissions, assisting with proofreading, refining translations, and putting the final touches on the manuscript. Stivaliss Licona Merino assisted in proofreading the Spanish transcriptions. Ben Olguín took the lead in translating the texts of Spanish-language correspondence, which he was able to complete with the assistance of Lilia Rosas and the insight of Raúl Salinas. For all the time, hard work, and dedication of the above people to this project, many, many thanks! UT Press editor Theresa May and the Director of the Center for Mexican American Studies at UT Austin, Professor José Limón, deserve thanks for believing in the project. Also at UT Press, Leslie Tingle, Allison Faust, and David Cavazos deserve special thanks for getting the book in shape for publication. We also wish to thank everyone who was so gracious in granting us permission to publish their correspondence with Raúl—for their courage to share and for their willingness to be part of something larger than themselves so that others may better understand the experiences of and insights about Chicano history, culture, and politics that this book documents.

Finally, we would be remiss if we failed to acknowledge the staff at Resistencia Bookstore, Casa de Red Salmon Press, and Red Salmon Arts who over the years have volunteered countless hours in keeping the doors open to this legendary base of cultural and political resistance: René Valdez, Toni Nelson Herrera, Alan Gómez, and Lilia Rosas.

raúlrsalinas and the Jail Machine

Raúl Salinas and the Poetics of Human Transformation

PRISON WAS NOT A PLACE FOR DEFEAT, it was a place for study, for preparation. Fidel Castro wrote while in prison: "What a tremendous school this prison is! Here I have rounded out my view of the world and determined the meaning of my life. I don't know if it will be long or short, fruitful or in vain, but my dedication to sacrifice and struggle has been reaffirmed."

—Assata Shakur, *Hauling up the Morning*, 4

. . . UN PROCESO DE TRANSFORMACIÓN MENTAL; see it occurring, feel it surging within, it's at once amazing, extremely difficult to grasp, painful and frightening!!!

—Salinas letter to Joseph Sommers, November 4, 1971

FROM 1957 TO 1972 Raúl Salinas spent approximately 12 years in four of the most notoriously brutal prisons in this country: Soledad State Prison (California), Huntsville State Prison (Texas), Leavenworth Federal Penitentiary (Kansas), and Marion Federal Penitentiary (Illinois). Just as there is a clear relationship between his pre-prison experience of social marginalization and his eventual incarceration, there is also a direct link between his prison experience and his development as a writer responding to the real conditions of his existence, in and outside of prison. This transformation led him initially to engage his fellow convicts, and eventually prison authorities, friends, and political activists in the outside world.

Spanning a period covering more than a decade, the nucleus of this collection is comprised of work previously published in prison newspapers and journals as well as letters to family, friends, allies, and organizations. But this collection includes not only Salinas' own words but also letters written to him from outside and within prison, as well as daily logs of the 1972 Marion Prison Strike, political manifestos, and two in-depth interviews conducted with Salinas after his release—one immediately following his release and the other twenty years later, on the occasion of Stanford University's acquisition of Salinas' archives.

As the documents herein will demonstrate, the process of transformation that Salinas underwent, one that he writes about with so much emotional fervor in the second epigraph above, was a process that was both solitary and communal. The emotional, spiritual, and political substance of this transformation is mapped out in his writings and makes his life one worthy of study, one that offers us lessons about society and the human capacity to persevere, adapt, and rebuild oneself. As documentation of one man's transformation from "social criminal" to an agent of social change, this collection is an invaluable "hidden transcript." Though Salinas is renowned in certain literary and political circles, he is not so exceptional a figure that he is known by all. Rather, what we have here is a portrait of someone who is exceptional in his ability to be representative of a good portion of the more than two million people currently caught up in the criminal justice machinery of this nation.

The publication of these writings makes a contribution in multiple arenas simultaneously. This work is both literary and historical in nature, providing us first-hand insight into a tumultuous period of this nation. From the inner sanctum of some of our country's most notorious iron cages, this work shows that though isolated, often severely cut off from human contact for extended periods of time due to solitary confinement, Salinas and fellow prisoners found ways not only to sustain communication but to systematically cultivate meaningful relationships and alliances with those involved in facilitating change in a society experiencing the upheaval of the civil rights and anti-war movements.

Since 1968 Salinas' writing and activism have earned him international recognition as a spokesperson for a diversity of political causes, ranging from prisoner rights and national liberation struggles to gang intervention and youth arts advocacy. He first received acclaim for his literary work in 1969 when he was a prisoner in Leavenworth Federal Penitentiary in Leavenworth, Kansas. Since then, in addition to being widely anthologized, Salinas has published three collections of poetry: *Un Trip thru the Mind Jail y Otras Excursions* (Editorial Pocho-Ché, 1980; Arte Público Press, 1999), *East of the Freeway: Reflections de mi pueblo* (Red Salmon Press, 1995), and *Indio Trails: A Xicano Odyssey thru Indian Country* (Wings Press, 2006). In 1994 Salinas' personal archives, dating from 1955 to 1994, were obtained by Stanford University.[1]

A biographical overview of Salinas' life helps to illustrate how he is both representative and exemplary in his contributions to prison literature and social history.

From Pachuco to Pinto: A Biographical Sketch of the Artist as a Young Man

Raúl Salinas was born in San Antonio, Texas, in 1934 and raised in East Austin, where he attended Catholic primary school and public high school through the eleventh grade. In interviews he has noted that he was a good student; he was clearly capable of mastering his lessons, but he was also a young rebel who often rejected strict rules and behavioral guidelines. His father left his family when he was very young, and he credits his grandmother and mother with teaching him Spanish and nurturing a love for literature in him. During his childhood the city of Austin's racial segregationist policies were being codified and enforced, thereby assuring that East Austin would be comprised exclusively of ethnic minorities. The Spanish-language names of downtown Austin streets bear testimony to an area that was predominantly Mexican until residents were forced to move to a less desirable hilly area east of the central business zone. The construction of Interstate 35 in the 1960s, a highway that functions as the barrier between downtown and the East Side, only concretized an already existing dividing line. It was within the barrios of this consciously marginalized community, comprised of several African American and Mexican neighborhoods, that Salinas first learned his "place" in society. Though there were tensions between the Black and Chicano communities at times, there was also overlap, cultural exchange, and camaraderie. As an adolescent Salinas was drawn to the many famous nightclubs in East Austin's Black community, where he thrived on the live rhythm and blues and jazz played there. This music, along with the Mexican *corrido, conjunto,* and *orquesta* traditions, was an important cultural and artistic influence in his life, one that would eventually manifest itself in his music (he played saxophone) and poetry.

When Salinas dropped out of school at age seventeen, unable to see its relevance to his future, he went to northern California and picked fruit for several years in the fields surrounding San José. It's important to note that Salinas "came of age" in 1952, the same year that John Clellon Holmes published in the *New York Times* "This Is the Beat Generation," one of the first articles to identify this nascent literary movement. Though situated in the Southwest, Salinas identified with the rejection of cultural and social conventions promoted by the young artists associated with the Beat movement. Like them, he had headed toward California looking for a way out of the oppressive conventions and expectations of society and family in the post-war boom period. Unlike the Beat poets, however, he was not college educated, not middle class, and not part of the white mainstream (though he did have a close relationship with his white stepfather, Samuel "Posey" Hill, and Melba Schumann, a white elementary school Spanish teacher). He could, however, identify with the Beats' street sensibility, their embrace of open literary forms, and their down-and-out stance. As a streetwise young man, he continued to find himself drawn to non-conventional, non-mainstream music venues, and he, like Malcolm Little, soon developed a hipster lifestyle that included the consumption and selling of drugs. At this stage in his life, Salinas embodied a culturally specific counter-cultural pachuco lifestyle, one that had its variants in other minority communities as well as in the margins of mainstream culture. While not radical, these cultural practices did resist the ideological and cultural conformity promoted in the 1950s. These "rebels without a cause" searched for individuality and alternatives in their rejection of mainstream American values and culture.

Busted through a state drug sting operation in 1957, Salinas was convicted in a Los Angeles County court of "violating the health and safety code for sale and possession of marihuana." He was sent to Soledad State Penitentiary, aka the "Gladiator School," later that year. Not counting his adolescent stints in juvenile detention centers, Soledad would be his first home behind bars, where he would remain for three years. It was here, a place with few distractions and few options for entertainment, that he began to write extensively for the first time. In addition to correspondence with family and friends, he began to experiment with poetry. Elsewhere I have examined in detail how these poems represent Salinas' early efforts to reflect on his individual life and demonstrate his embrace of literature, poetry in particular, as a therapeutic vehicle for identifying and transcending wounds inflicted by individual circumstances.[2]

Salinas' early literary influences in prison were those that he could get his hands on. Not surprisingly, what was most available to him was similar to what he had access to in the educational system, primarily British and American anthologies. In these he was particularly attracted to the likes of Emerson, Longfellow, Whitman, Williams, and e. e. cummings. And just as he was attracted to these poets who explored the dynamic relationship between society and the individual, he was also profoundly impressed by the politics and poetics of Latin American writers he discovered in this period. In the Spanish-language poems of Latin Americanists like Federico García Lorca and Pablo Neruda, his developing aesthetic was exposed to a wider range of expression, and the social critique of these politically engaged writers was the most explicit he had encountered.[3]

In 1959 Salinas was released from prison on parole. He was to remain out until November of 1961, when he was again busted on possession of marijuana, this time in Austin. He was sent to Huntsville State Prison, where he stayed until May of 1965. In Huntsville he joined the choir, which was the organizational unit that brought him together with other prison "intellectuals," men who enjoyed reading books, magazines, and newspapers, keeping up with current affairs, and exchanging ideas. This same group became part of the core that formed the production team of the monthly prison newspaper, *The Echo*. The editor of *The Echo*, Bart Edwards, soon learned of Salinas' in-depth, first-hand knowledge of jazz and convinced him to write a jazz column ("Quartered Notes"), which became a regular feature for a year and a half, until he was paroled. These early writings were penned under his childhood name of Roy Salinas; not until he was in Leavenworth did Salinas reclaim his birth name of Raúl, and later, inspired by e. e. cummings, he began using the lowercased, one-word raúlrsalinas, to sign his work. In November of 1964 Salinas wrote an editorial in *The Echo* that was excerpted and commented upon in *The Beaumont Enterprise* on Christmas Day of that same year. A critical examination of President John F. Kennedy's drug policy, "So much mystery, so much misunderstanding" was Salinas' first extra-prison acknowledgment as a writer. In this period, Salinas began to develop a journalistic style and identity that would be more fully realized in a subsequent period of incarceration. Upon release from Huntsville in 1965 he was still a novice poet, but his identity as a writer had begun to crystallize as a result of his reviews of the jazz scene, his first published poems in *The Echo*, the op-ed essay in *The Beaumont Enterprise*, and his numerous letters to family and friends, which he has always considered part of his literary production. But Salinas' literary output at this stage in his life remained linked to his confinement. After his release from both Soledad and Huntsville, his writing ceased; back on the streets, his attention and skills were diverted elsewhere.

When Salinas was sent to Leavenworth on a felony drug charge in 1967, he initially continued to be involved in illicit drug trade in prison, but here he met Ramón Chacón, a convict from South Texas who introduced him to the writings of Ernesto "Ché" Guevara and Frantz Fanon. He also met Standing Deer (alias Robert Wilson)[4] and Rafael Cancel Miranda, a Puerto Rican *independentista* who had been imprisoned for participating in a 1954 armed protest in the chambers of the U.S. Congress in order to draw attention to the colonial status of Puerto Rico. Through his interaction with these men and others, Salinas began to question his involvement in the drug trade and organized crime. More importantly, he began to see how race and class functioned in prison and the outside world to keep people from discovering constructive solutions to individual and group empowerment. In his "extra-literary" endeavors we can see his intellectual development—including the acquisition of language and legal skills. For instance, his relationship with Cancel Miranda and Oscar Collazo[5] helped him hone his knowledge of Spanish, learn about the Puerto Rican independence struggle, and begin developing an international perspective that enabled him to better comprehend the historical ravages of colonialism on his own community. In seizing control of their education, Salinas and his comrades underwent a radical transformation that involved reading works by leading intellectuals of Third World independence movements. This is evidenced by the lists of books and magazines they read; letters requesting specific titles are contained in Salinas' archives. As he and fellow convicts became more aware of the systematic disempowerment of ethnic minorities and working-class people in the United States, they began to order political literature from the outside, such as *The Guardian, Grito del Norte, P'alante, The Black Panther,* and *The Militant* to further their education and consciousness-raising. Thus the abundance of political literature in the "free" world during this time of social unrest in the United States became their educational texts.

Moreover, a multiracial cohort of convicts interested in exploring racism, class analysis, and national liberation began crystallizing. These convicts were brought together by the shared experiences of prisoner abuse, such as inadequate health care, guard brutality, disproportionate sentencing of people of color, unfair parole board reviews, indeterminate sentences, and the illegal blocking of prisoner access to legal materials (law books and documentation regarding their cases, in particular) that would enable them to challenge their incarceration. Their emerging commitment to prison reform required that they seize control of their education and begin to challenge the denigrating practices of prison culture. Racism, violence, and the exchange of contraband were destructive elements of this culture, and prison guards actively fostered these practices for their individual gain as well as for a means of prisoner control. A divided population whose hostilities were directed at one another rather than at prison authorities was preferable to a united population who recognized its own manipulation and the injustice of the legal system. In banding together in a multiracial alliance that raised questions about social justice, these prisoners became more than just teachers to one another; they sought to forge a safe house within the prison, one that rejected prisoner-on-prisoner violence, the domination of the weak by the powerful, and racism. As is seen in the collection of writings in section 1, Salinas' journalism experienced a decided shift in this period. Perhaps even more fascinating than this shift from music and sports to political analysis, is the way his transformation was documented in his letters

(section 2) as he underwent a spiritual, intellectual, and political metamorphosis.

Within the multiracial alliance of fellow prisoners, unification did
not mean that they failed to recognize the importance of validating
and "recovering" group culture and history. Rather, Latinos, Blacks,
Native Americans, and whites sought to understand the specificity of
violence, injustice, class inequality, and white supremacy for each
group. In 1968, a group of Chicano convicts arranged to have a
course titled "The Cultural History of the Southwest" taught by Francisco Ruiz of Penn Valley Community College in Kansas City. What
had been an informal education process became formalized as they
assumed control of their education and turned an institutional con-
straint into a political opportunity. This course lasted two years and
had a consistent presence of 25–30 students. It was from this class that
the newspaper *Aztlán de Leavenworth* was produced. *Aztlán's* first
issue was published on Cinco de Mayo 1970. Each issue contained
photos of the students in "The Culture History of the Southwest,"
with an article by a student on Chicano-Mexican history and culture,
political editorials, reports from other prisons and prisoners, as well as
updates on ex-prisoner activities, reports on visits by students, faculty,
or cultural artists, and a poetry and art page. It was in the inaugural
issue of *Aztlán* that Salinas' signature poem, "Un Trip Through the
Mind Jail," was first published and widely distributed.[6]

Salinas became a clerk in the education department during this
period and was elected by his peers in this emerging cadre of organizers as the editor of *Aztlán de Leavenworth*. Chicanos Organizados
Rebeldes Aztlán (CORA)[7] was centrally formed out of this group and
became the organizing vehicle for prisoner rights issues. The ideology
of CORA and thus of *Aztlán* was shaped by Third World anticolonial
movements and the cultural nationalism of the Chicano Movement. In
the first issue, an unsigned editorial explains the paper's philosophy by
referring to the National Chicano Youth Liberation conference in
Denver where *El Plan Espiritual de Aztlán* was penned[8] as an effort to
provide a political and spiritual focus for the Chicano Youth Movement. The lead editorial, written by Salinas, notes that the conceptual-
ization and the production of the paper was a group effort and had
two primary goals: "to Destroy and Rebuild." Unlike the often ideo-
logically inconsistent counter-cultural stance of many of the Beat

poets, the context and conditions of Salinas' confinement shaped him into becoming a "rebel *with* a causa" in an era rife with revolutionary potential.

It can be argued, then, that the value of Salinas' literary work lies not only in some traditional notion of "good writing," but in its value as a critical voice from within the depths of the penal system, a voice that is not so much exceptional as it is representative. It is representative inasmuch as his pre-prison life and his incarceration are all too typical of the prison population; his experiences of social disenfranchisement, undereducation, participation in the lumpen economy, and migrancy and other forms of displacement are indicators of experience and social location that are shared between him and many other prisoners. Because his post-prison life is marked by the linkage between his political involvement and his identity as an author, it is clear that Salinas' entire corpus of writing needs to be taken into account in order to understand the influences and direction of his writings, for they defy any single generic structure.

As is evidenced by Salinas' work included in this collection, it is the circumstances of his writing that matter as much, if not more, than the form, style, or "quality." Taken as a whole, this mixture of genres across time and space testifies to the enormous potential for transformation of *all* prisoners, given the right circumstances and commitment. From a post-1990s perspective, one can hardly examine a body of writing that is at once autobiographical, politically insurgent, interventionary, and representative, and which taken collectively reveal the experience of *conscientización,* without giving serious consideration to the genre of *testimonio.* The *testimonio*-like nature of Salinas' *oeuvre* can be instructive.

Outside the Prison Machine

Salinas gained his release in November of 1972 with the help of faculty and graduate students at the University of Washington at Seattle. Unable to return home to Texas or California due to parole restrictions, Salinas chose to be exiled in Seattle where his friends Joseph Sommers, Tomás Ybarra Frausto, Antonia Castañeda-Shular, Elda Cisneros, and Armando Mendoza lived and worked. He secured work at the university, received financial aid, and became a UW freshman at the age of 38. Immediately following his arrival, he joined a multiracial, Latino-led coalition of community groups intent on assuming control of an abandoned school building. Successful in their effort, they formed El Centro de La Raza. Within a year he was teaching courses in Chicano literature as an adjunct faculty member at UW. He also entered the still-emerging Chicano literary movement as he attended the first annual Flor y Canto at the University of Southern California and numerous other literary festivals in the Southwest.

As a student, Salinas immersed himself in the Native American fishing rights struggle in the Seattle-Tacoma region, working with the Nisqually/Puyallup peoples. After attending school for three years, he began working fulltime at El Centro de La Raza. It was here that his international vision and his ideas regarding Indian-Chicano unity were cultivated. In 1975 he traveled to Cuba for the first time as a member of El Centro. Later that year, as a staff member of El Centro's Indian-Chicano Education Project, he met and worked with AIM member Leonard Peltier. Though not in the forefront of AIM's battles on the Pine Ridge reservation in 1975, Salinas provided tactical support from Seattle. In 1976 he was co-coordinator of the Trail of Self-Determination, a seven-month cross-country educational caravan led by the Survival of American Indians Association, whose purpose was to offer an alternative perspective on the U.S. bicentennial. They arrived in D.C. on July 4 of that year. In 1977 Salinas co-founded the national Leonard Peltier Defense Committee. Four years later he would be selected as part of an International Indian Treaty Council delegation sent to represent Leonard Peltier at a Human Rights Symposium in Geneva.

In the latter half of the 1970s, Salinas also began to travel regularly to San Francisco. If Seattle became his political base, the Bay Area became his literary one when he began working with Editorial Pocho Ché to publish some important early works of Chicano literature. His first book, an early classic of Chicano literature, *Un Trip through the Mind Jail y Otras Excursions*, was published in 1980. Salinas' collaborations with Alejandro Murguía and Roberto Vargas, both of whom were directly involved with the Sandinista national liberation struggle in Nicaragua, broadened his knowledge of and participation in the International Solidarity Movement.

In 1981, after completing the terms of his parole with the Texas

Department of Corrections, Salinas moved back to Austin. Here he secured work teaching critical media studies courses through Mexican American Studies at the University of Texas at Austin and was involved with the League of United Chicano Artists (LUChA). Almost immediately he established Resistencia Bookstore/Casa de Red Salmon Press at his home in a shotgun storefront on Austin's East Side. The store remains open to this day, though it has since relocated to the city's near south side. In 1985 Salinas moved to St. Louis for a year to head the national office of the Leonard Peltier Defense Committee. As part of his ongoing work with the International Indian Treaty Council, Salinas traveled to Nicaragua, Libya, Cuba, and Panama. He continues to work on their behalf, and has, more recently, made trips to Chiapas, Mexico, as well as Vieques, Puerto Rico, in their name.

From 1989 to 1992 Salinas worked as a youth counselor with South Austin Youth Services. This work led him to become a specialist in gang intervention and conflict resolution, skills he continues to practice and speak on both formally and informally. Salinas' return to Austin presented him with the difficult challenge of continuing his role as activist, political spokesperson, and people's poet in an environment where he was known to have more savvy about the streets than political insight. He thus had to learn how to negotiate his old identity and relationships with his new direction in life.[9] A popular poet and speaker on social justice issues at universities and political and cultural venues, Salinas has always been lesser known and lesser appreciated in his home community. But this fact needs to be balanced with the reality that his has been a strong and steady cultural and political force in Austin, especially through Resistencia Bookstore, a haven for emerging writers and young leftists seeking guidance from an experienced activist. Resistencia has been home base for local chapters of AIM, the Leonard Peltier Defense Committee, the Comité en Solidaridad con Chiapas y Mexico, SOY (Save Our Youth) arts program, a read-in of *Live from Death Row* (part of the Free Mumia Campaign), as well as numerous ad hoc political issues committees addressing local, state, national, or international crises.

In addition to publishing his third volume of poetry, having his archives acquired by Stanford University, and seeing *Trip through the Mind Jail* reissued by Arte Público Press, Salinas has produced two spoken-word CDs[10] that have allowed him to showcase the musical dimensions, jazz in particular, of his work.

The goal of this brief profile of some of the more important moments of Salinas' prison experience has been to illustrate how his political consciousness was shaped in relation to his prison experience as well as the larger context of anticolonial struggles and the civil rights movement. His immersion into political activism as a prisoner continues to shape his poetics even as the cacophony of jazz and beat influences are more harmoniously synthesized in his most recent spoken word texts.

Salinas' contributions as a cultural worker are wide ranging. Today, in addition to conducting grant-sponsored youth writing workshops, he teaches courses from time to time at St. Edwards University and maintains a busy schedule on the reading circuit. Additionally, he has won many accolades for his work, including Best Supporting Actor in a Comedy by the Austin Circle of Theaters, the Guadalupe Cultural Arts Center Distinguished Writer Award, the Luis Reyes Rivera Lifetime Achievement Award, and the 2004 National Association for Latino Art and Culture (NALAC) Lifetime Achievement Award. His work with youth and his many contributions to community arts have been acknowledged in a Senate Resolution from the State of Texas.

Against the Jail Machine: Salinas' Contributions to Prison Literature and Social History

In the second edition of his groundbreaking study of prison literature, H. Bruce Franklin states that Jack Abbott's release and re-imprisonment following the publication of his collection of letters to Norman Mailer (*In the Belly of the Beast*) effectively captured readers' fascination regarding the penitentiary's impact on convicts. Franklin summarizes Abbott's thesis by asserting that "our penal institutions force each prisoner to become either a broken, cringing animal, fawning before all authority, or a resister, clinging to human dignity through defiance and rebellion" (xiii).

Prisoner rights activists within and outside the walls confront a conservative popular discourse that pathologizes prisoners and emphasizes the punitive dimensions of imprisonment over its reformative potential. In contrast to this denigrating and often dehumanizing discourse, in leftist studies of prison literature it is common parlance to refer to the prison experience as an educational one, as is evidenced by Assata Shakur's words in the opening epigraph. The analogy made between incarceration and education hinges upon the notion that, in isolation from the larger social world, many prisoners develop, discover, or refine their political consciousness. In contrast to the perceived disconnection of the university ivory tower from society, where the primary function of education is to reproduce the managerial class that preserves the status quo, the politics of knowledge in prisons often functions to produce counter-hegemonic intellectuals. Ironically, this re-education about the social circumstances that lead to incarceration takes place under brutal conditions in which the worst social forces and prejudices are intensified. This otherwise invisible spiritual and moral process of *conscientización* that many prisoners undergo, a process that precipitates a new way of seeing and acting in the world, is made tangible by Salinas' writings during his years of incarceration. In these works we witness Salinas' transformation from "social criminal" to political activist—a transformation that eventually led to his punitive transfer from the Leavenworth, Kansas, federal penitentiary to the control unit of a Marion, Illinois, federal prison in 1971. As many activists in the anti-war and civil rights movements began to face the threat of counter-intelligence programs (COINTELPRO) and other forms of government repression, convicts involved in prison reform work were also labeled as "dangerous" and subsequently marked for special repressive measures, including punitive transfers to specially designed behavior modification units. Franklin has noted that there are two overlapping groups of prison authors: "the political activist thrust into prison, and the common criminal thrust into political activism. The distinction between these two groups tends to dissolve as the definition of crime, from both sides of the law, becomes increasingly political" (242). Salinas' transformation and subsequent transfer illustrate the degree to which the prison system fears, and thus finds it necessary to contain through super-repressive means, organized and politically conscious prisoners.

Upon reading Salinas' *oeuvre* it becomes clear that his writing functioned as a tool of resistance against psychological and physical containment. More importantly, in describing his prison experience, Salinas also often refers to it as an educational one, with each move to another institution portrayed as a different and progressively more difficult degree program. This radical transformation that many prisoners undergo is often lost in popular accounts of the prison experience. Prisoners in contemporary literature and film are almost always rendered reductively by the Hollywood film industry. In popular films of the Chicano prison experience, such as *American Me* and *Bound by Honor* (aka *Blood In, Blood Out*), the representation of prison resistance is always articulated in continuing forms of criminality (drugs, sex, violence, organized crime, etc.), and a search for identity is often framed as a struggle for or against racial supremacy. Lost in these sensationalized representations are the kinds of consciousness-raising and inter- and intra-group alliances made inside and outside of the prison, particularly during the civil rights movement and prison rebellion years that frame the time of Salinas' incarceration. The intensified racism systematically fostered in prisons operates to thwart the development of an oppositional consciousness among prisoners by exploiting pre-existing social divisions. However, as much prison literature demonstrates, this struggle for survival and power need not be overdetermined. Originally a prisoner of social crimes (narcotics possession and distribution), Salinas' prison experience exemplifies the ways in which a convict is transformed by and transforms the Prison Industrial Complex.

Both in the context from which it emerged and now, Salinas' writing needs to be seen as an intervention in the ahistorical and often dehumanizing popular discourse surrounding prisoners and crime that all too often preempts any critical discussion of the faults and limitations of the criminal justice system. As part of a prisoner rights movement, he and his cohorts began to forge a radical cultural praxis that linked issues of identity with notions of power and justice, and thus cultural practices and "cultural studies"[11] became vehicles for education and mobilization. Salinas' poetry, journalism, letters, and political archives reflect a diligent, protracted, yet deliberate process of *concientización,* a feature that undermines the framework of pathology that stamps the popular representation of prisoners.

Few would argue that prison literature is not political, fraught as it is with issues of power. Most prison literature is testimony to the author's struggle to retain dignity and sanity in a context that forces a convict to conform or resist. Much of this literature can be said to have a similar intention as *testimonio* literature, whose goal is to render the "often invisible" abuses of power visible as it seeks to realize a politics of solidarity. In this regard "the artistic achievement of this literature [must be approached] with an aesthetic radically different from most aesthetics applied in the university and the university-dominated cultural media. In truth, it may not be going too far to say that the prison and the university provide the contradictory poles defining the field of aesthetics . . ." (Franklin, 235).

Prison literature, especially that which might be labeled "protest" literature, is by definition speaking from the margins. The issues of location and politics are important for here the function of literature becomes crucial. As Georg Gugelberger has argued with regard to *testimonio* in *The Real Thing: Testimonial Discourses in Latin America*, reading and teaching prison literature is imperative, or should be. Situated at

> the cross roads of all the discourses of institutional battles in recent years: postcolonial and/versus postmodern; genre vs non-genre; interest in autobiography; the function of the canon; authenticity/realism the debates on subalternity; discussions on authorship; othering discourse; margin/center; race/class/gender; minority discourse; Third World writing; questions of disciplinarity." (7)

And I would add issues of self-representation, violence, and social control among others. Moreover, though it doesn't share the same status as *testimonio* in these pro-penal legislation days, prison literature, like *testimonio,* runs a similar risk of being romanticized or reduced to mere art (or evidence of "culture," "intellect," or humanity from an unexpected source) and de-politicized when it is ripped from its context.

The politics of knowledge, culture, identity, and representation remain crucial to the creation of a body politic that is invested in creating a more humane society. Salinas and his comrades in struggle sought to acquire a knowledge of politics, find individual and collective fulfillment, and advance human liberation. In doing so, they found it necessary to systematically undermine and counter a dehumanizing and divisive prison culture.

The Jail Machine in the Twenty-First Century

It is this systematic process of dehumanization that is at the core of the notion of the prison as a machine intent on cranking out neatly packaged "good" citizens, no matter the cost to one's sense of personal dignity. Whether these human warehouses are called correctional institutions, reform schools, behavior research or modification centers, adjustment centers, penitentiaries, prisons, or jails, the U.S. Prison Industrial Complex has but one goal: to isolate, contain, and modify the bodies, minds, and spirits of its residents to accept "their" subordinate place in society. This philosophy is predicated on the notion that prisoners are defective human beings who have proven their antisocial nature through their crimes.

In 1972 a backlash against the prisoner rights movement was initiated that is directly responsible for the proliferation of prisons and prisoners in this country. Todd R. Clear, a professor at John Jay College of Criminal Justice in New York, notes: "Beginning in 1972, the prison population started a pattern of unrelenting growth in annual increments (from a base of around 200,000), lasting for over a generation and continuing today." The result is a 500 percent increase in incarceration, and more than 2 million inmates in prisons and jails, with the burden of the increased incarceration falling most heavily on poor African American and Hispanic communities.[12] According to a fact sheet from The Sentencing Project, "There are now 6.6 million Americans incarcerated or on probation, or parole, an increase of more than 258 percent since 1980."[13]

With the world's most imprisoned population (690 per 100,000 population), the United States must come to terms with a policy gone awry. As we witness the incarceration of huge sectors of entire populations—Black males have a 29% chance of serving time in prison at some point in their lives; Hispanic males have a 16% chance; white males have a 4% chance; 46% of prison inmates in 2001 were black and 16% were Hispanic[14]—we must understand that we have created policies that are undermining our future and exploit and further magnify social prejudices against people of color, youth, the poor, and the undereducated (68% of state prison inmates have not completed high school; 36% of jail inmates in 1996 were unemployed prior to entering jail; 64% of jail inmates in 1996 had monthly incomes of under $1,000 in the month before their arrest).[15]

Perhaps the most important purpose served by the publication of this collection will be its contribution to an increased understanding of the human potential that lives behind the walls of prisons. Put another way, it is my hope that this collection will help undermine the mask created by a discourse of dehumanization that the mainstream media and political, legal, and judicial officials have imposed on this segment of our society. We must acknowledge prisoners as members of the human family, as our fellow citizens, if we are to rectify the social conditions that create their incarceration. We must be willing to ask what is wrong with a society that is so ready, willing, and able to disregard so much human capital. What does our current political economy of incarceration say about the nature of the freedom of which we would deprive others?

Today, with few exceptions, there is very little public attention given to the ever expanding Prison Industrial Complex as a significant portion of our population, most of whom are very young, are incarcerated for longer periods of time with little regard for rehabilitation. They are victims of a judicial system hell-bent on addressing the symptoms of a society gone awry and not the underlying causes that drive people to live outside the law. What we can learn from this collection of writings as well as the work of many other prison writers, is that in the same way that prisons serve as a microcosm for the larger world, it is also true that insights into human nature, the enormous capacity for love and justice, can transcend even the most repressive circumstances. Perhaps we can learn to foster those qualities, those virtues, and in our own way, contribute to the formation of a more just society.

Organizational Structure

raúlrsalinas and the Jail Machine is organized into four major sections that are designed to enable readers to follow the trajectory of Salinas' transformation as a writer and emerging activist-intellectual. With this purpose in mind, each section represents a particular genre of writing that, more or less, is organized chronologically. In section 1 we begin with Salinas' journalism because though he did write letters to his family during his earlier period of incarceration in Soledad, few of those early letters to family have been saved. Moreover, it is only after Salinas started contributing to *The Echo* that he began to forge a "writerly" identity that would shape his presentation of himself and his experience in ways that are self-reflective and less formulaic. His journalism, like his letter writing, documents an evolving sense of self and society. This critical sense of self shapes not only what he writes about but also how he writes. Yet, even from his first jazz column in January 1964, we see that Salinas was already aware of the role of music in expressing social discontent and the importance of an avant garde for innovative forms of expression. Presented here are nine of fourteen of Salinas' jazz review columns. A significant span of time elapsed between the Christmas 1964 overview of Kennedy's drug policy and the first issue of *Aztlán de Leavenworth* published on May 5, 1970. By 1970 Salinas had undergone a major ideological transformation due to his contact with political prisoners in Leavenworth, his extensive reading, as well as his educational and organizational experiences obtained through CORA. His contributions to *Aztlán, New Era,* and *Entrelíneas* demonstrate a major evolution of his political consciousness during his time at Leavenworth.

In section 2, "Flying Kites to the World," we gain insight into Salinas' most intense period of transformation through his correspondence with a wide array of people. A kite is prison slang for any type of written correspondence. Kites that reach the outside world are one means for a prisoner to send some part of himself over the forty-foot walls surrounding most prisons. The term also signifies a prisoner's sense of isolation and his tenuous relationship to the outside world, one subject to all manner of whimsical interruptions, be it censorship or getting "lost" in transit. Because receiving and sending correspondence was under intense scrutiny, and often a privilege subject to revocation by prison authorities, and because correspondence with the "free world" was the most reliable means of establishing and maintaining relationships with non-prisoners, these letters reveal many dimensions of a complex human being undergoing personal and political change.

Salinas' letters to politicians, activists, family, and friends involve careful negotiations between his former life and his current self. These relationships are often paradoxical: they reveal someone who is simultaneously fragile and intense, someone seeking connection and commitment even as he expresses deep uncertainty and fears. They are letters fraught with newfound power and cautious restraint. The selections included here are intended to provide a multifaceted view of Salinas, as he communicates with immediate family and strives to connect to activists, academics, lawyers, politicians, journalists, cultural centers, and political organizations. His candor and acute political insight, as well as his emerging reputation as a poet, command respect from his audience. Many recipients of his letters formed lasting friendships with him. We are fortunate to have here some exchanges which illustrate the intensity of his dialogue, analysis of his situation, reflections and reports from progressive social movements on the outside, and Salinas' meditations on his radical metamorphosis. The letters are by and large organized chronologically, though there are four sets of exchanges with individuals that I have grouped together since there is a revealing strand of dialogue in each one that merits concentrated attention. Also included is correspondence with prison officials and other legal documents outlining Salinas' life as seen by "official transcripts" of his prison experience. These documents making up his prison dossier, in and of themselves, tell us little about Salinas' personal growth and transformation. Rather, the flattening out of his life that occurs here is presented as a means of reminding us of how a meaningful life can be lost in institutional bureaucracy. Comprising the bulk of the collection here, these letters began with exchanges with his family in 1968 and end in 1974, a little over a year after Salinas' release from Marion.

"Flying Kites to the World" is followed by section 3: "The Marion Strike: Journals from 'el pozo.'" The daily log of activities and statements about the strike reproduced here offer a harrowing first-hand look at prisoner resistance to institutional brutality carried out by guards and the draconian regulations defining the nation's most notorious control unit at the time. As noted in a 1992 report by the Committee to End the Marion Lockdown, the term "control unit" was first coined at the United States Penitentiary (USP) at Marion, Illinois, in 1972 and has come to designate a prison or part of a prison that operates under a "super maximum security" regimen. Marion was opened in 1963, the same year Alcatraz was closed. Designed to be the new "most repressive" prison, the Bureau of Prisons designed the facilities and programs at Marion with the intent of being able to control the most dangerous and most politicized prisoners in the country.[16] After implementing a behavior modification program entitled CARE (Control and Rehabilitation Effort), in the late 1960s the BOP began transferring the nation's "most dangerous prisoners" to Marion. Raúl Salinas and several other prisoners were moved from Leavenworth to Marion in April of 1972. This transfer signaled official recognition of Salinas as a dangerous mind, not for the social crimes for which he was originally sentenced to prison, but for his activism from within prison that marked him as a disruptive agitator. Describing it in vivid detail, a press release about the strike, transported out of the prison under cover on August 5, 1972, documents the initial events leading to the strike and provides an introduction of sorts to the daily log of "The Marion Story," as the strike came to be called by besieged prisoners. This daily log of developing events was maintained from July 15 to November 3, 1972. The materials in section 3 complement the story of Marion as told in the press, by journalists and prisoners alike.

Finally, the collection ends with two post-prison interviews of Salinas in section 4. The first took place almost immediately after his release and illustrates a critical mind preoccupied with his contributions to the prisoner rights movement by way of exposing inhumane behavior modification practices of the federal government. The second interview was conducted by Ben Olguín and myself upon the occasion of Stanford's acquisition of the Salinas archive. This is twenty-two years after his release, and though his experiences had broadened immensely, the poet's sense of purpose, his world vision, as well as his artistic sensibility were more finely honed, not dulled, by the years of struggle, resistance, and transformation.

This project was made possible by the preservation of Salinas' archives as part of Stanford University's Special Collections. What appear here are materials that tell an important story, one that extends beyond Salinas' own life. Every effort has been made to transcribe and present these materials in a manner that preserves the integrity with which they were originally created—even though they were created in conditions that were less than ideal. Some of these works, particularly the newspapers, letters, and journals, now exist as faded and torn mimeographs, typewritten or carbon paper copies, and letters handwritten in pen or pencil. Our goal was to present these with as little editorial alteration as possible in order to respect and preserve the context and circumstances of their production.

A consistent motif in Salinas' creative work is that of the journey. The travels and travails of his own life are grist for an extraordinary tale. This person's singular journey from individual alienation to rage to resistance is linked to social movements that occurred inside and outside of prison, and thus his story is also our story. And we must claim it as such if we are to embrace the belief that justice is a realizable vision, not merely a lofty ideal.

Notes

Significant portions of this introduction are derived from my 2003 essay "The Re-education of a Xicanindio," published in a special issue of *MELUS* titled *Literature and the Idea of Social Justice*.

1. The acquisition of this collection was facilitated by Ben Olguín and myself on Salinas' behalf. Roberto Trujillo, Stanford Special Collections Acquisitions Specialist, made the creation of this collection possible. His invaluable work in securing the preservation of the private papers of many Chicana and Chicano authors cannot be overstated.

2. Mendoza, "The Re-education of a Xicanindio," 54–55.

3. One of Salinas' prison journals is a notebook containing typed copies of all his favorite poems, which he reproduced from an unidentified 1958 Latin American anthology of literature.

4. In 1979, Wilson was unsuccessfully solicited by the U.S. government to "neutralize" Leonard Peltier in Leavenworth. See Matthieson, *In the Spirit of Crazy Horse* (pp. 374–381) for details of this plot.

5. Collazo was a member of a Puerto Rican commando group that stormed Blair House and attempted to assassinate Harry Truman in 1954.

6. This poem was originally dedicated to Eldridge Cleaver, a dedication that Salinas withdrew when Cleaver's political commitments changed (Mendoza, "Some Reflections on Twenty Years of *Un Trip Through the Mind Jail y Otras Excursions*," p. 3).

7. See Section I, note 1, for a fuller explanation of the history of the name of the group and its two names.

8. The prologue was written by Alurista, and the remainder of the document was a collaboration among conference participants. Alurista's pivotal role as author of the prologue was not initially known to prisoners.

9. A point I made in the afterword to *East of the Freeway*, Salinas' second collection of poems, and one which Salinas speaks directly to in a fall 1973 letter to friends at an Austin bar, included in this collection.

10. *Los Many Mundos of raúlrsalinas* (2000); *Down the BEATen Path* (2002).

11. I realize this is an unconventional reference to an academic mode of inquiry that was not yet a critical force in the United States; however, as I will illustrate later, it is a useful reference because the culture classes in prison became a site of critical inquiry on the relationship between knowledge, power, public institutions, and the social order. Thus, I would argue that cultural studies practitioners have much to learn from prisons as a site of radical re-education.

12. This figure includes 1.3 million in federal and state prisons. More than 630,000 are in local jails. "Facts About Prisons and Prisoners" (online publication, visited 12/12/04).

13. Ibid.

14. Ibid.

15. Ibid.

16. See "From Alcatraz to Marion to Florence—Control Unit Prisons in the United States" (undated pamphlet, p. 2).

YO Y MI PRIMO JUANILLO,
AT METZ PARK - AUSTIN 53

TWO FRIENDS FROM ANOTHER BARRIO
CLEMENTE & AMADO SORIANO. THIS
WAS TAKEN AT XMAS' 53 WHILE
AMADO WAS ON FURLOUGH FROM
LA CORRE. CLEMENTE WAS LATER
MY CELL PARTNER IN HUNTSVILLE.

"...IS TO SAY THAT MIDGETS, JUNIORS, HIPSTERS, CHAVALONES, VETERANOS, LOW RIDERS, PACHUCOS..."

GREETING NEWBORN SIS —
ACABADO DE LLEGAR FROM "LOS
TRAISA,NOS" IN CALIFORNIA
LATE 40'S

VATO LOCO W/SIS SOME YEARS
LATER AT NEFITA'S CANTON
ON HIDALGO STREET ———
AUSTIN EN LOS '50'S

Photo album from Salinas' youth

Salinas as a young man in San José, California (1952)

Salinas at Metz Park in Austin, Texas (1953)

TO WHOM IT MAY CONCERN:

> In Re: Roy Salinas
> 2605 Hidalgo St.
> Austin, Texas

Roy Salinas was raised in Austin, Texas and attended school here. He is seventeen (17) years of age. He works for a Baking Company during part of the year and works in a harvest field during the remainder of the year.

While he has been in trouble as a juvenile, these offenses occurred some three years ago. He has never been sent to a reformatory.

I believe that he has been doing his best in the past three years to be a useful citizen and I believe that he has no disqualifications that should keep him from serving with the Navy or other branches of service.

Yours very truly,

Bob Long,
District Attorney

BL/elh

Travis County D.A. letter certifying that Salinas is fit to join military (December 6, 1951)

Salinas and group discuss issues related to prison publications (1964). Photo courtesy of Dept. of Special Collections, Stanford University Libraries.

Salinas in cell, Huntsville State Prison (circa 1964)

Christmas Pageant, Chapel Hope Choir, Huntsville, Texas (December 1963). Salinas is in front row, fourth from left.

Salinas with grandmother Gabriela Hernández Gil (circa 1965)

Salinas' arrest in Austin as part of a federal drug sting (photo from Austin American-Statesman, *April 1967)*

Salinas' Journalism

In November of 1961 Salinas was arrested while attending a Ray Charles concert at Palmer Auditorium in Austin for possession of marijuana. He was subsequently sentenced to five years and transferred to Huntsville State Prison, where he stayed until May of 1965. In Huntsville he joined the choir (see related article following these columns), which was the organizational unit that brought him together with other prison "intellectuals," men who enjoyed reading books, magazines, and newspapers, keeping up with current affairs, and exchanging ideas. This same group became part of the core that formed the production team of the monthly prison newspaper, *The Echo*.

Under the encouragement of his peers, Salinas authored a jazz column entitled "Quartered Notes" over a span of sixteen months (January 1964–April 1965). These selections originally appeared in *The Echo*. Raúl Salinas, at that time, wrote under the byline of "Roy Salinas." The Anglicization of his name first occurred in school, but it was later adopted by him. In his early twenties he often used "Roi."

These reviews of the jazz scene are significant for a number of reasons. On the one hand, they document the profound influence of African American culture on Salinas' aesthetics—an experience that was an integral part of his youth in East Austin, where Black music was a thriving and powerful, if often underacknowledged, force. Moreover, they illustrate his attentiveness to the jazz world as it was written about in newspapers and magazines. His columns are clearly influenced by the journalistic style of such renowned jazz critics as Ralph J. Gleason. But this is no mere mimicry here, for Salinas worked hard to research every column under extremely restrictive conditions. Though Salinas had begun to experiment with poetry and short story writing during his incarceration at Soledad State Prison, this writing ceased until he was in Huntsville. The columns are his first efforts at journalism, and they thus mark his development as a writer for a public audience.

It was in Huntsville that Salinas began to forge an identity as a writer with an audience. With the publication of an editorial in *The Echo* that was noted by a local newspaper, Salinas began to see the power of writing. In his subsequent period of incarceration, the subject matter of his journalism assumed a decidedly political tone, even as he continued to write about culture. Increasingly, as he was exposed to literature that assessed the role of culture and nationalism and the role of the intellectual in revolution, Salinas conscientiously embraced his role as a writer on behalf of social change.

Articles from *The Echo*, Texas State Prison, Huntsville

(aka the Walls Unit)

Quartered Notes • *January 1964*

BY ROY SALINAS

THE REVOLUTIONARY CONCEPTS of the avant garde have always managed to raise more than a few eyebrows in each respective phase of the arts. As jazz writer Don Hackman so aptly stated, "Revolutions in art, like revolutions in society, inevitably affect the lives of everyone."

Whether it be the action painters in art, the *chosisme* (thingishness) novelists in literature, the "new wave" screen writers in motion pictures, or the "new thing" exponents in modern jazz, the experimentalists are still at work.

In 1958, an obscure young Texan armed with a white plastic saxophone and a bagful of original compositions invaded the studios of Contemporary Records; and the sounds that came about through this recording session were completely devoid of any ties with the more accepted forms of conventional jazz.

IF THE RADICAL BIRTH of bop had stood the jazz world on its ears (and it did!), then this new iconoclastic music was more astounding. The album bearing these innovations was appropriately titled *Something Else!*

Almost overnight Ornette Coleman, the saxophonist mentioned above, became the center of a controversy that divided musicians into two camps. The advocates who championed this new arrival—among those being John Lewis of the Modern Jazz Quartet fame and the immortal Dizzy Gillespie, believed that this was a further extension of Charlie Parker's *New Directions* and Dizzy's *Things to Come*.

The opposing camp viciously attacked Coleman and vulgarly branded his music "anti-jazz." The critics also joined in the fray. Some hoped that by defending the "new thing" their names might be written in the history book of jazz should it become the next step in jazz evolution. Others simply wrote about the new thing as best they understood it.

THERE WERE OTHER listeners: the young musicians who would eventually emerge as disciples of this latest sound in modern music. They listened faithfully, hailed the new prophet, and religiously adopted his tenets; by the early 60's they were ready to go out and preach their scripture to the world.

The stunning music produced by these young rebels has been accused of creating unpleasant sounds to the ear and feelings of uneasiness because of the raw emotional expressions they deal with.

All manner of eerie grunts and shrieks are heard; the effect most widely employed is a haunting and agonizing cry of the human voice. If the message holds no validity in jazz because of the almost nihilistic moods of anger, despair, and indifference, it is for the listener to decide.

TECHNICALLY THE REVOLT is more evident. As is said of Coleman, "All logic, order, and continuity seem to be lost in his playing." He employs a complete freedom of improvisation without regard for chord structures or measure lines.

John Coltrane's approach is through his exploration as to the extent of scalar improvisations. Still other members eliminate or reject *all* harmonic or melodic devices, relying upon rhythmic patterns.

Can this be passed off as a lack of technique on the part of the musicians as some would have it, or is it a new path towards the development of jazz? While avant garde jazz has more opponents than supporters (or so the strongly voiced opinions would lead one to believe), it is interesting and paradoxical to note that it is becoming more of an accepted way of playing.

Perhaps the importance and logic of this current transition will not seem clear until another decade or two has passed. Then it will probably be recognized as an essential addition to the myriad schools of sound which make up the wonderful world of jazz.

■ ■ ■

Quartered Notes • *February 1964*

BY ROY SALINAS

THROUGHOUT THE PAST YEAR there were a great number of prominent deaths in all stations of life. Popes and Presidents died; Poets and Painters also died. And so, out of the midst of these luminaries, one death caused grief to fall on the music world.

Music lovers as well as musicians were saddened by the passing of Dinah Washington. Death paid its untimely call to her as she slept in the early morning hours of December 14. Thus another major jazz voice was taken from the music field.

From Dinah's teenage days with the Lionel Hampton band in the 1940's to her last jazz festival appearance, she always captivated the audiences wherever she performed. Her fans affectionately dubbed her "Queen of the Blues," and for very good reasons.

Her career was based upon a multi-faceted talent. First of all she was a blues singer, as evidenced in her recording of Bessie Smith tunes. As a jazz vocalist, she surrounded herself with such stalwart musicians as Maynard Ferguson and the late trumpet virtuoso, Clifford Brown. In the role of nightclub entertainer, she offered her musical charms in the popular idiom.

SHE RECORDED SEVERAL POP ALBUMS, some as duets with Brook Benton. Because of this pop-oriented style—developed during the years just prior to her death—she gained a much wider listening public, resulting in the tremendous accolades from her innumerable fans in the twilight of her career.

Personally, I enjoyed the Dinah who belted out "Evil Gal Blues" and "Salty Papa" in the greatest blues tradition. But I equally enjoyed her beautiful interpretations of ballads like "Cottage for Sale," a recording she made with a jazz group, hand picked personally by her.

I have always felt that an artist's stature in jazz can be measured not only by his contributions, but also by the influence he may have over the younger musicians. And Dinah surely influenced several of the new crop of vocalists: A slight tinge of the Washington style is obvious in the singing of Etta Jones, Nancy Wilson, and most certainly in the voice of Dakota Staton, especially in her first recordings. You could almost say that Dakota's rendition of "A Froggy Day" is a musical tribute to the "Queen."

DINAH POSSESSED other talents which were lesser known to the general public. She had an extensive knowledge of music, and she was also a very fine pianist.

This is what made up the musical character of one who definitely etched a profound mark for posterity in the annals of jazz history— "The Unforgettable Miss D."

■ ■ ■

Quartered Notes • *March 1964*

BY ROY SALINAS

THE GOATTEED FACE of Thelonious Sphere Monk, mischievously staring out from the cover of *Time* magazine (February 28), was surely a delight shared by all jazz lovers fortunate enough to see it.

The selection of Monk as cover subject, complete with Tyrolean lid, was a wise choice and one of those rare treats in jazz which occur, surprisingly enough, from *Time* to *Time*. As memory serves me, only two other jazzmen have been honored thusly: Duke Ellington and Dave Brubeck.

Not too long ago, the staff of *Time* held a banquet for all the eminent persons that have appeared as cover subjects. Kings and queens mingled with scientists, statesmen, and actresses. Picture, if you will, a similar affair in the future: Can you imagine the unique Monk, sporting perhaps a velvet beret, rubbing elbows with the cream of society? I can, simply because Monk has declared his artistry by skillfully carving a niche for himself in the granite mountains of jazz. With his bare hands!

MONK'S PORTRAIT STUDY is rewarding in that it will find its way to millions who are unfamiliar with jazz or its proponents. And who knows how many of his records they might buy or how many of his concerts they might attend?

The interpreters of Monk's provocative compositions are very few. His hit tunes and ditties that seem so simple on the surface are profound etudes in jazz. Soprano saxist Steve Lacy records mostly Monk tunes and is now writing along similar lines. Pianist Cecil Taylor is another emulator of his, and Miles Davis includes a Monk tune in most of his recordings.

When Monk plays his music, he is like a painter who stands away from his easel and slings paints at his canvas. But you can't object because of the beautiful colors he chooses.

THELONIUS HAS ALWAYS been considered somewhat of a weird and offbeat character, and his music has been described as the meanderings of a madman. Still, he remains an individualist, a prime requisite in the performing arts. Monk has yet to be swayed by the numerous schools and fads which have arisen since the advent of jazz. He lives in a wealthy land of dissonant chords, harmonic interplays, and rhythmic interpolations. From these he has never deviated.

As proof that Europeans are at the forefront of his admirers in recognizing him as a serious composer, a German jazz critic said that "his music is like *al fresco* painting; you can't take them with you, but if you like what you see, you'll be back, and with Monk's music, you will."

Then there was a recent Iron Curtain escapee who could only speak four words of English: "Hot Dog" and "Thelonius Monk!" What a tribute to bestow on a person.

■　■　■

Quartered Notes • *April 1964*

BY ROY SALINAS

TO START OFF this potpourri of jazz things, I must respond to several complaints hurled at this column, concerning the supposedly erroneous printing of a chick's name in February's article.

It seems that the wrath of some rock 'n' roll devotees was unintentionally evoked when this writer made mention of the late Dinah's influence on Etta Jones. The impression was that a major goof had been made in misprinting the name of one Etta James.

I hadn't the vaguest idea that this would be the end result, for I am not familiar enough with Etta James to write about her personality or music in "Quartered Notes." However, I have it from a reliable source (a hip little frog) that she is for real, and that her style is a cross between r 'n' r and pop music.

Etta Jones, on the other hand, is strictly a jazz songstress. Her repertoire includes such evergreens as *Don't Go to Strangers*, *If I Had You*, and *Look to Your Heart*. Acting as "confreres" of hers on some of these tunes are musicians of the caliber of guitarist Barry Galbraith and bassist Keeter Betts.

FOR VARIOUS REASONS, sound-alike names are a common occurrence in the entertainment field. Some are from respect and admiration for their more prominent namesakes, others are a means of enhancing their commercial appeal by the name association. Whatever the reasons, some very interesting mistakes are produced, if nothing else.

You'll find it's an interesting pastime trying to unravel the names of jazz personages as to "who's who." Dig: Lady Day, Anita O'Day, Ruth Olay, Nita Rae, Frances Faye, Rita Reys. Or how about Annie Ross, Rita Moss, and Lita Roza?

Then there are pianists Horace Silver and Horace Parlan and trumpeters Dizzy Gillespie and Dizzy Reece. If you really want to get hung up, try Red Mitchell, Whitey Mitchell, and Blue Mitchell! (Two bass-playing brothers and a trumpet man respectively.)

KUDOS, ALONG WITH a blues riff, to the University of Houston's KUHT-TV for their presentation of the fine modern sounds of *Jazz Casual* on Friday nights.

A WAILING AGGREGATION worth hearing are the "Houstonians" of Sam Houston State College. They blow mostly original compositions by students and music faculty members, plus arrangements of the compositions of nationally established jazz musicians. We just don't get to hear enough of them on Huntsville's KSAM.

■ ■ ■

Quartered Notes • *May 1964*

BY ROY SALINAS

ONE OF MY STRONGEST aversions—to the point of disgust—is directed toward people who try to emulate what, in their narrow minds, constitutes the hard-core jazz fan. In my opinion, this desperation to achieve a true hipster image only results in a sickening state of ultra-coolness: the epitome of sheer squaredom!

This attitude is more harmful to jazz than a mob of agitated public citizens, posing as reformers, crying out in defiance against the corrupting influences of jazz. In their attempts to become associated with the 'in' group—if there is such a thing—these misinformed (or uninformed) pseudo-hipsters go to extremes with their lies to others, who are in worse shape musically. Sort of a blind leading the blind gig.

A FEW DAYS AGO, I accidentally hit upon a conversation between a purported hipster and his intended victim. Soon, talk drifted around to the Newport Jazz Festival, and Hippy made this statement, "man, las' year's festival wuz the toughest since '38 . . . it say in *Down Beat*." This jarred me a little, and I tried to be helpful by explaining to him why this could not be so. However, no amount of coaxing could convince Hippy that he might've meant 1958. Or, that perhaps the jazzman's bible was guilty of a misprint. Oh! No, he remained unshaken and very dogmatic. Now, the ardent jazzophile—or one who makes such a claim—knows that in 1938, even Norman Granz' Jazz at the Philharmonic concerts were several years from existence.

Oh! Well, I saw no sense in blowing what might still turn out to be an interesting discussion of the subject so sacred to me. Besides, even jazz aficionados are entitled to mistakes now and then. What really sent me away fuming was Hippy's comment on the lack of recordings made by Bird in recent months. Isn't that tragic?

To Hippy and all those confused souls like him, who consider the false mask of hipsterism more important than a proper jazz orientation, let me inform you that Charlie (Yardbird) Parker died on March 12, 1955. Almost sounds archaic, no? It is no wonder then, that no one has heard any recent recordings of his . . . (logical?). On leaving that particular scene, my only regrets were for the poor unsuspecting parties: the hipster's audience. For in all sincerity, he really thought he was being schooled!

ON THE OTHER HAND, I am familiar with several persons whose knowledge of jazz is not very extensive, yet, I have a great deal of respect and admiration for them because they don't profess to be know-it-alls in the field. Their appreciation for the jazz idiom and other forms of music is so profound that it commands my respect. These people are not mere dilettantes who would don the cloak of jazziana for effect alone. Instead, they are serious and honest in their belief of jazz being a true art form.

If Jazz is indeed a major phase of the performing fine arts, how can we expect it to flourish as one, if the same people who embrace it, by the same token degrade it and display it for what it is not, by their conduct and affectations. How can we expect the layman or "square" to lend his support if all he has to go by is our inane and ridiculous behavior? A poetess friend of mine once wrote, "So blow me a jazz horn, let's be real and cry."

JAZZ IS A PRODUCT of our environment. Predominant in this musical environment is the African culture blended with the European influences. There are also traces of the latin culture inherent within its structures. But it is a *native* American product, nonetheless. One which we should not allow anyone to defile and desecrate . . . especially if we are to consider ourselves enthusiasts of modern jazz.

To the swinging Giraffe in the land of Bruins; we thank you for jazz clues, and of course, for digging us.

■ ■ ■

Quartered Notes • *July 1964*

BY ROY SALINAS

I FIRST SAW THE NAME of John Coltrane in print in the late 40's on a record label when he was a sideman for the great Dizzy's band. He had no solo space as I can vaguely recall. (Since I am limited for reference material, I must rely solely on memory.) Nevertheless, he was an integral part of the reed section of that exciting big band which also included James Moody and Cecil Payne. Moody and Payne were then more musically mature and tended to overshadow the budding 'Trane almost entirely.

When Miles Davis formed his quintet in late 1955, he selected Coltrane as second horn on the front lines from among the many hornmen on the jazz scene. Response from the jazz enthusiasts throughout the world was almost immediate.

'Trane had arrived, in the truest and most literal sense of the word. He showed a tremendous amount of promise as a major voice on the tenor saxophone, in spite of the fact that his tough competitor, Sonny Rollins, was then shaking up the jazz field forcefully and imposingly making his sound heard.

ANY FOLLOWER OF JAZZ knows that Miles is noted for his extended solos, of which no better example can be found than on his album 'Round Midnight. Two memorable tunes from that album can best serve the purpose of presenting a picture of how I hear 'Trane. The title tune has John biding his time and cooling it while Miles makes his overlong nocturnal excursion.

As soon as the trumpeter fades out, 'Trane unleashes his surging sounds like a man who has been waiting for his liberty so long that when he is given his freedom he feels he must make a lasting contribution of some kind to the world. And contribute 'Trane does, very generously and effectively. On Bye, Bye, Blackbird he executes such an attack as to convey the feeling of virility and desperate driving.

Along with the well known alto saxophonist Julian (Cannonball) Adderly, 'Trane locked horns with Miles Davis to make up the Miles Sextet. The exposure he attained as a result of this association was extremely rewarding.

After taking his rigorous training under the strict discipline and wise tutelage of such stalwart giants, he decided to try out his newly acquired wings. They were "bird" wings, at that, because it is obvious that he had heard and listened to the immortal Charlie Parker.

THE END RESULTS SHOW that the wreaths of laurel bestowed upon him were well earned. As a leader, with Miles' rhythm section, he displays some magnificent improvisational qualities. What he has to say is very well stated. He has swept the nation's jazz polls with an overwhelming majority. The new star on the jazz horizon has become a reality.

■ ■ ■

Quartered Notes • *September 1964*

BY ROY SALINAS

THERE HAS BEEN MUCH irrelevant material written about the true origins of jazz and its originators. Hours have been spent, or perhaps wasted, in argumentative discourses concerning the "disastrous" fusion of jazz with European classicism. "Jazz was doin' all right by itself," the diehards claim, "until 'they' came along and diluted it, labeled it, and stuck it in the concert halls."

If the results of the melding of sounds mean that jazz is being accorded the same level of prestige as the other fine arts then "they" (whoever they may be!) should be highly commended! Jazz has suffered long enough under a banner of notoriety as it stands. How fortunate the listener is in being able to hear this music played under such favorable and respectable conditions.

Ironically, the very people who blame the ethnic involvement for the lack of economic success, and question "their" capabilities to perform jazz for the same reasons, entirely dismiss the fact that the European influence is just as prevalent among the descendants of the originators of jazz. Within this area, some of the more modern swingers reside.

SURE, WE HAVE THE Lydian concepts of George Russell, the untouchable Lenny Tristano cult, and the atonalities with rustic lines of Jimmy Giuffre. But at the same time we also have the 18th Century fugue sounds of the Modern Jazz Quartet, and pianist John Lewis has undeniably listened very attentively to Johann Sebastian Bach.

Are we to put him down as being nowhere simply because we prefer the "cookers"? Certainly not! It is this variety and personal interpretation that adds to the magnificence of jazz. Therefore, I think it unfair to degrade a musician on the basis of his difference in culture or our lack of interest in his approach, if it be a legitimate and dedicated one. All members of the MJQ are alumni of the bop school *cum laude*, which makes them swingers of the highest caliber, capable of holding their own with any combo blowing today.

This properly organized cohesive unit attained a certain air of classicism and respectability when director John Lewis, vibraphonist Milt Jackson, drummer Kenny Clarke (later replaced by Connie Kay) and bassist Percy Heath donned for the first time identical white ties and tails.

LOOKING FOR ALL THE WORLD like symphony musicians, the MJQ began their extended programs of what has been termed "semi-classical jazz" or "third stream" music.

Some of John Lewis' original compositions which have become standard fare with enthusiasts the world over are the jazz fugues *Concord* and *Versailles*. A spontaneous interplay between Jackson and Lewis comes through marvelously on *Bluesology* and *Festival Sketch*.

With their roots stemming directly from the jazz tradition of America and their continued study and playing reaching into the European territories, there should be no fear of the outcome; and it will make for some beautiful music, too.

The importance does not lie in the mixture of the two, but in the transference and expression of classical music into the jazz idiom in a creative manner. And if this task can be achieved by any one group, the Modern Jazz Quartet would be an exemplary one.

■ ■ ■

Quartered Notes • *November 1964*

BY ROY SALINAS

ONE OF THE MOST POPULAR young vocalists on the current music scene is, by all indications, the lovely and talented Miss Nancy Wilson. Even within these confines she appears to occupy that lofty pedestal usually reserved for the "greats" only.

She seems to be enjoying the same amount of popularity as Ella, Sassy, and the swinging Anita O'Day. Such loyal interest expressed by the handful of faithful readers of this column led to the writing of this portrait of Nancy.

Nancy's first two albums, *Something Wonderful* and *Like in Love*, assisted by the excellent big band of Billy May, did much to enhance her career insofar as musical experience is concerned; they made a small impact in audience recognition. It wasn't until she recorded *The*

Swinging's Mutual with the George Shearing Quintet that she came into prominence as a singer of extraordinary capabilities.

Nancy's rendition of *The Nearness of You* showcases her electrifying and dynamic voice at its best. The freshness that she inflects into this popular ballad makes one feel as though he were listening to it for the very first time. *Green Dolphin Street,* a Miles Davis composition is given a bouncing workout. She does wonders with this familiar jazz "standard." Her phrasing is beautiful and her enunciation perfect.

IN THE NINTH annual Jazz Critics poll in 1961, she copped eighth place in the New Start Division of Female Vocalists. Again in 1963, she was voted into the thirteenth position among the other 12 established singers. A recent issue of Variety Magazine shows her latest album, *Today, Tomorrow, Forever,* has led a lengthy 15 weeks on the best seller lists. While in the single hits section, she has been ably represented for the past nine weeks by another best seller, *How Glad I Am.*

Now the question is, will success spoil her career in jazz? Some of the music critics believe she is leaning too far into the area of supper club, cocktail lounge pop vocalist; but to hear that magnificent set of pipes interpret *Never Will I Marry,* with the Cannonball Adderly group in a hard swing setting, is sheer loveliness.

Perhaps the tune most frequently associated with her is *Hello Young Lovers,* from the album of the same name. Nancy Wilson may not break any barriers in the jazz or pop fields, but she is nevertheless a groovy chick and we dig her.

SOME DAYS AGO I scuffled around until I found some of her sides and I was able to enjoy again the impressible and technically superb tonal qualities of her voice. The tremendous command of song that Nancy has "knocks me out" completely! With these marvelous implements of the trade, along with her charming goods looks, Nancy Wilson has secured her future in the world of music. She is loved by Southern Eskimos and Australian Shrimps, but alas, her drummer husband Kenny Dennis hangs tough at every performance of hers.

■ ■ ■

Quartered Notes • *December 1964*

BY ROY SALINAS

IN KEEPING UP WITH the rapid pace of the ever changing jazz spectrum, many people tend to overlook, neglect, and even cast aside the more sedate and settled musicians.

The well-informed buff who rushes to accept the sophisticated (?) sounds of *new thinger* Don Ellis, may forget Clifford Brown's lyrical beauty, or Fats Navarro's fleet inventiveness. Raving wildly about Archie Shepp and Ornette Coleman might make him oblivious of the warm, sensitive tenor of Ben Webster, the swinging Zoot Sims, and yes, the bluesy horn of Lou Donaldson. In embracing Les McCann's earthly diggings of the soul-funk variety, and Cecil Taylor's weird abstractions, many disregard the lovely pianistics of Oscar Peterson and the extremely tasty piano work of Hank Jones.

Call it nostalgia, romanticism, or whatever. Perhaps I'm just a hip old square (or is it square old hipster?). At any rate, the facility with which Hank Jones' hands builds those single note phrases and the splendid finesse he displays on the keyboards, never fail to tug at my emotions.

IN HIS MOST REFLECTIVE moods, I don't think I've ever heard anyone play more beautifully than Hank; not even Billy Taylor. And if I have, it was without a doubt, Art Tatum.

Born in Pontiac, Michigan, in 1918, Hank comes from a musically prominent family. With his brothers Thad (trumpeter in Basie's band) and drummer Elvin, he has been associated of late with jazzmen from the Detroit area.

Equally at home in any type jazz setting, Hank has been accompanist to Billy Eckstine and Ella. In the album *Somethin' Else!*—not to be confused with Ornette's recording which gives the proper spelling—with Cannonball and Miles, he weaves a pleasant musical pattern around the standard tune *Autumn Leaves* that conveys the mood very effectively. When the time comes to start cookin', he is most able and ready, as he does on the title tune of the same record.

HE IS ONE OF THE elder statesman in jazz who needs no assist from anyone in keeping abreast of the modern scene. Hank has arrived at his instrument and style through constant digging and steady work. He is quite deserving of the title—Jazz Giant.

Wishing all jazz lovers a Cool Yule and a Frantic First!

■ ■ ■

So Much Mystery, So Much Misunderstanding •
Thanksgiving Day, 1964

Dip the brush in mortal goodness . . .
Paint a picture free from hate . . .

Upon the easel of society there is a stark and sordid canvas. The portrait of Drug Addiction as painted by the stinging brushes and the lacerating palette-knives of the exploiters, the sensationalists, and the scandal-mongers.

Fortunately, the progress of modern medicine, psychology, and penology is helping to change that picture; the morbid colors are slowly fading away.

This social enigma is indeed a serious problem. Our institutions are overloaded with addicts. Many receive no treatment or help in curbing their affliction, aside from the daily existence of "doing time." Sen. Thomas J. Dodd, on the U.S. Senate floor said, "We have failed in psychiatric treatment methods; we have failed in medical treatment methods; and we have failed to eliminate narcotics addiction through punishment and correctional efforts."

Our late President John F. Kennedy was aware of this complex problem, when at the opening session of the White House conference on Narcotic and Drug Abuse, September 27, 1962, he said, "I do believe there is no area about which there is so much mystery and in a sense, so much misunderstanding . . . where there is so much difference of opinion."

But has it all been pure failure? How much of this mystery can we attribute to the refusal and lack of understanding of this dilemma? Or perhaps it would be more appropriate to call it indifference, which is worse.

If the criminal aspect is symptomatic, then the addiction itself is definitely a disease. Character defects come under the heading of mental disorders, which vary in degree. Yet addiction is ignored on a purely criminal basis. I strongly believe that any man is mentally unbalanced, who after spending 15 years in prison, heads for the nearest drug source available upon release. He should be placed under psychiatric care. What else can be expected of him if there are no means at his disposal to eradicate the monster that lies dormant in mind and body throughout his incarceration?

The addict is an isolated human wreck. Impregnated with selfishness and greed in his quest for euphoric relief—he is nonetheless a human being. One thing is certain, he needs help! He needs someone to communicate with in trust—someone who can help bring out his innermost feelings on his sickness and make him realize the worthlessness of it. Otherwise he will only keep that sickness at bay until he is free again.

The subject of narcotics is a touchy and not-too-pleasant topic for discussion. Instead of approaching the problem with interest, the general public shies away, because of the stigma that is assumed to be the penalty for sympathizing with the unfortunates caught in the clutches of this unfortunate disease.

As for the addict himself: his plea is not for pity, but for understanding and enlightenment. Most addicts are unaware of the motivational forces that contribute to their addiction. As a result of their receiving no training or guidance they despairingly yield to the malady.

The Harrison Act of 1914 viewed addiction as a law enforcement problem rather than a clinical one. In October 1961 the United States Supreme Court decided that to be in the physical condition of narcotics addiction was not a criminal offense. Perhaps the greatest and most effective asset in fighting the drug problem so far, is the establishment of Synanon House, a rehabilitation center in Santa Monica, California.

Since its beginning in 1958, Synanon has been very successful in its attempts to recondition human lives. According to Dr. Harris Isbell of the United States Public Health Hospital for Addicts at Lexington, Kentucky, the recovery rate there will be between 15 and 25 percent over a five-year period.

On the other hand, Synanon proudly boasts an 83 percent average. Some of these people, confirmed addicts with narcotic histories of up to 20 years, have managed to stay "clean" for the six years that

Synanon has been in existence. One of the main emphases after the withdrawal period at Synanon, is placed on the group therapy sessions. These sessions branch off into the realms of religion, psychology, and sociology, but since these people all have a common bond of addiction, their talks revolve mainly around this bond. The basis is still narcotics.

Authentic and realistic documentary films are being made to replace the outmoded and exaggerated strips. One of the old film's enhancing the public's misconceptions, portrays the addict as a 15-year-old caught shoplifting, with a supply of drugs in his pocket sufficient for a week. The truth is that with this amount in his possession, an addict couldn't care less about getting out of bed!

The other shows a man just released from prison, about to try drugs for the *first* time: His nose is running and he is trembling with the "chills." The old pro in this same film—the go-between—is craving for a "fix" to the point of hysteria. He is wearing a fancy overcoat, wristwatch and ring, as he asks his supplier for some drugs on credit! I don't delight in saying that I have seen addicts walk away barefooted after securing the necessary drugs for their habits, without even giving it a second thought! How absurd and mythical can we get?

Many of the opposers of the addict-as-patient concept, believe that any help extended to this "ruthless breed" will only result in their being pampered. Such pampering is the first impression torn to shreds at Synanon. The individual is subjected to merciless attacks of questioning by other members in the panel discussions, in order to break through his hardened armor.

These organizations and groups need support. People who are in positions to help should not hesitate to offer what is probably the most worthy and significant contribution in the molding and rebuilding of human beings for a better society.

Articles from *Aztlán de Leavenworth,* Kansas Federal Penitentiary

On the History of C.O.R.A. and *Aztlán*

IN THE EARLY PART OF 1970, the prison administrators of Leavenworth saw the need and importance of instituting Ethnic Studies in the educational department for the benefit of the diverse ethnic groups of this penitentiary.

In March of 1970, Professor Francisco H. Ruiz of Penn Valley Community College in Kansas City, Missouri, began teaching a Cultural History of the Southwest class for Chicanos. At various times he brought along graduate students and community workers to assist him in conducting said class.

A newspaper, which bears the title Aztlán, meaning "the lands to the North," assumed to have been the point of origin for the Aztec nation, came into existence with the first issue printed in May 1970.[†] To date, there have been four issues printed. With a rare exception, the material for the paper is strictly Chicano convict work. We do not solicit outside material, and only on one occasion have we featured an article by someone other than the Chicano population of Leavenworth. In this manner we try to stress the importance of originality and the nurturing of unknown hidden talents in the arts, poetry, journalism, publications work, and public speaking. Emphasis is placed on Higher Education as one solution to "the" problem.

Chicano-oriented films are brought in from time to time, such as "Yo Soy Joaquin," a filmed documentary of Corky Gonzales' epic poem of the same name. Also, "Delano," dealing with the farmworkers march to the state capitol at Sacramento in 1967.

In October of the same year, the class evolved into a combination of Chicano Studies and Cultural Group. A committee was formed (through general elections) as follows: Meme Duran, Chairman; Dickie Mena, V. Chairman; Pelon Avila, Recording Secretary; Dickie Pineda (Alberto Mares), Correspondence Secretary; Alberto Palomino, Programs Chairman; Ruben Estrella, Publicity Chairman; and raúlrsalinas, Editor. This committee held forth until April 1971, when their 6 month tenure was up. Then, the second committee was elected. These were the results: Dickie Mena, Chairman; Ramon Chacon, V. Chairman; Carlos Becerra, Recording Secretary; Jose Rubio, Correspondence Secretary; Hector Vargas, Programs Chairman; Tone Briones, Publicity Chairman; and raúlrsalinas, Editor.

The name C.O.R.A. (Chicanos Organizados Raza de Aztlán), submitted by Beto Gudino, was chosen for our group. We have been functioning now for 17 months. Our weekly meetings are conducted thusly: Friday nights from 6 to 9 p.m. Committee business & reports (correspondences, newspaper, grievances, etc.), then, one of our members is selected as main speaker for the evening. He is selected from the general membership and asked a week in advance to talk on whatever is relevant to the Chicano cause. Following this, outside guests are introduced. These may consist of students, professors, farmworkers, businessmen, local politicians and neighborhood counselors; both male and female. The last hour is devoted to lectures by the professor concerning the Castilian language, Maya & Aztec history, and Art & Literature of Mexico and the Southwestern United States. Our accomplishments are few but they are obviously noticeable. Our artists have participated in the Raza Art Festival in Houston, Texas and won awards at the religious art show at Leavenworth penitentiary. The painting of one our brothers is being used on an album cover of a popular recording star's music. Their paintings have appeared on local TV and videotape. Our writers are also gaining an audience outside. The poets have been quoted extensively and one is in the process of having several poems published in an Anthology of Chicano Literature which will be published by Prentice-Hall and one by Knopf Publisher later on in the year. Our newspaper has been acclaimed *the* best publication in the Chicano Press Association, both in prison and out. We have been quoted in the *Guardian*, *The Village Voice*, *La Raza*, *Con Safos*, *Entrelineas*, and the Cabinet of Spanish Speaking Affairs in Washington, D.C. We now have 20 Chicanos enrolled in the college program, and many more in the High School level.

† *Editor's Note:* This unpublished essay was written by Salinas in early March 1972 to document the formation of this important Chicano prisoner group. Beto Gudino actually proposed Chicanos Organizados *Rebeldes* de Aztlán for the group name. This name was accepted in principle, but the group adopted Chicanos Organizados *Raza* de Aztlán as its "above ground" name so as not to draw unwanted suspicion upon themselves from prison officials.

■ ■ ■

Aztlán's Statement of Philosophy • *Número 1, Año 1, 5 de Mayo de 1970*

Aztlán: "the lands to the north." The legendary site assumed to have been the Aztecs' point of origin in their mass exodus south to Tenochtitlan, which today we know as Mexico City.

The theories regarding the geographical location of these fabled lands are many. Yet, should one combine these theories, one would find that a number of them fix the site well within the boundaries of the Southwestern United States.

At the National Chicano Youth Liberation Conference held in Denver in March of this year, it was decided that (among other things), indeed, the Southwestern states would henceforth be recognized as the nation of Aztlán.

The Chicano convicts of Leavenworth number approximately 400. By no mere coincidence, the greatest percentage of us come from the aforementioned area.

It is with this spirit of our ancestors deeply rooted within us and a pride in our homestates, that we consider ourselves, behind prison walls, true representatives of Aztlán. A miniature nation is, perhaps, more appropriate.

Therefore, in good faith and for a true cause, we feel justified in having chosen *Aztlán* as the title for our newspaper.

Like everything else that has gone into making the existence of this newspaper possible, the selection of the title was a group effort. It goes

NÚMERO 1   LEAVENWORTH, 5 DE MAYO DE 1970   AÑO I

AZTLÁN --"the lands to the north". The legendary site assumed to have been the Aztec's point of origin in their mass exodus south to Tenochtitlán, which today we know as México City.

The theories regarding the geographical location of these fabled lands are many. Yet, should one combine these theories, one would find that a number of them fix the site well within the boundaries of the Southwestern United States.

At the National Chicano Youth Liberation Conference, held in Denver in March of this year, it was decided that (among other things), indeed, the Southwestern states would henceforth be recognized as the nation of AZTLÁN.

The Chicano convicts of Leavenworth number approximately 400. By no mere coincidence, the greatest percentage of us come from the aforementioned area.

It is with this spirit of our ancestors deeply rooted within us and a pride in our homestates, that we consider ourselves, behind prison walls, true representatives of AZTLÁN. A miniature nation is, perhaps, more appropriate.

Therefore, in good faith and for a true cause, we feel justified in having chosen AZTLÁN as the title for our newspaper.

Like everything else that has gone into making the existence of this newspaper possible, the selection of the title was a group effort. It goes without saying, that the suggestion for an Aztec motif with corresponding designs were selected in the same manner for obvious reasons.

The two figures on either side of the title represent Tizoc, an Aztec king (A. D. 1481-1486). They are found sculptured on the Stone of Tizoc, which is in the National Museum of México City. The stepped border designs surrounding the figures and title is taken from pictures of Aztec ceramic pottery.

The goals of our newspaper are twofold: to Destroy and Rebuild. To destroy the myth of the worthless Chicano; the misconception of his non-productivity; the prejudice that exists, for lack of understanding, in the minds of many; the inferior feeling which we may, or may not, be possessed of. To rebuild the image of ourselves in the eyes of others; the dignity to face the world as Chicanos and Men; the sense of pride in who we are. And, finally, to establish communication among ourselves and with our people, wherever they may be. We can accomplish these goals because: SOMOS AZTLÁN!

AZTLÁN -- "las tierras hacia el norte". El sitio legendario que se presume fue el punto donde se originó el éxodo de los aztecas hacia Tenochtitlán, la que hoy conocemos como Ciudad de México.

Las teorías tocante a la posición geográfica de estas fabulosas tierras son muchas y variadas. Sin embargo, si combináramos todas estas teorías, encontraríamos que la mayoría de ellas fijan bien el sitio dentro de la emarcación del sudoeste de los Estados Unidos de Norteamérica.

En la Conferencia Nacional de la Liberación de la Juventud Chicana celebrada en Denver, Colorado, en marzo de este año, se decidió, entre otras cosas, que los estados del sudoeste de los Estados Unidos de Norteamérica serían reconocidos como la nación de AZTLÁN.

Los convictos Chicanos de Leavenworth somos alrededor de cuatrocientos. Pero, no por mera coincidencia, la mayoría de nosotros procedemos de las tierras antes mencionadas.

Con el espíritu de nuestros antepasados tan profundamente enraizado dentro de nosotros, y con un sentido de orgullo de nuestros estados nativos, aun dentro de estas paredes y barras nos consideramos verdaderos representantes de AZTLÁN. Pudiéramos decir, quizás, que formamos una pequeña nación.

Por lo tanto, con buena fe y verdadera causa creemos más que justificado el haber escogido AZTLÁN como nombre para nuestro periódico.

Como todos los pasos que se han dado para hacer posible la existencia de este periódico, la selección de su nombre también ha sido un esfuerzo colectivo. De más está decir que la decoración azteca en el título fue seleccionada en la misma forma por razones obvias.

Las dos figuras dibujadas a cada lado del título son de Tizoc, rey azteca (1481-1486) Se encuentra esculpida en la piedra de Tizoc, que está en el Museo Nacional de la Ciudad de México. Las cenefas, alrededor de las figuras y el título, fueron tomadas de retratos de vasijas de cerámica azteca.

Los propósitos de nuestro periódico son dos: Destruir y Reconstruir. Destruir el mito de la poca valía del Chicano; el falso concepto de su falta de productividad; el prejuicio que existe, por falta de comprensión, en las mentes de muchos; los sentimientos de inferioridad de los cuales podemos o no estar poseídos. Para reconstruir la imagen nuestra ante los ojos ajenos; la dignidad de enfrentar el mundo como Chicanos y Hombres; un sentido de orgullo en quiénes somos. Y, finalmente, para establecer comunicación entre nosotros y con nuestro pueblo, en donde quiera que estemos. Nosotros podemos lograr estos propósitos porque: ¡SOMOS AZTLÁN!

PARA AZTLÁN   DE OSCAR J. VIGLIANO.

AZTLÁN ha despertado. No ha despertado por el ruido de la casualidad, sino por el ruido, más fuerte, de la necesidad. Todos te conocíamos, AZTLÁN, pero no sabíamos cómo llamarte. Eras como un hombre admirado por el barrio entero, pero por miedo o por respeto no nos acercábamos a hablarte. Miedo porque hay quien te cree peligroso, respeto porque nosotros los que te conocemos sabemos que lo mereces. Hoy nos reunimos con fervor de hermanos. Tú nos unes. Aun en las horas negras del pasado la Raza no te olvidaba, la Raza siempre te admiró, te necesitaba. Pero la Raza sí fue olvidada, fue ingultada, fue defraudada, maniatada y hasta a veces...encarcelada. Tú nos unes. Quizás un nuevo horizonte se Levanta, quién sabe dónde. Nosotros lo buscamos, Te necesitamos, AZTLÁN. Aztlán quedarán aunque sea por un segundo, los crímenes cometidos y los no cometidos, los castigos, las justicias y las injusticias, los horrores, todos "esos" recuerdos. Queremos volar contigo, AZTLÁN, y contigo soñar, pero soñar realidades.

Muchos estamos presos, algunos de nosotros mismos, otros de otro destino. Unos con sentencia, otros sin. Unos con uniforme, otros sin. Ahora AZTLÁN se ha despertado y nos une a todos fuertemente. Juntos queremos hablar, queremos gritar, queremos aprender, queremos escuchar, queremos enseñar, queremos OFRECER. Que por medio de AZTLÁN dejemos a los cuerpos encerrados y hagamos volar a nuestras almas, que son libres, por las inexploradas alturas de la esperanza.

First Issue of Aztlán de Leavenworth *(May 5, 1970). Courtesy of Dept. of Special Collections, Stanford University Libraries.*

A Trip Through The Mind Jail

for Eldridge

SUPLEMENTO - PAG. UNO - AZTLÁN - LEAVENWORTH
5 DE MAYO DE 1970

LA LOMA
Neighborhood of my youth
demolished, erased forever from
the universe.
You live on, captive, in the lonely
cellblocks of my mind.
Neighborhood of endless hills
muddied streets--all chuckhole lined--
that never drank of asphalt.
Kids barefoot/snotty-nosed
playing marbles, munching on bean tacos
(the kind you'll never find in a café)
2 peaceful generations removed from
their abuelos' revolution.
Neighborhood of dilapidated community hall
---Salón Cinco de Mayo---
yearly (May 5/Sept. 16) gathering
of the familias. Re-asserting pride
on those two significant days.
Speeches by the elders
patriarchs with evidence of oppression
distinctly etched upon mestizo faces.
"Sons of the Independence!"
Emphasis on allegiance to the tri-color
obscure names: Juárez & Hidalgo
their heroic deeds. Nostalgic tales of war
years under Villa's command. No one listened,
no one seemed to really care.
Afterwards, the dance. Modest Mexican
maidens dancing polkas together
across splintered wooden floor.
They never deigned to dance with boys!
The careful scrutiny by curbstone sex-perts
8 & 9 years old. "Kingie's bow-legged,
so we know she's done it, huh?"
Neighborhood of Sunday night jamaicas
at Guadalupe Church.
Fiestas for any occasion
holidays holy days happy days
'round and 'round the promenade
eating snow-cones---raspas---& tamales
the games--bingo cake walk spin the wheel
making eyes at girls from cleaner neighborhoods
the unobtainables
who responded all giggles and excitement.
Neighborhood of forays down to Buena Vista--
Santa Rita Courts--Los projects--friendly neighborhood
cops n' robbers on the rooftops, sneaking peeks
in people's private night-time bedrooms
bearing gifts of Juicy Fruit gum for
the Projects girls/chasing them in adolescent heat
causing skinned knees & being run off for the night
disenchanted walking home affections spurned
stopping stay-out-late chicks in search of
Modern Romance lovers, who always stood them up
unable to leave their world in the magazines pages.
angry fingers grabbing, squeezing, feeling,
french kisses imposed; close bodily contact, thigh &
belly rubbings under shadows of Cristo Rey Church.
Neighborhood that never saw a school-bus
the cross-town walks were much more fun
embarassed when acquaintances or friends or relatives
were sent home excused from class
for having cooties in their hair!
Did only Mexicans have cooties in their hair?
¿Qué gacho!
Neighborhood of Zaragoza Park
where scary stories interspersed with
inherited superstitions were exchanged
waiting for midnight and the haunting
lament of La Llorona---the weeping lady
of our myths & folklore---who wept nightly,
along the banks of Boggy Creek,
for the children she'd lost or drowned
in some river (depending on the version).
i think i heard her once
and cried
out of sadness and fear
running all the way home nape hairs at attention
swallow a pinch of table salt and
make the sign of the cross
sure cure for frightened Mexican boys.
Neighborhood of Spanish Town Cafe
first grown-up (13) Argmout
Andres,
tolerant manager, proprietor, cook
victim of bungling baby burglars
your loss: Fritos n' Pepsi-Colas---was our gain

you put up with us and still survived!
You too, are granted immortality.
Neighborhood of groups and clusters
sniffing gas, drinking muscatel
solidarity   cement hardening
the clan   the family   the neighborhood   the gang
Nomás!
Restless innocents tattoo'd crosses on their hands
"just doing things different"
"From now on, all troublemaking mex kids will
be sent to Gatesville for 9 months."
Worry home from la corte
khakis worn too low---below the waist
the stomps, the greña with duck-tail
-Pachuco Yo-
Neighborhood of could-be artists
who plied their talents on the pool's
bath-house walls/ intricately adorned
with esoteric symbols of their cult:
the art form of our slums
more meaningful & significant
then Egypt's finest hieroglyphics.
Neighborhood where purple clouds of Yesca
smoke one day descended & embraced us all.
Skulls uncapped--Rhythm n' Blues
                    Chaile's 7th. St. Club
loud negro music-wine spodee-odees-barbecue-grass
our very own connection man: big black Johnny B------.
Neighborhood of Reyes' Bar
where Lalo shotgunned
Pete Evans to death because of
an unintentional glare,
and because he was encuadre,
only to end his life neatly sliced
by prison barber's razor.
Duran's grocery & gas station
where drunkenly stabbed Julio
arguing over who'd drive home
and got 55 years for his crime.
Raton: 20 years for a matchbox of weed. Is that cold?
No lawyer no jury no trial i'm guilty.
Aren't we all guilty?
Indian mothers, too, so unaware
of courtroom tragi-comedies
folded arms across their bosoms
saying, "Sea por Dios."
Neighborhood of my childhood
neighborhood that no longer exists
some died young--fortunate--more rot in prisons
the rest drifted away to be conjured up
in minds of others like them.
For me: only the NOW of THIS journey is REAL!
Neighborhood of my adolescence
neighborhood that is no more
YOU ARE TORN PIECES OF MY FLESH!!!
Therefore, you ARE.
LA LOMA---AUSTIN---MY BARRIO---
i bear you no grudge
i needed you then..identity..a sense of belonging.
i need you now.
So essential to adult days of imprisonment,
you keep me away from INSANITY'S hungry jaws;
                    Smiling/Laughing/Crying.
i respect your having been:
My Loma of Austin
my Rose Hill of Los Angeles
my West Side of San Anto
my Quinto of Houston
my Jackson of San Jo
my Segundo of El Paso
my Barelas of Alburque
my Westside of Denver
Flats, Los Marcos, Maravilla, Calle Guadalupe, Magnolia,
Buena Vista, Mateo, La Seis, Chiquis, El Sur and all
Chicano neighborhoods that now exist and once
existed; somewhere....., someone remembers.....

                    raúlrsalinas
                    14, Sept.-'69

Salinas' signature poem as it first appeared in Aztlán *(May 5, 1970). Courtesy of Dept. of Special Collections, Stanford University Libraries.*

without saying, that the suggestion for an Aztec motif with corresponding designs were selected in the same manner for obvious reasons.

The two figures on either side of the title represent Tizoc, an Aztec
king (A.D. 1481–1486). They are found sculptured on the Stone of
Tizoc, which is in the National Museum of Mexico City. The stepped
border designs surrounding the figures and title is taken from pictures
of Aztec ceramic pottery.

The goals of our newspaper are twofold: to Destroy and Rebuild.
To destroy the Myth of the worthless Chicano; the misconception of
his non-productivity; the prejudice that exists, for lack of understanding, in the minds of many; the inferior feelings which we may, or may
not, be possessed by. To rebuild the image of ourselves in the eyes of
others; the dignity to face the world as Chicanos and Men; the sense of
pride in who we are. And finally, to establish communication among
ourselves and with our people, wherever they may be. We can accomplish these goals because: SOMOS AZTLAN!

■ ■ ■

Music for the Masses • *Número 1, Año 1, 2 de Febrero de 1972*

> . . . Revolutionaries will come to sing the song of the new
> man with the authentic voice of the people.
> —Ernesto Guevara de la Serna

Music, as part of a people's culture cannot be appreciated (nor
respected) if an understanding of it is lacking. An understanding of
those components in various forms that go into the execution of a
song.

True, Chicano music, like all western world music, has an undeniable link with European tradition. Not so much in the Germanic, as in
the Spanish vein. That is to say, Villa-lobos, rather than Bach. Still,
there is a unique quality to the Chicano form of art-song. This quality,
we can proudly proclaim, stems from the Indio side of our noble,
hybrid race.

The forms of Chicano music range from Spanish classical music,
enjoyed principally by the aristocrats, to *Rancheras* (country & west-

ern), which are so much a part of the plebeian working masses. From the sophisticated boleros and *Ritmos Tropicales*, to the *Corridos* and *Tragedias* (ballads & folk songs) which flourished during the Mexican Revolution of 1910–1920.

Today, our people in Mexico and the united states interpret all idioms of the music, including jazz and rock. This is possible, primarily, because of the respect and sympathy we maintain for the myriad and diverse cultures that abound in the world.

However, this is not sufficient. Now, we need/demand/require that the same respect and understanding be accorded our music . . . Latin, Spanish, Mexican, CHICANO music! Especially, when we are invited to perform.

To accomplish this end—effectively and harmoniously—it is necessary to institute two requisites: of the musicians, it is expected that they practice, study and rehearse their repertoire to as near-perfection as possible. Of the english-speaking audiences, it is demanded that they open up their ears and . . . listen! If they do so, then our music will become their music too.

But, most people don't listen . . . or they do so with preconceived negative notions; as evidenced by the review which appeared in the Kansas City Star, concerning the music of EL CHICANO. The article was totally lacking in understanding, as prejudice oozed out from under the subtle guise of hipness.

We pintos at Leavenworth heard much more than the conservatively stuffed ears of one Jerry Kohler. EL CHICANO, the latin/jazz/rock conglomerate from East L.A., first came on the national scene with the version of Gerald Wilson's "VIVA TIRADO," in an album by the same name VIVA—TIRADO (Kapp Records KS3632). This phenomenal musical group played an afternoon concert on the yard of this prison on Tuesday, August 17, 1971. And, it was an unforgettable experience. After a half hour video tape interview with Aztlán staff and C.O.R.A members, they set up an array of electronic equipment under the hot Midwestern skies and played!

Because they were promoting their latest release, entitled REVOLU-CION (Kapp Records KS 3640), most of the selections played were from this album, although they did play several which are not included in that recording. With their opening number, "Keep Moving On," they did just that to the crowd, as we got an audial taste of the

"Brown Sound." This is what they call their particular music: "THE BROWN SOUND".

Technically speaking, the music of EL CHICANO is not original in the sense that they invented it, nor do they lay claim to as much. Instead, within the context of their sound, we hear the hypnotic Afro-Cuban beat, the soft strains of the Spanish boleros and the driving energy of american rock. Another unique facet of this group is the manner in which these diverse musical influences are merged, then filtered through, interpreted and expressed through the medium of the soul of these barrio youth.

The sextet is composed of Bassist-Leader Freddie Sanchez, Organist-Pianist Bob Espinoza, Guitarist Mickey Lespron, Drummer Johnny De Luna, Conga Drummer Andre Baeza, and the lovely Ersi Arvizu—La Chicana—on the vocals and assorted percussive instruments (maracas, guiro, cecerro, claves). As if there is one catalyst which fuses this group into the musical entity that it is, without any doubt, it is Baeza and the bombarding sounds of his congas. He drove the group and the audience to its highest levels of intensity, with running commentary between numbers.

On "Viva La Raza," the shy and frail, pony-tailed, bespectacled guitarist Mickey Lespron becomes a righteous bad monster! And though a press release from their recording company lists among his influences Freddie King by way of the late Wes Montgomery, his eclecticism shone through radiantly in his tribute to another late guitarist, Jimi Hendrix. Mickey went into a stoned out frenzy on this killer jam, then he began to caress the electric goddess with his teeth! During this extreme output of raw energy, his pony-tail came undone and his flowing mane covered his wire glasses completely, but he continued hooking up phrases one after another; sounds chasing sounds, becoming one in split infinitesimal seconds, far out into space.

Coming down from this musical high was no easy task. As if to cushion the ride, the tempo slowed down. On stage came the Brown Barrio Princess of Song. Wearing brown, calf-length lace-up boots, and brown hot-pants, Ersi also wore a white poncho with red and green border, which was knitted especially for her, as a gift from the pinto population. Unlike that lame reviewer (?) for the K.C. Star, this audience knew what was happening when the intro was laid down on "Sabor a Mi" (A Taste of Me). Nothing resembling schmaltz; much more, it was mood music, the kind heard throughout the barrios of Aztlán and Mexico. This is land, a far cry from the heart of america. Needless to say the soft, tropical rhythm interplays behind Ersi's dusky, throaty voice, literally mesmerized us in sound.

There were other, equally soul-soothing, moments. One that endeared the gracious vocalist to her listeners was when she dedicated a very tender and moving song to her brown brothers and other hip peoples who recognize our struggle. The title of her tune was "Te Adoro" (I Adore You) and more than a love song, it was sheer poetry full of compassion. When she ended the song, she lowered her head and remained thusly for an eternity into seconds. When she did raise up to face the stunned prisoners, there were tears streaming down her cheeks. No schmaltz here, Mr. Kohler; just some good old latin soul— Con Alma!

This was followed by some soul-tinged number of the Tina Turner/Sly Stone variety, complete with unrestrained vocal abandon, frenetic gyrations, and complete freedom of the human voice. Heat generated prevailed.

Some familiar tunes were here too. "Cubano Chant" was given a very hip interpretation, as was Martin Denny's "Quiet Village." The last two tunes were definite Chicano statements. One was "Chicano Chant," or as we know it, "El Grito." Andre Baeza, at this point said, "we call our thing "THE BROWN SOUND," because we are brown dudes from the barrio. We call our group EL CHICANO, in the singular sense, because we function as a unit, a vehicle to present Chicano people to the world. Our music is not limited to brown audiences, it is meant for all the people who care to dig it." As he went into a conga barrage with "Don't Put Me Down (cause I'm brown)," Bob Espinoza's wailing organ enhanced the power of Baeza's narration. They got a thing going between them that left the prisoners in an uproar as screaming organ interwove with staccato conga offbeat patterns. Comments voiced around the joint immediately following the performance, and for days/weeks/months after, were as numerous as they were different.

And there were the usual questions among *some* listeners as what evaluation, if any, to apply to the music heard. There were a few who in this new dawn still questioned the validity of the group's sound. You know, the "they stole our music" bunch. As if music gave a damn who played it, just as long as you ain't jiving. I know a black poet doing more Dylan Thomas than Langston Hughes (Never Don L. or Leroi) and I appreciate him nonetheless. Those sideline critics, non-musicians just didn't hear what was laid on them, out front. One thing is certain, EL CHICANO has that intrinsic quality which appeals to the listening tastes of all audiences. And yes, many influences can be heard in their sound, as was said before. That they readily, and without hesitation, pay musical and verbal tribute to these influences is what's important to us as Chicanos. And for those folks who still cling to conditioned thoughts about EL CHICANO employing *their* music, whoever *they* may be; relax. We can't afford to play the MAN'S game.

These musicians' experience as a downtrodden people helps them to create and interpret, rather than to imitate. Besides, the social implications were quite obvious, if one only dared to pick it up. At any rate, and for the most part, nothing less than appreciation was expressed for EL CHICANO'S memorable concert by the convicted masses of Leavenworth.

Chicanos in this society (or that one) need to create for themselves and their people the artistic arms necessary in our struggle for liberation. One way is to break the controlled media barrier. This too, is what EL CHICANO is about. Prior to May of this year, according to our limited sources, no Chicano Press Association paper had given them any coverage. Now, they have been written about in Papel Chicano, a Houston publication, and El Tecolote of San Francisco, plus a mere mention in a couple of others. The L.A. Freep gave them the most extensive review to date, and this only days after the East L.A. desmadre. On their tour through the Mid West, the only radio advertisement came from KBEY, a rock underground station in Kansas City, Mo. Sad to say, the only "Mexican-American" program in the area panicked behind the group's name! And to you hip and/or Raza entrepreneurs place your bread on a winning team. Should they by any chance charge a high price for their music (as has been implied in some quarters), it will be a wise investment. Rest assured that their efforts will be expanded generously, for worthwhile causes.

A perfect example of this is the fact that half of their performances are benefits for La Raza. After the show here, they were scheduled to appear at Basin Street-West in San Francisco, at which time they would make a side trip to San Quentin. Whether they played at "Q" is not known, since on their scheduled date an overly publicized tragedy occurred at that prison. Their benefit concerts which the group has performed have been: a panel discussion at the University of California–Irvine Campus entitled *"The Chicano and the Legal System,"* for which they furnished the music on May, 3 1971. After their impressive Leavenworth appearance, they played at La Semana de La Raza in San Antonio on September 11 & 12. There have been concerts in Albuquerque and Houston, also.

As convictos, who aren't always thought of as humane creatures we'd like to express our sincerest gratitude to the people who made the show possible: the Parra brothers—Bob & Fred—whose *Mexican-American Organization for Progress* sponsored the sextet in Kansas City; the insistent Prof. Francisco H. Ruiz, who teaches our Cultural History of the Southwest Class, for realizing the social value of bringing a dynamite group such as this into the penitentiary; the keepers of the keys for opening the front door; and, mostly to what came in, once the doors were opened: EL CHICANO. Those competent makers of the "Brown Sound," who rendered us an unforgettable afternoon. Who filled the void with some moments that will sustain our tormented hearts and should for a long time to come . . . and then some.

raúlrsalinas
Austin/Aztlán

"Editor's Notes," caricature by Carlos Becerra, Aztlán

■ ■ ■

Editor's Notes • *Número 1, Año 2, 2 de Febrero de 1972*

BY RAÚLRSALINAS

All graphic illustrations, cartoons, pen & ink drawings in this issue—except when otherwise noted—are the original creations flowing from the Boss Rapidograph pen of the multi-talented artist, Carlos Becerra. Carlos is an instructor of Spanish, promising oil painter, and excellent caricaturist. He is a valuable asset to the family of Aztlán artists. This is a highly competent draftsman from San Anto, who merits much attention. More of his imaginative work will be featured in future editions of Aztlán. Here is a dude who bears watching, and perhaps, worth sweating out, at the front door. CPA Publications—pick up!

Workers in this issue not credited elsewhere: Ramoncio Lozano, Hawaiiano, Fred Bustillo, Maique, Juan Adams, El Chato, Montecalvo, and all who will be helping to wrap-up this edition.

Well, we made it through this first year without losing all of our marbles: 1972 is THE year for many brothers and sisters in the slams. Much happened with the PEOPLE in 1971; both good and bad. Especially, in the final hours.

Tragedy occurred in the prison camps. Penal Reform became a fashionable, but empty term. Particularly was it favored by politicians. Attica brought everything out front. The existence of the bastilles was personified. A tender warrior fell in Q.

Chan's axe unleashed. Jack Venable's guitar was stilled. Latest news front the Coast, saddening. Alfonso "El Pache!" Alvarez, is no more. Before his death, this dedicated brother from Flats/Los, had made some gigantic strides; a magnificent transformation. He was wholly totally involved; committed to the betterment of La Raza and all the common people. Most of us didn't know him personally, but we felt his spirit, nonetheless. There had been some correspondence between us and La Raza. Por Los Pintos, an organization he helped to establish. Que Aguite!

Compa had his thoughts recorded, other Boricua's not as fortunate. Talamantez & Pinell vegetate in H section, Reies ever struggling. Second level of socio-political awareness is some spooky. John S. basks in the sun, PUN needs the SUN. Ericka is breathing fresh air, sister A.Y. D., cannot. Do YOU know the way to San Jose?

Under the "Circus Tent" the pornzines got star bill. On the other hand, Tania, A/2 Sun, Chicano Manifesto, Vladimir Nikolai L., and Brother G.J.'s kites were not featured due to uptight delay, temporary internment, and plain old paranoic screwtiny. Ex-alumnus Ramon Tijerina taking care of business: Teatro de Aztlán troupe member, co-editor-"Piramide del Sol" and something-or-other in the Art Dept. at Jacinto Treviño College at Mercedes TX. In Seattle, Rene has arrived. In Austin, Alma Canales continues her struggle for La Raza Unida Party and for the people—with a fierce dedication. In San Anto, el Mario coming through, loud and clear. There is much work to be done, yet. Madness reigns in the ZOO . . . and elsewhere, also. INSANITY MAY BE JUST AROUND THE CORNER!

■ ■ ■

Repaso • *Número Uno, Año Dos, 2 de Febrero de 1972*

Esta edición de *Aztlán*, da empiezo (¿comienzo?) al segundo año de existencia a nuestra publicación. Es de aquellas, recordar aquel ayer cuando se expresaba la necesidad de una "voz," para la clase de Historia Cultural de Sudoeste—cual se inició en esta prisión en febrero de 1970, bajo la instrucción del Prof. Francisco H. Ruiz y su asistente, Oscar J. Vigiliano.

Nunca nos imaginamos, cuando se nos dió el permiso, de lo que encontraríamos en el proceso de hechar a rodar nuestro papiro. Todavía llevo fotografiado en la mente, el grupito de tres individuos, que se reunieron sobre un cafecito negro, a discutir la formación de la publicación colectiva: *Aztlán*.

Se habían leido una serie de articulos en el periódico *La Opinión*, titulados *Aztlán: Cuna de los Aztecas*, y sobre esta información, cual los tres poseían, se sugerió el nombre *Aztlán*. La Conferencia Nacional de la Juventud Chicana, celebró su segundo año en Denver, Colorado; donde se documento El Plan Espiritual de Aztlán, y ésto sirvio para afirmar concretamente la decisión.

Tan pronto se pusieron de acuerdo en el nombre del periódico,

empezó la maquinara a caminar con mas rapidéz. Uno de los camaradas cursaba una clase de antropología, sobre los indios de
norteamérica, y en su texto llevaba en la portada una esculturita del
rey Azteco, Tizóc. Allí mismo, con tinta emprestada, por detrás de un
calendario, se dibujó el primer modelo del "masthead" que ahoy porta
nuestro papel, *Aztlán*.

 Como llano en fuego, se extendió el "alambre" por las galerías,
corredores y yarda de esta horrendo canton. Se solicitaba palanca en
forma de asistencia, escrituras, ensayos, pensamientos, arte, poesías,
etc. La llamada—a según se ha visto—no fue en vano. Con una
maquinita tipográfica, de modelo antíguo (que hasta la fecha, con
excepción rara, todavía usamos) convertida en Chicana, se fue trans-
formando el material escríto a mano, en columnas listas para la
imprenta. Se utilizaban los momentos y lugares para trabajar, cómo y
dónde se presentaran. Ya se hacía un trocito en la escuela por las
noches; en el "law library", sitio de recreo, y la oficina del capellán
católico, por los sábados y domingos. ¡Que recuerdos!

 Se realizó el primer número, con fecha de Cinco de Mayo pero no
salió hasta quince días después. Así de esa, manera fue como sigueron
publicandose los siguientes números; espóradicamente.

 Los contribuyentes en esta edición inicial consistían de trece pintos
y un carnal de "la libre". Este fue el asistente del profesor de nuestra
clase Historicultural. Como sólo tuvimos un "press run" de 500 ejemplares, y no esperabamos tener tan buen éxito, de pronto se hizo
exhaust el *supply* y llegó a considerase, por alguien mas que nosotros,
un "collector's item". Se nos permitieron 4 páginas, con un suplemento, en las cuales se incluyeron artículos sobre nuestra relación
hacia el concepto de Aztlán; solidaridad por el Habanero; darditos por
el compa Boricua; con poco arte y poesías, también. Los mensajes de
los carnales cubrían varios temas distintos. De Califas, nos aconsejaba
El Meño que ya era tiempo de "alivianar la concha"; de Denver, que
nos pusieramos a analizar la situación de nuestra gente en la lucha por
los derechos humanos. Hubo otros mas mensajes sobre la cultura e
historia.

 Dos semanas después de que *Aztlán* pegó a la calle, se formó un
"Workshop", para discutir ideas sobre futuras ediciones de nuestro
recién-nacido papiro. Las reuniones se efectuaban los jueves por las
noches.

El segundo número se propuso para el 26 de Julio, para dar reconocimiento a la lucha de nuestros camaradas del Caimán. Pues, otra vez pasó lo de antes. La prensa no rodo hasta septiembre 1970. En éste número, ya se estaba desarrollando conciencia socio-política en las mentes de las personas envueltas en nuestra clase y periódico.

Para el tercer y cuarto números de Aztlán ya se refería a los sucesos del movimiento Chicano; las muertes en los barrios, la opresión, y los problemas del tercer mundo. Los pintores/artistas también comenzaban a expresar sus ideas, a según ellos comprendían los problemas sociales, políticos, y económicos.

En el curso de este año pasado, hubo "cachúques", disgustos, y mail-entendimientos. Pero, esto es lo natural; adémas, al mismo tiempo se estaba realizando el progreso de *Aztlán*. Nuestros pintores, poetas, y escribanos fueron dandose a conocer através de sus esfuerzos dirigidos al mejoramiento de la Raza Chicana. Los papiros de la prensa Chicana nos dieron su apoyo con usar y reproducir varios artículos dibujos nuestros.

Una de las revistas Chicanas que mas dió exposición a los pintos del Once en general y los contribuyentes en particular, fue *Entrelíneas*. Tal revista es publicada por el Prof. Ruiz y sus redactores han sido muy generosos con su apoyo y asistencia en nuestras labores literarias/artísticas.

Así es que llegamos a este punto; batallando con las distintas personalidades, dando luz a talentos ocultos, dispertando conciencia, comunicando con los nuestros en el otro lado del paredón, participando, y aprendiendo a trabajar juntos para el alcance de una meta común. Esperamos qué con éste numero, la dedicación aumente; para tumbar las barreras de ignorancia, indiferencia y apatía; que existen en el mundo entero. He aquí nuestra contribución.

Review (translation)

This issue of Aztlán begins (starts?) our publication's second year of existence. It's amazing to recall those days when the call for a "voice" was being made, for the Southwest Cultural History course—which was begun in this prison in February 1970, under the direction of Professor Francisco H. Ruiz and his assistant, Oscar S. Vigiliano.

We never imagined, when we were given permission, what we

would encounter in the process of rolling out our little paper. I still have the image in my mind, the little group of three individuals, that met over a cup of black coffee, to discuss the formation of the collective publication: *Aztlán*.

They had read a series of articles in the newspaper *La Opinión* entitled "Aztlán: Birthplace of the Aztecs," and with this information that the three possessed, the name Aztlán was suggested. The Chicano National Youth Conference celebrated its second anniversary in Denver, Colorado; where the *Spiritual Plan of Aztlán* was written, and this served to concretely affirm this decision.

As soon as they agreed on the name of the newspaper, the mechanism began to move with more speed. One of the brothers was taking a class in anthropology, on the indians of North America, and on his book the cover had a little statue of the Aztec King, Tizóc. At that moment, with borrowed ink, on the back of a calendar, the first draft of the "masthead" that our paper now sports, *Aztlán*, was drawn.

Like a prairie fire, the news was "wired" throughout the tiers, corridors and yard of this horrendous home. We sought support in the form of assistance, writings, essays, thoughts, art, poems, etc. The call—as one has seen—was not in vain. With a little mechanical typewriter, an ancient model (that to date, with rare exception, we still use) converted into a Chicano machine, we began transforming handwritten material, into print-ready columns. We found the time and place to work, however and whenever they presented themselves. We did a little in the school at night; in the "law library," recreation yard, and the Catholic chaplain's office, on Saturdays and Sundays. What memories!

We finished with the first issue, with the date of May 5th but it did not come out until fifteen days later. This is the way that the other issues were published: sporadically.

The contributors in this inaugural issue consisted of thirteen Chicano convicts and a "freeworld" brother. This was the assistant to our Cultural History professor. Since we only had a "press run" of 500 copies, and did not expect to have so much success, the supply quickly was exhausted and it came to be known, by someone other than us, as a "collector's item." We had four pages, with a supplement, in which were included articles about our views about the concept of Aztlán; solidarity with the people of Cuba; props for the Puerto Rican brother; with a little art and poetry, too. The messages of the brothers covered various topics. From California, [El Meño] advised us that it now was time to "get our heads straight"; from Denver, that we begin to analyze the situation of our people in their struggle for human rights. There were other messages about culture and history.

Two weeks after *Aztlán* hit the streets, a "workshop" was formed, to discuss the ideas about future editions of our newly born little paper. The meetings were conducted on Thursday evenings.

The second edition was scheduled for the 26 of July, to recognize the fight of our brothers from Cáiman [Cuba]. But, the same thing happened as before. The press did not roll until September 1970. In this issue, the socio-political consciousness of the people involved in our class and newspaper was already starting to develop.

By the third and fourth issues of *Aztlán* we were already referring to events in the Chicano Movement; the deaths in the barrios, oppression, and the problems of the third world. The painters/artists also began to express their ideas, and their own analysis of the social, political, and economic problems.

In the course of this past year, there were blunders, disagreements, and misunderstandings. But, that is normal. Nevertheless, we were succeeding with *Aztlán*. Our painters, poets, and scribes were being recognized for their efforts to improve the Chicano People. Newspapers from the Chicano press gave us their support by using and reproducing our various articles and drawings.

One of the Chicano journals that featured the convicts of the Eleventh in general and its contributors in particular, was *Entrelineas*. That journal is published by Professor Ruiz and his editors have been very generous with their support and assistance in our literary/artistic endeavors.

That is how we arrived at this point; struggling with distinct personalities, bringing hidden talents to light, raising consciousness, communicating with our own on the other side of the wall, participating, and learning to work together towards a common goal. We hope that with this issue, the commitment grows; to tear down the walls of ignorance, indifference and apathy; which exist throughout the world. Here is our contribution.

■ ■ ■

Articles from *New Era,* Kansas Federal Penitentiary, Leavenworth

New Era, Now Era • *Fall 1970, 4–5*

NOTE FROM THE EDITOR

A PRISON IS A PRISON is a prison, to paraphrase Gertrude Stein or whatever literary giant may have uttered such a phrase, in regards to the rose.

Insofar as loss of freedom is concerned we must admit, that with the coming of the technological age, some changes have occurred—slow though they may have been in arriving. But not enough. We feel that more changes are necessary and should, therefore, be forthcoming.

The prevailing atmosphere of Leavenworth, which both keeper and kept seem to be hung up in, is one of a distinct stagnating and dehumanizing nature. The archaic and passé concepts of notoriety which this massive cage has wallowed in and enjoyed for so long, have become a myth.

Leavenworth today is witnessing the arrival of a new type of prisoner; one who isn't haunted by the specter of his prodigal predecessors of days gone by. One who doesn't scurry into the gloomy caverns of idleness and self-defeat at the mere fact that he has arrived at a prison which has the reputation of being the most infamous of all, in this country. In this "with it" generation, that is all so meaningless.

Here, one could stop and wonder: what criminal came first? The

Certificate of Merit

American Penal Press
Newspaper Contest
1970
FIRST PLACE

Best Sports Story

"Sometimes, Champs Turn Up in the Strangest Places"

Awarded to

Raul Salinas

New Era, U.S. Penitentiary

Leavenworth, Kansas

Howard R. Long, Chairman

Department of Journalism
Southern Illinois University
Carbondale, Illinois

New Era

fall 1970

Member Of Penal Press Of America
Member Of International Penal Press

underwood

Above: Facsimile of First Place Award presented to Salinas by the American Penal Press for Best Story. Award included three-year scholarship to Famous Writers School.

Fall 1970 issue of New Era *Magazine (artwork by Rubén Estrella)* slicked-up Hollywood type, who spoke out of the side of his mouth: Or, the average guy who got uptight about something and took the only way out he knew? Because, after all, isn't that what the game of life is all about? Acquiring as much as possible? The only requisite to that, however, is that you choose the proper methods; that makes the difference. Our only affinity with the ghosts of past felons is, that they were unfortunate men, much like ourselves, who were doing time under, perhaps, worse conditions.

The *New Era* has been in existence for 53 years, with one exception, a fallow season of two years when its absence was sorely lamented. Throughout its duration, *New Era* was intent on reflecting the most creative ideas and achievements of convicts in hopes of bridging the gap between prisoners and free society.

Also, it strove to inform the outside world in regards to convicts' problems, their endeavors towards social adjustment and productivity. By advocating peace and equality, it sought to help in a minor way to lessen indifference and biases. Finally, to motivate and inspire self-expression of all Leavenworth prisoners, allowing each the opportunity of offering his ideas for publication.

A few months ago, the importance of these objectives and the magazine's existence was reaffirmed—the end result being the very issue before you.

As it has been so aptly stated by the top man on our sequestered totem-pole, *New Era* is intent on promoting the convict; his problems and his needs. The problems and needs of today's prisoner are the same as they were 53 years ago. The only difference is in the approach to the solution.

"This is the Dawning of the Age of Aquarius," sang that beautiful cast of the stage production "HAIR." And so it is, that with the ushering in of the *New Era* into the Aquarian Age, we also usher in the "Now Era." With all emphasis and concern placed on today.

> And tomorrow . . .
> PEACE,
> Raúl Salinas

■ ■ ■

Sometimes, Champs Turn Up in the Strangest Places •
Fall 1970, 42–45

The game of handball originated in Ireland and was introduced in the United States about 1810. Today, this country can boast to having the most expert players in the sport, which functions under the regulations of the U.S. Handball Association and the Amateur Athletic Union.

The game can be played either single or four-wall version. Both are as disparate from one another as they are from the European version, which is in itself more like hockey: something else!

The four-wall variety, played in an enclosed court utilizing the ceiling as well, is where Paul Haber reigns as king. In this particular game, the player holds his ground to take the serve and drops back for the kill. The single-wall version differs in that the player drops back to take the serve and rushes in for the kill.

Here at Leavenworth we have the single wall type and, quite naturally, we also have a man who is king of our confined court.

On June 16 of this year, Paul Haber, USHA national singles champion, entered the walls of Leavenworth to give an exhibition of the athletic skills which have gained him his title. His visit was under the auspices of the prison's Recreation Department.

If the cry, "Hey Irving, action!," can bring all the Brooklyn handball devotees running to Avenue P and Fourth Street on any given day, so does "game time!" instantly bring out the convicts en masse, here.

When Paul arrived, he was immediately escorted to the West wall of the big yard which serves as our handball court. With an experienced eye, the Champ surveyed the breadth and length of the pockmarked wall that appears to have been used for executions by firing squads many years ago. Warming up, Paul prepared to show the eager spectators what champs are made of.

Exhibition or not, in order to give the Champ a suitable opponent, one must come up with a player of some merit. The men who frequent our court chose Sammy Chavez as the man to be pitted against Mr. Haber. The men were introduced and after their warm-up, both champ and opponent were ready.

Sammy, our man on the court, is a native of Albuquerque, New

Mexico. Never once having played in the free-world, at thirty years of age, he is a fourteen year veteran of the prison handball circuit. He has been Leavenworth Champion for six consecutive years. On Memorial Day, he copped honors in the A class of both the pink-ball and the black-ball divisions. Along with these laurels, he also won the Best All-Around Handball Player of the Year Award, in 1967.

The first thought in Sammy's mind was that he had to really work out, in spite of the fact that Haber was used to playing a fourwall game, as opposed to the prison's single wall court. Somewhat uncertain as to what lay ahead, Sammy was nevertheless, determined to win. Or, at least give his best showing for his people—the prisoners who are his superfans.

After it was agreed they would play the best two out of three, the game got underway. While the first game was in progress, Sammy was unable to pinpoint his opponent. He began making deliberate shots just to see what the Champ's comeback would foretell. Obviously, Paul's reactions implied he was a ready player. Haber has been known to come on like a whirling dervish whenever there is a ceiling involved, but here, he ran into a bit of difficulty; at this penitentiary the sky is, literally, the limit! All through the first game they checked each other out. The final score was 21–11. Haber's comments to Sammy, after the first game were, "You've got a helluva' game! You should think of competing when you get out. There's good money in it. All you have to do is practice the four-wall game for awhile."

After a short rest period, the second game commenced. The two men played hard, but evidently our Sammy was the better man. True, the Champ just came in for an exhibition game, but with such a reputation you just don't give up everything! The final score in the second game was 21–8, with Sammy taking both games. Up went the rallying cries of "more!" from the faithful followers. Sammy was in fine form.

Here, stemming from some skeptical source, the question might arise, "is Sammy really that good?" That question can be answered in many ways, and at the same time, not answered at all. Those of us who know Sammy, feel he can take on some of the greats Paul has played with in his time. As to whether Chavez is capable of holding his own on the streets, it can't be known, because prison is the only place he's had the opportunity to develop his athletic abilities. Perhaps, when he is released, if he's given the chance, he can become as good as, or better than any champion at the four-wall version. But, until that time, the answer is as moot as the question should be.

The crowd was really rallying behind Sammy and wanted to witness some more. Here at the penitentiary, you just don't utter the cry of "game time!," and expect the guys to sit still after two games going one way. So more action.

The Champ and Sammy (or should I say, the Champ and Paul) decided to play some doubles. Two fine West Coast products were nominated. Haber chose as his partner another of our outstanding players: Johnny Van from Pittsburgh. Californian Freddie Hockenberry from Los Angeles, our number two man of Leavenworth's decaying handball court, teamed up with Chavez. They played two games, both teams winning one each. Sammy displayed the very best sportsmanship manners, as did the others. And although Paul lost the match, he won in that he's now more enlightened and highly impressed with the playing abilities of a convict, who, in his estimation, has all the qualifications of playing with the best handball players around. He gained an insight into a man who, because of his present situation is considered different, but who played just like any other opponent.

Upon departing, Paul again told Sammy, "you've got a good game. When you get out, you can play partners with me anytime you like." Asked by some of the spectators, "Well Champ, what do you think of him now?," his answer was: "He can play in my league, anytime." He also said he'd definitely be back.

When Sammy was asked if he thought the Champ would tighten up his game on a singlewall before he returns for a rematch, he replied, "He may. If he does, he'll be ready next time."

Then he grinned. "But so will I."

■ ■ ■

An Essay on Semantics in the Joint • *Spring 1971, 25*

Convict or inmate, which are "we"? At the moment, there seems to be a semantical storm abrewing among some circles of the penal press hierarchy. Ruling this confined estate as if it were an escritorial fiefdom must be a drag. Or so I would imagine.

*Winter 1970
issue of* New Era
*Magazine (artwork
by Rubén Estrella)*

The controversy revolves around the issue that the terms "convict" and "convicted felons" conjure up a bad image in the mind's eye of society. Not only that, but it has been decreed that these terms are also in very poor journalistic taste, as opposed to the supposedly more respectable term "inmate."

I refuse to accept that opinion. The grounds on which that idea is rejected are stated here and now.

According to Funk & Wagnall's Standard College Dictionary, the terms are defined thusly:

convict (kon'vikt) n. 1. one serving a sentence in prison 2. one found guilty of a crime.

fel-on. (fel'en) n. one who has committed a felony.

in-mate (in'mat') n. 1. one who is lodged or confined in a
prison, asylum. hospital, etc. 2. an inhabitant 3. one who
dwells with another or others.

After giving the above definitions much thought and careful study,
one can only deduce that a convicted felon is a convict. A convict is he
who is doing time in a penitentiary. That, and only that! The inmate,
on the other hand, can be a convict, a mental or medical patient, and
assorted other little etceteras. To stretch the inmate thing a bit further,
he is also one who lives permanently in a fixed place. Permanently?
And finally, a person who lives with one or more people. Like a man
and wife, perhaps?

But, let's face it, these are merely book definitions, which really no
one adheres to. There are other definitions. The man on the streets has
his too. For instance, if you are corresponding from prison with some
prospective employer, he will undoubtedly refer to you as an inmate,
or whatever you're into, as inmate training. However, if your
encounter with him is over his desk, while he examines a job application in which you've honestly listed your arrests, he will (if he is
biased) inform you that due to a standing company policy they do not
hire ex-convicts. Bear in mind that this is even after you've paid your
debt, when you are a former-past-no more resident of any penal institution! The definition varies according to the condition of one's mind.

Getting into a more familiar territory, the milieu of the individual
whose collective appellation is here in question, the definitions take on
an entirely different meaning. And tone. The "convict," as defined by
a select group of "reliable sources," is one who has the strong set of
principles concerning his conduct toward his fellow prisoner. He has
enough sense to not involve himself in another's personal life. He
knows who he is, where he is, and what is expected of him. The
inmate assumes a superior posture to the common prisoners. He identifies more with authority than with his pent-up peers. He is many
other uncool things.

But, for the sake of objectivity, all of the definitions cited above are
just that: definitions. It is only what is in the mind of the beholder that
determines their value or their damage.

Labels, after all, are just labels. I certainly didn't baptize myself "convict." But someone did. And I don't care. However, I would just as well prefer to be called a tricycle, or watermelon, or carnival, or any such groovy items; because in reality, they are just labels, terms, definitions.

By placing so much importance on such minor issues as what to call prisoners, our keepers create major problems, which are in reality, meaningless and time-consuming.

Time is wasted which could be spent discussing, and quite possibly, resolving some of the more significant issues, like better educational facilities, more effective methods of treating drug addicts, eradication of archaic and barbaric laws, and the implementation of modern concepts in the field of penology in general. To concentrate on such matters they must first have clear minds, free from the unnecessary clutter of whether to call a place of confinement a correctional training facility, corrective treatment center, or simply a penitentiary.

By worrying less about semantics and more about the important problems of our nation's prisoners, they will become more effective as crusaders for what should be our common goal.

¡Un coraje!

Article from *Entrelíneas*, Penn Valley Community College, Kansas City, Missouri

Portrait of an Artist • *Vol. 1, No. 5–6, pp. 3–5*

By RAÚLRSALINAS

> *Artist! Dare,*
> *as you pass your brush*
> *across the skies*
> *to paint the canvas of*
> *the universe.*
> *Allow your palette to embrace*
> *Humanity . . .*

A PEOPLE'S ARTIST molding his talents through the sufferings of prison and all of its dreary landscapes. This is Rubén Estrella. Born in San Antonio, Texas, on August 5, 1944, he has seldom been outside his native city—with the exception of annual trips to the cotton fields on the migrant circuit—and to prison.

The product of a broken home, the artist grew up in the care of a doting grandmother and domineering uncles. Throughout his formative years, Estrella felt—firsthand—the plight of the migrant farmworker, as well as the oppressive forces of poverty. In his teens he lashed out against these forces, physically and otherwise. Today, he bears the physical and emotional scars of this rebellion.

Art always fascinated him. In school he did pencil sketches which never failed to catch the eye of other children. One teacher in particular showed a fleeting interest in him, however, nothing materialized. Perhaps this was due to the fact that, at that time, his subject matter consisted solely of hideous monsters and ogres, drooling at the mouth, with sharp fangs exposed.

On his arrival at Leavenworth Penitentiary, Rubén was impressed by the many prisoners who whiled away their time by painting. Immediately, a whole new world opened up for him. In these early days, he made no distinction between original work—which is rare—and copy work reproductions. More than anything, he seemed obsessed mostly with colors. Estrella lunged desperately into art, which proved quite therapeutic. For through art he found some outlet to the deep scars of his youth, plus the fresh wounds of incarceration, which he fought to eradicate. His first pictures in oil were similar to the pencil drawings he had done in school: winged devils perched on bare trees, as if waiting to devour whatever passerby happened to come along. Of these early efforts, two still remain in the artist's personal collection. For an entire year, he was engaged in a chaotic struggle and his works showed the struggle.

In this prison art colony he found artists, who, like himself, were disillusioned and frustrated. Alone, he had to nurture his creative talents, relying on energy from within and encouragement from less than a handful of patron-friends. Inspiration was not easily found.

After he had been painting for a year, he began to acquire some of the much-needed confidence. He dabbled in landscapes and portraits, with portraits taking up most of his interest. It was at this time that Estrella met Rufus Guevara, a highly talented artist, palette-knife virtuoso, and severe art critic. Being a strict disciplinarian, Guevara was not lavish with his praise. In heated discussions, he would point out, not what had been accomplished on canvas by the novice Estrella, but rather what he had failed to develop fully, into the overall composition. In spite of the conflicting artistic temperaments of both seasoned veteran and young neophyte, Estrella fell heir to a very definite influence.

In the Spring of 1969, the artist entered two pieces in the 1st Annual Religious Art Show held in the prison chapel; one, a simple portrait of a nun; and one of an army chaplain kneeling in prayer on a war-torn battlefield. The latter picture won honorable mention. In the fall of the same year, he sold four paintings at fifty dollars each at the Annual Leavenworth Art Show.

Estrella started reading all he could about painting, painters, and the art world in general. He became engrossed with the technique of contrasting lights and shadows, as employed by Rembrandt. The experimentation period had its beginnings around this time. He branched out into other media, such as acrylics, water-colors, and pastels. One of his first acrylics, a nude bust with an overly-strong Modigliani influence hangs in the very private collection of a friend, because he does not consider it one of his better pieces.

The first piece to gain some measure of public recognition outside of prison, was a remarkably sensuous study of Ché Guevara in four moods. Whereas the piece has a very slight imbalance to its composition, the splendid use of umbers, ochres, and deep greens strategically placed (two faces of the late guerilla fighter in full light, one in partial light and shadow, and the fourth one in complete shadow) indicates he had learned his few lessons well.

Through his portraits, rendered with sensitive feeling, he captures as much of the person's essence and soul, rather than just an exact likeness. One of these, "Guerrillero Yaqui" (replete with rifle, knife, and bandoliers), depicts an aging warrior with much fight still left in him, fondling a small, crude, wooden cross around his neck. The background colors appear as if the subject were inside a cave with a campfire producing the light. This is a very direct, gripping work. Bubbling over with an overwhelming sense of accomplishment, Estrella immediately went to work on "El Carnalito," one of his most expressive canvasses to date. It shows a small Chicano boy with baggy jeans, scuffed shoes, oversized belt flapping loose, and unkempt hair. He is standing full length in the middle of what could be a wheat field or an empty sandlot playground. On his face is an expressive, wistful look mixed with a seeming ambivalence. The thumb of his right hand is hooked in his pants pocket. The left hand is also stuck in his pocket, but there is a definite outline of his tiny knuckles, signifying a clenched fist.

When Ethnic Studies were instituted at Leavenworth, Prof. Francisco Ruiz and guest lecturer Oscar Vigliano saw Estrella's work and were extremely impressed by its excellence. As a result of the effect that the artist's paintings had on these gentlemen, there followed a televiewing of the three pictures on a short community video program in Kansas City.

Equipped with these basics in art, Estrella went to work on the staff of NEW ERA, the inmate publication at the federal penitentiary. For his debut issue, he painted a creation entitled "Rebirth", a roughly built-up figure who appears to be desperately trying to get out of an enclosing crypt. The depth that is portrayed is enhanced by an extended gigantic hand completely out of proportion with his body. There is a look of anguish on its face. It is not definable as either man nor beast, but certainly some type of creature. This painting won top honors in the American Penal Press Contest of 1970, resulting in a three year scholarship to Famous Artists School.

Through the Chicano Press papers made available to the Chicano group, Estrella had the opportunity to keep abreast of the struggling Chicano Movement and the artists emerging from the same. He became more concerned with the social conditions of his people and gained a strong sense of dedication towards contributing his share to their aspirations.

The police riot following the anti-war moratorium in East L.A. on August 29, 1970, moved him to express his anger on canvas. His finished product was a fiery, brilliant red-yellow-orange abstract impressionistic piece entitled "Whittier Blvd.—1970." It vaguely depicts the area going up in flames, with some helmeted, heavily-equipped figures engaged in violent activity, while other figures are sprawled throughout the entire breadth of the canvas. There is an intense feeling of burning heat and the mood created is one of extreme agitation. Viewing the impressionistic shambles of the shops and stores on fire, is to catch a glimpse of the artist's incendiary personality. Very complex and tormented. But truly an artist.

To Estrella the term "Chicano" is simply himself. Like most people of his ilk (the lower-class worker) the term has ever been a part of him. Although the term and concept have been embraced quite fiercely in the late 60's and early 70's by the people of Mexican descent, particularly the students, to most people in the Southwest it is no novel word. And contrary to what sociologists and educators may say, the artist never suffered from the proverbial cliché "identity crisis." He knows he is Chicano; always has been. In his native Texas, he was constantly reminded of this. Therefore, he paints, like his Spanish and Indian predecessors, according to his moods. And whether he is creating thematic "ethnic" canvasses or interpreting life from an artistic plateau, his Chicano soul forever bares itself. His art can be defined as protest art, if any definition is necessary. For his palette screams a deplorable socio-political condition.

As a child Estrella remembers, that outside of an occasional yearly field trip to an uptown art museum, the children of the Chicano communities were rarely exposed to art in any manner. Because of this, it is his contention that natural artistic talents among Chicano youth never fully, if ever, developed.

The artist envisions the creation of "Casa de las Artes" in the barrio where he grew up. This would consist of an art studio-gallery-workshop wherein Chicano artists could create canvasses, murals, sculptures, poetry, and music. A place where these creations could be viewed, read, and heard by the common everyday people: Chicanos and non-Chicanos alike, the young and the old, a place for teaching children and whoever else expresses the desire, to paint, to write, to sculpt, and to play music. This would, according to Estrella, be approached from all aspects. First, an initial introduction to the respective tools required whereby people start dabbling by getting the feel of clay, fingerpaints, oils, charcoals, etc. Then, basic instructions and eventually individual tutoring and study of traditional historical art and artists, to murals in the contemporary idiom; a center where philosophic ideas could be exchanged between artists; techniques learned from one another, and finally Creative Arts Festivals planned with the community in mind. Once having realized this project, the artist, and artists, could leave and go out to set up similar centers throughout Aztlán . . . and the United States.

This is Rubén Estrella's main goal. A self-sustaining, self-determining art commune which is very close to being a reality. The need for such can best be summed up in his own words:

> We need more Chicano artists to express the feelings of our people, who can also interpret life as ARTISTS, from our own dual-cultural perspective. But most important is that we allow children the opportunity to express their natural—untainted— desires, through the medium of creative arts.

Among his many works have been portraits of Leila Khaled, Joan

Baez, Faye Dunaway, Dionne Warwicke, Charles Manson, Ché Guevara, Otis Redding, and a small, but very powerful oil of Mexican musical genius Agustín Lara, which in this writer's estimation should hang in the Agustín Lara museum, if there is such a place, or one is in the offing.

In the early part of this year, he donated three pieces to the Raza Art Festival in Houston, Texas. These consisted of "Whittier Blvd.— 1970," previously mentioned, and two others. One, a portrait of an aged man with weather-beaten face, outdated coat, bearing a pin displaying the black eagle, symbol of the farmworkers' struggle, his wrinkled hand, finely detailed, resting on an open page of the bible. He called this one "El Chavista." The third in the set was a semi-surrealistic work depicting a young man looking out from the inside of a bare room, as he sits on the steps, shirtless with a Virgen Guadalupana tattooed on his back, holding back a tattered screen door with his foot. Far out into the picture as if in another room, but definitely outdoors, is a misty image of a split-level home which could very well be the "Heights" or any suburbia. On the wall, hung from a rusty nail is a huge, life-size pocket watch.

Very recently he painted an action portrait of a vocalist hometown friend, who in turn thought enough of the work to grace his latest album cover with it. The album is "Young, Gifted and Brown," by Sunny and the Sunliners. In this year's Religious Art Show, the artist copped 1st prize for an acrylic study on the classic "Madonna and Child" theme. This was ably portrayed by a Vietnamese mother with child in arms, look of hunger and desolation in their eyes. Another major work of his, also done in the medium of acrylics is "Futility," which was used for Winter 1970 issue of *New Era* Magazine. The piece was entered into this year's Penal Press Contest, for which results are not yet in. Now, Estrella is in the process of doing a book cover and illustrations for a volume of poetry written by another friend of his. He also did a gouache poster which he donated to La Raza Unida Party in Texas, hoping they can use it for propaganda purposes in their political campaigns. All these services that he renders to "La Causa," are not done for political gain, but instead as humble offerings from C.O.R.A., the Chicano Culture Group at the U.S. Prison at Leavenworth.

At the present time he is trying to secure permission from the proper authorities to paint a historical mural of his concept of Aztlán, portraying the mass exodus south and the founding of Tenochtitlán. These would, if approval is granted, be placed alongside those of Gen. George Washington crossing the Delaware and the signing of the Declaration of Independence which hang in the prison's learning center. In his lonely prison cell, the 27 year old Rubén Estrella lives . . . to paint.

Salinas and friends in yard at Marion (1972)

Salinas with friends in yard at Marion (1972). Photo courtesy of Dept. of Special Collections, Stanford University Libraries.

Salinas and Rafael Cancel Miranda at Marion (1972)

Members of C.O.R.A. in Cultural History of the Southwest Class, Leaven-worth Prison, 1971

Salinas at editorial desk in Leavenworth (1970)

Salinas and friends in cell in Leavenworth (circa 1971)

Painting of Salinas by Rubén Estrella (circa 1969)

Flying Kites to the World

LETTERS, 1968–1974

T he correspondence that follows offers unique insight into the innermost fears, hopes, passions, and intellect of a mind and spirit undergoing change over a period of years. The letters included here are only a small portion of the overall collection in the Salinas archives. Though Salinas wrote to his family in former periods of incarceration, few of those letters are part of the archive. In fact, perhaps it was Salinas' growing awareness of the need to document his life through his correspondence, as well as his involvement in the prison publication enterprise, which gave him access, that led him often to use carbon paper to make copies of his letters. But, as one sees in reading his letters, the material conditions were not always controllable, particularly when he was placed in segregation and limited to use of a #3 pencil stub as a writing instrument. Still, this did not prevent him from communicating to the outer world.

As with his journalism, one can chart Salinas' political and spiritual development in his letters. Though it is clear that his family and friends had already taken notice of his creative talents and sought to encourage him to write and publish, it is also clear that his writing flourished as he became steeped in the prisoner rights movement through C.O.R.A., other consciousness-raising activities, and the Chicano prison publications efforts at Leavenworth. Furthermore, his role as editor placed him in a unique position to respond to inquiries from the outside world. Because many of these inquiries were about his work that had begun to receive notice in political and academic circles, Salinas' very personable responses allowed him to cultivate authentic relationships with several people. An examination of the

more extensive correspondence between Salinas and four of his inter-
locutors found near the end of this section reveals the dispersed and
diverse community he established through an honest exchange of
ideas and feelings. This extended, and perhaps imagined, community
was one strategy of survival because it enabled him to feel connected
to life outside the walls. Moreover, he also used his position as editor
to solicit cultural and political organizations not only to take up the
cause of prison reform but also to send publications, meeting minutes,
and any information that would aid prisoners in feeling connected to
political movements in the "free" world.

Despite having embraced the use of lowercase letters for his name
to de-emphasize his ego as an engaged writer and social critic, Salinas
was unafraid to challenge his correspondents, particularly those in
academic and political circles. His extensive knowledge of the role of
the artist in revolutionary struggle fostered by the writings of national
liberation movement intellectuals from all over the world is apparent,
particularly in his well-aimed barbs at academics and his perception of
their limited commitment to a political cause. It is also clear in reading
his letters that the influence of Third World intellectuals had begun to
cultivate an internationalist perspective in him as he made it clear on
more than one occasion that the Chicano movement was only one
phase of a larger working-class struggle.

In addition to an emerging and deepening commitment of the
author to the struggle for justice and equality, we also see in his letters
much anxiety about his pending release, about what his role in the
world will be in the post-prison years, particularly in relationship to
his family and community in the aftermath of his transformation. The
transformation itself is cause for anxiety, though it clearly brings with
it a sense of empowerment and purpose. His many ways of identifying
himself, besides his name and politicized farewells, indicate a growing
sense of clarity about this role: from *preso* (prisoner), to his number
(#83908-132), to *editor*, to *poet-soldier*. One can sense early on that,
as he says, the pen would become his finest weapon with which to
wage war against injustices inside and outside of prison.

■ ■ ■

February 24, 1968

Dear Roy,

I just got your painting and its beautiful! I've hung it in the living room over the stereo. you'll never believe the story that goes with it though! Your friend said that he got here at five till six this morning, so he decided to visit awhile to call at Carmen's. At about seven he rang. Richard answered, and asked him to speak English! Anyway, Carrie was at work so Ricky called her, then she called us. When he called, your friend didn't leave his name or anything. All I knew was that there was a guy at the Bus Station with a painting for me. So off I went! I found him standing right inside the door & I asked him if he was the guy with the picture from Roy. After we found out who was who, we had to open the package so that he could get his painting out. He said it was for a little girl. Does he have kids? He sure was a sweet guy! He spoke very highly of *you*! And I was proud of the way he did talk about you! He said you were fine, and that you were going to school! What are you taking? I guess you know I'm waiting for you to finish your novel! You may think that I'm kidding, but I'm not! In all seriousness, even your friend said that you're too bright to be in the situation you're in! So, if you haven't already started, why not *get* started. Nowadays, the Literary field has been stretched to such communities that with your talent, I have no doubt that you'll make it! Please don't think that I'm trying to sell you on something foolish! It's just that you have talent & I'm not the only one who has noticed! I don't know if you remember a guy named Johnny Mayfield or not, but he said you were the greatest artist he'd ever seen! Of course J. Mayfield isn't much of an authority. But all your friends & even Mom has said you are talented, so think about it.

Say Roy, do you remember that tape you made about an alto sax player? I believe you called him "Bird." I found it a few nights ago, & Vince & I listened to it all the way thru! Vince really like it too! He made me label it & put it with the rest of our tapes! I was kind of shocked because he has always been what the High School crowd calls "straight" (square). He never liked Jazz, The Underground party, Pop art or anything. He's a purely *work* type of guy. We have problems sometimes in our communication and ideas because of it, but I love him and he *does try* to understand me and I try, too. But that's why I was shocked when he said he really liked your tape!

Before we were married I tried everything to get him into a coffee-house here in town, but he wouldn't budge. Now, he likes it! This place is real cool! Everyone sits around on the floor discussing anything you'd like. You drink black coffee, listen to oriental music, play oriental board games, or just sit by yourself. It's really great! Like I said, before we got married he didn't like it & *now*! WOW! Well I want to get this in today's mail. We're going to Mexico tonite so I'll probably write you Monday & fill you in. Be good!

> All my love,
> Sis
> PS Don't forget your novel &
> write soon
> Carolyn

■ ■ ■

July 9, 1968

Dear Roy,

Your last letter was really an experience! I must agree with you on your cause, the fight for legalization of pot. Although not quite as experienced as you are, getting "stoned" is a fad all high school swingers must pass through, and *then* try for successful lives (swingers as opposed to straights!) I do believe my letters to you will go no farther than Leavenworth legal channels and yourself. For the simple reason that I am no longer swinging, but being a full time innocent straight. I suppose the fact that I'm not a total stranger to your world has more than surprised you. Never fear, though, my dear brother, although sometimes I regret it, I prefer living legally until the time Leary and the rest of the "live" world are given complete legal freedom on "smoking." You say you are able to turn me on to the underground? A subscription perhaps? Please send more details. Do you remember the "mag" "Night Beat"? (not sure that's the name) The one with my picture in it? Do you think I could get it back? I'd like to show Vince I'd rather dance than cook! (not really). Just plain conceit!

Now to the nitty-gritty. Do I plan on racing also? The answer is, yes dearest. In fact, I have, since your last letter, won two trophies of considerable class and size! I took a picture of Carmen with one of them because I hadn't won the other one yet. But, as you probably have guessed by now, I have about 4 rolls of undeveloped film just lying all over the house . . . but . . . someday . . .

As far as Carmen finding herself another man . . . she's got lots of friends but her heart belongs to Daddy! So never fear, if you ever decide you want her for your own again, I'm sure she'll be more than willing!

This will be all for now, it almost supper time. Venson says "hello" and so does mom and dad. Did mom or Carrie tell you that Dad was real pleased with the Father's Day card that you sent him? Mother told me that he wants her to buy him a frame for it.

Anytime you are ready send your paintings. We'll be glad to keep them for you.

Love as always,
Sis [Carolyn]

■ ■ ■

1968

Dear Dad, How have you been doing? Mom and Carolyn went to Houston Friday because they were going to see Clara get married on Saturday. I'm in cub scouts now and I've learned a lot of new things. We might go to California this summer and see Aunt Terry and Uncle Norm. I wonder when you are coming home, cause the other part of the house is almost finished. I wish you could come down for Christmas so you could have fun with us. By the way I hope you are glad about this, on my report I got "E"—excellent and they all were "S" for satisfactory. And Momo and Popo and Carolyn and David are all alright. And so are we.

Love always,
Your son
Lawrence

■ ■ ■

10-25-70

Dear Brother Roy,

How are you doing? I hope things are going all-right for you. I want you to know that I was (am) very proud when I saw what you had written, but I also want you to know that I always knew you could do it. I was just wondering *when* you would do it. I honestly believe that you've got a lot more to give, and I hope you'll give it to your fullest capacity. I'm very sorry on the other hand—to hear that communications between yourself and the family have become almost nil. Actually, if I had known of it, I would have written sooner. Heaven knows, I had all the time in the world to write while I was carrying David—but I'm sure you understand that my state of mind was a bit unstable, and therefore, my letters would be full of nothing but chaotic depression. Not too amusing, huh? *Now,* that my time is nothing but hectic minutes, hours, and days, I'm sitting here trying to steal a few minutes to write you a decent letter. I'm going to try to keep it up this time, but my past writing record shows all too clearly that I'm not too dependable. All I will say for now is be patient because I really do have my hands full nowadays. I have no time I can really call my own because my life belongs to David now. He's my purpose and reason for living—and living is a 24 hour job. I wish that you could see my little boy—he is so beautiful and innocent and so full of wonderful happiness—I love him more than life! (Not that I ever really *loved* life—it's just a saying) I'm sure that you know what I'm trying to express to you. Mom and I had his picture taken in the hospital when he was three days old, but, I haven't received them yet. The representative said it would take 3 weeks for me to get them—which means they should be here sometime next week. It almost makes me sick— the fact that I have to send you a picture—because I want you to see him yourself as the real little person he is. Don't misunderstand me, I'm not putting you down for being where *you* are —It's where *I'm* at—or—where my head is at. I *know* you love me, and I know you'll love David and I want him to have all the love this world has to give. I realize I'm hard to understand when I talk this way but bear with me, maybe someday I'll be able to bare my heart to you, *then*, maybe, you'll be able to understand me. Until then . . . Have you heard from Mom yet? I hope you won't hold it against her if you don't, because we've both hurt her a hell of a lot, and I'm afraid we won't stop until God takes her away from us. Anyway, she knows that too, and I think she feels that if she doesn't write, it will keep her from getting hurt just one more time. Do you understand? Women have a bad habit of letting their hopes build up, only to have them crushed over & over again—and that's exactly what she's trying to avoid with both of us. But, she'll always love us, no matter what, so please forgive her for *seeming* indifferent. I hope there is no limit to how many pages I write—if there is you'd better let me know, because as you can plainly see, I always manage to ramble on and on without ever really saying anything!

ALL MY LOVE ALWAYS,
Carolyn

■ ■ ■

12-29-70 [1]

Querido Hermano

There is a small group of Chicanos sitting around a fire in Palo Alto, California on this night. We have come together from various parts of the country. Lubbock, Texas; Seattle, Wash, and Los Angeles. We sang (off-key) for about an hour, ate a delicious meal de frijoles, arroz, tortillas y chile. Afterwards one of the more perceptive members of our group read us a beautiful moving poem, written by you. We've decided to write and tell you how much we enjoyed your poem—words are inadequate all I can say is—¡Te aventaste!

María Elda Cisneros
de Mendoza

Hermano—

Su poema nos llevó al lugar donde vivimos y crecimos. A mí me volvió a un campo de labor donde los señores siempre daban discursos el 16 de septiembre y el cinco de Mayo. Gracias por haber expresado tan claramente y con tanta sensibilidad y entendimiento lo que sentimos.

[*Your poem took us back to the place where we lived and grew. It returned me to a labor camp where the men always gave speeches on September 16th and the 5th of May. Thank you for having expressed our feelings so clearly and with so much wisdom and understanding.*]

Antonia Castañeda Shular

Dear Brother—

We read your poem tonight and were very much inspired. I don't know the scene myself but you made it real to me. I hope you keep on writing more—

Thank you,
Tish Sommers

Querido Hermano Salinas,

El grupo de chicanos a que se refiere María Elda incluye a un par de "fellow travelers." Los recuerdan y las sensaciones que figuran en la superficie del poema que acaban de escuchar; creo que significan más para nuestros amigos Chicanos que para nosotros nos indentifiquen en el significado esencial debajo de la superficie; creo que su poema es una expresíon artística de unas experiencias que, si no las hemos vivido explícitamente, las podemos sin embargo entender. Y al entender nos sentimos armados e impulsados a luchar para que no se repitan.

Gracias, y que le vaya bien.

[The group of Chicanos to whom Maria Elda refers includes a pair of "*fellow travelers*." The memories and feelings that appear in the surface of the poem that we have just heard, I believe that they signify more for our Chicano friends than for us who identify the essential significance beneath the surface; I believe that your poem is an artistic expression of certain experiences that, if we have not personally experienced, we can nonetheless comprehend. And by understanding we feel capable and compelled to fight so that they are not repeated.

Thanks, and all the best,]
Joseph Sommers

Carnal

Se me enchina el cuerpo cada vez que leo tus poems / out of my skull with the pulsating emotion / los rostros de imagenes de nuestra sociedad / you sing con el cora abierto que me toca . . . you speak la verdad de las verdades (the history of nuestra gente) outside (and inside the walls) Erasing all those circles that contain us / You bring y siembras semillas de liberacíon en muchas mentes jovenes that are in barrios and campos are beginning to move.

Con todos mis poros abiertos I read your message and cannot contain the joy / alegría deseperacíon en la esperanza.

If it would be possible / I would like to get your pinto publication and maybe get on your mailing list.

Con sus palabras como lluvia lenta o tempestad de calavera sonientes, con tus ideas me bañas de sentimientos / recuerdo la amargura y el amor de nuestra lucha. Venceremos porque recordamos pero aun podemos empezar / because our hatred is but love misplaced because la causa is just and because it is time for us to make history or time will make history of us.

[*My body trembles every time that I read your poems* / out of my skull with the pulsating emotion / *the traces of images from our society* / you sing with an open *heart* that touches me . . . you speak *the truth of truths* (the history *of our people*) outside (and inside the walls). Erasing all those circles that contain us / You bring *and nurture seeds of liberation in many young minds* that are in barrios and *fields* and are beginning to move.

With all my senses heightened *I read your message and cannot contain the joy* / happiness and desperate hope.

If it would be possible / I would like to get your *pinto* publication and maybe get on your mailing list.

With your words like a soothing rain or a tempest of smiling skulls, with your ideas you shower me with feelings / I remember the bitterness and the love of our struggle. We shall triumph because we remember, we can still begin / *because our hatred is but love misplaced because* la causa *is just and because it is time for us to make history or time will make history of us.*]

Hasta la victoria siempre,
Tomás Ybarra-Frausto

■ ■ ■

María Elda Cisneros de Mendoza

Estimada carnalita:

Your letter could not have arrived at a more opportune time. It served to alleviate the mental anguish of the moment. Moreso, it was the most thrilling event of the new year; one that merited a prompt reply. Unfortunately this was not possible. 1971 came on wild and hectic, which left me beset with local problems. Palomino may have explained it in more detail. Que no? At any rate, your letters arrived and overcame the constriction of prison life. i'm free again!

The vivid description you provided me with, of the group's get together, became a real part of me. The meal, needless to say, made my mouth water; especially the tortillas y chile. Que saboreada! It's been a few calendars now. Your off-key singing came through so clear, it evoked a fraternal chuckle from me. Thank you for being so generous in sharing this moment with me. It was sorely needed.

It pleases me muchly that you enjoyed my poem, because it's your poem. It also belongs to everyone who can identify with it; see themselves in it. Such was the intended goal, to present a personal experience which the reader could then transform into a universal experience. A life experience; the Chicano experience! At the risk of seeming vain, might i ask who the perceptive person who read the poem was? Could it, perhaps, have been that illustrious maestro . . . , el Sr. Mendoza?

Again, thank you for everything. Hope to see "you-all" sometime in the not-too-distant future. Until that day, give my fondest regards to your entire group. You and Mando receive the very best from all of us. Palomino suggested that i include a carbon copy of each letter. Here's our publication, too.

Sinceramente,
raúlrsalinas

■ ■ ■

Antonia Castañeda Shular

Querida 'Toña:

Moments before your letter arrived—encompassing all my emotions—my situation was worser than worse. Local problems! Now the absurd realness of jail is no more, for the time being; as i transcend into the *warm* reality of that small gathering in Palo Alto . . .

Please understand that by your kind words, you have outright burglarized my embittered heart and tendered it into the sweet wine of carnalismo . . .

You are much thought of within the pinto circuit. We feel as though we know you and the others personally. i have drawn from Palomino, all of the wonderful stories regarding the people and activities on the *Isla.*[2] There was no doubt in my mind that someday, soon, we would be corresponding. Ever since we learned from Mando that you were with Quinto Sol, i became jittery (malías) with anxiety. Not having made the initial move, i'll cop to the charge of laxity and negligence.

Your comments about "Trip . . ." transporting you back in time to the labor camps of your youth, served to further extend the communion of "*OUR*" experience. Que loco! Really, those places were too much, huh? Cotton and tomato patches, beet fields y toda la cosa. Wow! Y luego a la polkita el sabado, a disipar las penas. Que no? [*And then the Saturday Polkas, to soothe the mind and body. Right?*]

You know, i've been trying to capture the exact mood of embarking "a los trabajos," on those migrant caravans, in short story form. However, a lack of discipline has resulted in its not evolving past the fragmented, outline stage. So, it remains buried somewhere in my uncatalogued, unsystematized files.

Listen, i understand your boss (if such be the case) has a bad rep of not answering mail promptly, if at all. Some of the carnales have made an attempt at corresponding with him to no avail. Why is this? The one piece i've read of his, tells me he is a heavy dude. And, i'm told, his publications are all "de alta calidad."

Como su carta fue la primera que trate de contestar, y viendo que en la situacion en que me encontraba no me permitía escribir en español, en fin, decidí comunicar en gavacho.

Para terminar, agrego que mis intenciones al salir, son y serán de visitarlos para satisfacer uno de mis mayores deseos; conocer a cada uno de ustedes, que juntos se unieron para ayudarme a robarles un día a mis carceleros. Saludos de todo aquí y gracias mil.

[Since your letter is the first I have tried to answer, and given that my situation did not allow me to write in Spanish, finally, I decided to communicate in English.

In closing, I might add that my intentions upon release are and will be to visit you all to satisfy one of my greatest wishes; get to know each and every one of you, who together united to help me steal a day from my jailers. Regards from everyone here and many thanks.]

raúlrsalinas

■ ■ ■

Sr. y Sra. Joseph Sommers

Apreciable amigo y hermano:

La reunión ya mencionada, se me está muy bien grabada en el pensamiento. Nunca jamás la olvidarle, porque ustedes han hecho posible que yo haya sentido la proximidad de esos momentos alegres.

Y bienvenidos, "fellow-travelers", si hubiera mas gente como ustedes, la lucha en el camino hacia la victoria no sería tan dificil. Si, es posible que los recuerdos y sensaciones tengan mas significado para la Raza. Pero, el poeta (a según mi parecer loco) no debe limitar su público audiente, ni sus lectores. Al contrario, la labor del poeta (Chicano) a de ser de hechar su historia a los vientos para que todo el mundo—incluso fellow-travelers—la oigan y así lleguen a comprender la verdadera historia de la experiencia Chicana!

En conclusión, quiero decirle que las gracias las merece usted, por su generosidad. Por su interés en el recluso, el Chicano y la humanidad entera. Sin mas,

Su atento amigo y servidor

[Respected friend and brother:

The aforementioned meeting, is strongly etched in my mind. I will never forget it, because you all have made it possible for me to have felt the proximity of such joyous moments.

And welcome, "fellow-travelers," if there were more people like you, the struggle toward victory would not be so difficult. Yes, it is possible that the memories and feelings have more meaning for the Chicano people. But, the poet (according to my crazy view) should not limit his public audience, nor his readers. On the contrary, the work of the (Chicano) poet should be to throw his history to the winds so the whole world—including fellow travelers—hear it and in that way can come to understand the true history of the Chicano experience!

In conclusion, I want to say that you are the one who deserves thanks, for your generosity. For your interest in the imprisoned, the Chicano and humanity as a whole. For now,

Your faithful friend and
servant]

Dear Mrs. Sommers:

You people have overwhelmed my entire being. What more can i say? i am deeply honored. You are endowed with rare gifts: compassion & a love for humanity. The world needs more people like you. Thank you, i *must* continue writing.

Respectfully,
raúlrsalinas

■ ■ ■

Tomás Ybarra-Frausto

Compa:

tus palabras llegan / hacia mi / como agua fresca / de cantaro. / como astros / brilliantes que iluminan / la obscuridad de esta inmensa pajarera. / derritiendo en instantes numerosos / las rejas de / amargura y soledad.

as for my writings, / sólo son clamores que brotan del fondo de la experiencia / como asucenas sofocadas por hierbas malas.

it is possible / all our joint publications are enclosed / would enjoy a permanent correspondence, arrangements can be made / have taken the liberty of sending the Sommers' letters and publication to you / hope you can see them entregarselos.

No pierdo la esperanza de conocerlos pronto / mi labor esta ya determinada / this has been the complete turn-on / el poeta lo eres tú!

[*your words reach me like fresh water from an earthen jar. Like brilliant stars / that illuminate / the darkness of this immense birdcage / melting continuously / the bars of bitterness and loneliness.*

as for my writings, / they're just rantings that blossom from experience / like lilies suffocated by evil weeds.

it is possible / all our joint publications are enclosed / would enjoy a permanent correspondence, arrangements can be made / have taken the liberty of sending the Sommers' letters and publication to you / hope you can see them *give them to him.*

I have not lost hope of meeting you all soon / my work is now clear / this has been the complete turn-on / the true poet is you!]

Hasta la liberación,
raúlrsalinas

■ ■ ■

Feb. 2, 1971

Austin

Dear Roy,

So glad to receive your letter and sorry I am not a good letter writer. I am plain lazy. We are all fine. A few problems with "Naner" of course. I'm biased but I think it is not all her doing. Just one of those things. Like Uncle Manuel used to say "El distino de cada criatura," I suppose it means "Each child's destiny." Richard on the other hand was nominated as most handsome or something (not sure what) but he had to have his picture taken, & yes Mom's had to chauffer him, to Scarborough's to the photographer's. But then he is the "brain" of the family. He gets very angry & embarrassed with "Naner" and was sort of throwing it up to Carmen, but I got hold of him and told him his mother was proud of him but they were all her kids and she could not love one less, for her mistakes, so he piped down. Carolyn also tries to help with them in her own half-mature way. Last night she let Rick drive her V.W. home, she rode with him, then drove back home. Of course it's about 2½ blocks away. My own news is that for 2 Sundays I have been interpreting the readings and gospel in church (for the Deaf). Oh, I'll admit the first Sunday *I blew it*, I was so embarrassed, as I have to stand to the right of Father inside the altar rail and facing the people. Wow! The first time I barely got thru the readings, but last Sunday I even signed the sermon. Unbelievable huh? Of course I still take sign language classes at every opportunity. I finished one course about 2 weeks ago and will start again Feb. 25th. We pay $1.00 per lesson for 10 or 15 weeks. Pay also in advance of course. Carolyn helps by encouraging me, & Carmen by babysitting with Davidcio when Carol works nights & I have class. Popo on the other hand gets a little perturbed, talks about how old we are, etc., but my mama taught me "you are never too old to learn" and old people need something worthwhile to do, & this Deaf bit is *my thing*. This Sunday Larry sat up front and when I started signing I saw his little face looking at me—I told him after mass that when I saw him I felt more relaxed and boy! was he proud—the minute we got home he told Popo—Paul Samniego, Carol, and anyone who would listen "Momo says it helped her seeing me sitting there, it relaxed her." *That's your son!* He also helps me at Deaf C.C.D. He will read what's on the overhead projector—this way I don't have to turn my back on my class, he reads & I sign. Some help, huh? So you see son, tho' there are some things I can't bear to think about such as "if only so & so," yet I have to count my blessings including one that my son as far as I am concerned is a good son & I love you. My grandkids are a joy to me. I love them all, so what more can I ask. If Carmen gets perturbed don't judge her too harshly—it's a big load to raise children by oneself especially in this day and age. Negro Ortiz stopped by yesterday—came down for his boy's graduation. He is doing fine. Works in grocery store in Plainview, helps with teenage C.C.D. in church—said tell you hello.

Love from all, Mom

■ ■ ■

June 21, 1971

Sr. Jose Angel Aguirre
Austin

Estimado Carnal:

This letter serves as an attempt to establish some sort of communication between you and us. We heard that you had raised from TDS and that you were now situated in the Austin area again. Then, when a copy of Ya Mero (McAllen) reached our nethermost (and i mean nethermost) confines, we were delighted to see your glowing countenance gracing the first page photo of a rally in South Tejas. We felt the vibes surging through our beings to see you involved in el movimiento de nuestra gente [*our people's movement*]. Or was the trip south, multi purpose? At any rate, we derived a tremendous boost in morale. So much so, that we decided to contact you and let you know about our commitment to La Causa.

In March of '70, Prof. Francisco Ruiz from K.C., MO, began teaching a Cultural History of the Southwest class. From the git-go, it proved to be beneficial for all concerned Chicano convictos. Two months later, our most cherished newspaper, Aztlán, came into existence. By late Oct., we elected a "mesa directiva" [*board of directors*] for a culture group for which the name C.O.R.A. (Convictos Organizados Raza de Aztlán) was chosen. The 1st "mesa" had a tremendously successful 6 month tenure, at which time a second mesa was elected.

Our weekly juntas are conducted on Friday nights from 6 to 9 p.m. and they run thusly; mesa business & reports (correspondence, newspaper, grievances, etc.), then a pinto is selected to be main speaker for the nite. Aqui se puede aventar el camarada, a segun su nivel [*Here is when a comrade can get down, according to his ability*]—politics, education, revolucion, whatever. Just so it is pertinent to the Chicano cause. Despues se introducen los visitantes de la libre—carnales militantes, Chavistas lechugueros, tios tacos, professors, y estudiantes. Aveces hay peliculas del calibre de "Huelga en Delano" y "Yo Soy Joaquin." Al final, el profe nos da una hora de lecturas en la lengua castellana, y historia de los mayas / aztecas y literatura mejicana. Por medio del papiro estamos en contacto con todos las pintas de Aztlán, safando el animal aquel te platique! De allí, nichis, carnal! [*Afterwards the freeworld visitors are introduced—militant brothers, Chavez Union organizers, uncle toms, professors, and students. Sometimes there are movies like "Strike in Delano" and "I am Joaquin." Finally, the professor gives us an hour of lessons in Spanish, and history of the Mayas / Aztecs and Mexican Literature. Through the paper we are in contact with all the prisons of Aztlán, excluding "that beast" I told you about before. From that place, zip, brother!*] But you know that out front, no? Naranjas!

And you, how have you been faring? Ya 'ubo con el tubo, o siempre siempre? We sincerely hope you are living in peace, Jose; you owe it to yourself. We (you & us) both know that life has shown us its cruelest side. Let's not help it along any more than what we already have in the past. We can utilize what we have experienced through the years, for the betterment of our people. We hope you don't think we're preachin' in any way, compa; al contrario, ya nos estamos poniendo mss radical que la chingada [*bro; on the contrary, we are becoming even more fucking radicalized*]: We have become more aware in a social & political respect. We are able to see much more clearly the ulterior motives behind a lot of the shuck that's been put on us for so long. We feel it could / should stand some change.

One important point in revolutionary thought is that one cannot work within the system and hope to accomplish social change. Well! that's not exactly where our heads are at. With all due respect to that line of thinking, we feel that one can work within the system and be effective for the better. However, it is going to take people like us (sure-enough-hope-to-die tecatos-vatos locos-pintos) who have suffered the gravest injustices meted out by the tribunals of the land. We think we can be revolucionarios in this sense becoming so well-equipped and qualified that we are able to penetrate the system. We must get our stuff together and infiltrate the same institutions that have contributed to our oppressive state. This, whether it is as neighborhood counselors, lawyers, teachers, politicians, and even as artists / poets / musicians; so long as we have the interest of our people at heart. Of course, it is going to be an arduous task. One that will require much discipline on our part. Discipline, dedication and study will, in our estimation, bring about the New Chicano, capable of determining his own destiny.

Let us hear from you and the Austin scene. Information on the paper printed there under the name of Echo (or is it Eco?). Do keep in touch. Saludos de los homies y todos los Chicanos de C.O.R.A Aztlán / Leavenworth.

> Hasta la liberación,
> raúlrsalinas
> editor

■ ■ ■

September 9, 1971

EL CHICANO
c/o Aztec Productions
Los Angeles

Queridos Carnales y Carnalita:

We were overwhelmed by the tremendous flow of energy and good vibes that you gave out during your performance here last month. Our initial intentions were to get this letter off immediately after you left. However, being caught up in the daily struggle that we are, it was not possible until now.

Needless to say, there are Chicanos here (todos!) who walk the yard with a certain sense of pride in the fact that you laid it down to the people here, what we're all about. Gracias mil!

At this time, we are into *Aztlán* #4, which should be ready by next week. Unfortunately, it was already prepared for printing when you folks arrived so that now we will shoot for a "special" issue on the musical happenings of "El CHICANO." Hopefully, by the end of this month.

Enclosed you will find our entire output of publications, with the exception of New Era #1, which has been depleted; the only one we had left was given to Ersi (naturally) on THAT day.

To this date we have not heard from you again, we are concerned. What has been transpiring with the group since Aug. 17? Ese, Baeza, we almost got into a good rap, no? How is your carnal in Q doing? Incidentally, the interview tape turned out fairly good, sound was a bit off. A ver what we can work out. More on that later. Look out por El Mickey, he's a heavy little dude.

What we are all anxious for is to know when you will be touring out towards the wilds of Kansas/Missouri again. Any time soon? Let us know what can be arranged in regards to photos, a couple of jams and some charts.

Reciban ustedes y "La Barrio Princess"—en el espíritu de Aztlán— un fuerte abrazo de Carnalismo from *all* the Pintos Chicanos de C.O.R.A./*Aztlán*/Leavenworth.

> Hasta la liberación,
> raúlrsalinas

■ ■ ■

November 4, 1971

Estimado Prof. Sommers:

El día siguiente, después de haberle contestado al Ybarra, recibí una copia de su carta al Prof. Ruiz. Me puse a escribirle una notita de explicación, cuando me llegó su muy amable carta, incluso el preface, introducción, y table of contents pages. Dias después, también recibí carta de Toña. Del Tomás solo una form letter (cual contesté) acompañando los permisos. Se ha conformado el niño. ¡Alegría total! [*The day after I responded to Ybarra, I received a copy of your letter to Dr. Ruiz. I sat down to write him a note of explanation when I received your very nice letter, with the preface, introduction, and table of contents pages. Days later I also received correspondence from Toña. All I got from Tomas was a form letter (which I answered) along with the permissions. This kid is satisfied. Pure joy!*]

Antes de continuar más adelante, le admito que mi carta a Tomás fue escrita en unos de mi momentos más enfermos. ¿Que no fue el Oscar Wilde el que dijo algo tocante al "prison air being so foul only poison weeds grew there? Por ahi va. [*Before continuing any further, I must admit that my letter to Tomas was written during one of my most ill moments. Wasn't it Oscar Wilde who said something like "prison air being so foul only poison weeds grew there?" Or words to that effect?*] As a consequence, i kinda' let out my frustration on him. i still feel i was right, however, and it's a very real part of me. You know, deprived of most everything, one gets to expecting overly much, and at the time, i wasn't taking into consideration your personal responsibilities.

La verdad es que estoy en un proceso de transformación mental; [*The truth is that I am undergoing a process of mental transformation;*] i can see it occurring, feel it surging within me, and it's at once amazing, extremely difficult to grasp, painful, and frightening, to say the least! There are some enlightening moments, though, and that is when i partake and drink deep.

Esto junto con la cosa *Attica* y la muerte del camarada Jackson alla en Quilmas, me agrava la mente. Me canso tanto a veces. Todo parece ser tan inútil. [*All this combined with the* Attica *thing and the death of comrade Jackson over there in Quentin, it weighs heavily on my mind. I get so tired at times. It all seems so futile.*] Nothing seems relevant, anymore, other than an all-out confrontation between the common people and the MAN. La publicación (*New Era*) aquí, for instance, ¿qué bien voy a hacer, escribiendo [*The publication (*New Era*), for instance, what good will I do, writing*] empty treatises on Penal Reform, which no responsible person will act upon, as they should. Or, trying to enhance (some more) the myth of rehabilitation. It just ain't that time of day anymore, Profe. Otro ejemplo: Hace unos días un camarada salió de aquí, volvió a liberar (un Gavacho a un Chicano) a uno de los nuestros, [*Another example: a few days ago a comrade got out of here, returned to liberate one of ours (a white dude helping a Chicano)*] from the camp outside the wall y despúes se llevó un avión a Cuba [*and later took a plane to Cuba*].

De eso se trata hoy en día, todos estudiando; concentrando en liberar (literally) a los presos y reclusos del mundo. Y la orientación que se está llevando acabo, too much! Cuba y Chile ya no son localidades geográficas que uno ve en mapas. Ahora ya se sabe que es posible llegar allá, si eso se desea. Se habla de los campos de entrenamiento por los desiertos del Amman, Jordán y en las provincias de Korea al norte. Sobre todo ésto, sigue la batalla propia. Yo, personalmente, no me considero terrorista, quizas ni guerrillero, porque, let's face it, we haven't even fought yet. Me considero capaz de hacer un sin número de actos que sean necesarios para el bienestar del pueblo o en defensa propia. Pero mi arma es la pluma, arma que empiezo a conocer un poco más cada día. Mi labor (a según la veo en mis ratos locos), es la enseñanza de los niños; la propaganda por nuestra gente. Estoy reteansioso de salir a dar de mí lo todo, como nunca la ha hecho. [*That's how it is these days, everyone studying; concentrating on liberating (literally) all prisoners and captives of the world. And the development that we are undergoing, too much! Cuba and Chile are no longer mere geographic locations that one sees on maps. Now we know that it is possible to get there, if this is what we wish. There is talk about the training camps in the deserts of Amman, Jordan, and in the provinces of North Korea. Amid all this, our personal struggles continue. I, personally, do not consider myself a terrorist, perhaps not even a guerrilla because, let's face it, we haven't even fought yet. I consider myself capable of committing any number of acts necessary for the well-being of the people or in self defense. But my weapon is the pen, a weapon I am getting to know better each passing day. My task (as I see it in my crazy moments) is the education of youth; advocacy for our people. I am super-anxious to get out and give it my all, like I never have done.*]

Su visita a Chile ha de haber sido una experiencia allencompassing. He tratado de absorber todos los detalles. Me imagino la actividad que ha de haber en la gente misma, viviendo el desarollo socialista. El Perú (con excepción de una poema u otro del Vallejo y Abril) nunca me ha interesado, simplemente porque no lo conzco; ni en escrituras. Al momento, la novela no me interesa. Me encuentro concentrado en *SALIR!!* [*Your visit to Chile must have been an all-encompassing experience. I have tried to absorb all the details. I can only imagine the excitement among the people, living within the development of socialism. Peru (with the exception of a poem or two from Vallejo and Abril) never interested me, simply because I don't know it; not even its literature. At present, I am not interested in the novel. I find my self focused on GETTING OUT!!*] But you can understand that, no? Por cierto muy poco me ha interesado la novela, a través de los años. Mas bien prefiero la historia, biografías, la poesía, y los ensayos. [*To be honest I have had very little interest in the novel over the years. I much prefer history, biography, poetry, and essays.*]

Oh, i've read a novel or two, but aside from Saroyan, Steinbeck & Faulkner, la novela americana, nomás no [*the American novel, no way*], i am partial to F. Scott Fitzgerald & Sinclair Lewis, if only for their self-destructive streak. As for Hemingway, and all the rest, later! It wasn't until the Beat movement of the late '50s produced its *literature*, that i got back into the novel. Parecen tener mas significancia para mí las escrituras del Camus y el Kafka. De los latinos, he leido a Azuela, Rulfo, Fuentes, etc. Ahora pronto al Vasquez, Rivera & some from the Quinto Sol stables. [*I think the writings of Camus and Kafka have more significance for me. Of the Latinos, I have read Azuela, Rulfo, Fuentes, etc. More recently, Vasquez, Rivera & some from the Quinto Sol stables.*]

Tocante la profesora Franco, me gustaría saber más de ella. Fíjese, que tengo otro profe que (adopté) se interesó del "Trip . . . ," e hizo un estudio, o ya sea critiqué sobre el poema, para un literary journal de la universidad de Venecia en Italia. [*Regarding Professor Franco, I would like to know more about her. Check this out, I have another prof (I adopted) who got interested in* "Trip . . . ," *and made a study, or a critique of the poem, for a* literary journal *from the University of Venice in Italy.*] Me mandó el papel y después de unos cuantos futile attempts a traducirlo del italiano al ingles [*He sent met the paper and after several* futile attempts *to translate it from Italian to English*], I had to take it to my Puerto Rican comrade (caso del '50 [*whose case is from '50*]), who did a magnificent job of translating it from the Italian into Spanish. Perhaps I can send you a copy, if you wish.

Lo que usted quiera mandar, le aseguro que será bien recibido y bien utilizado. No tan solo por mi, sino por mis camarads también. Lo que si le voy a pedir directamente es ésto: al momento se me ha perdido mi profe [*I assure you that what you want to send will be well received and well used. Not just by me, but by my brothers, too. What I will ask you directly is this: to date I have lost my prof*] between the U. of Conn, & the U of Wyoming, where he went to teach a summer course "Innocence in American & European Fiction." Le agradecería mucho si me pudiera asistir en hacerlo locate. Se llama Glauco Cambon. A veces es muy dificíl escribír de aquí, y en otras ocasiones (abajo de ala, como ésta), se es posible expresar todo a todo. [*I would really appreciate it if you could help locate him. His name is Glauco Cambon. At times it is very difficult to write from here, and on other occa-*

sions (underground, like this), it is possible to express everything about everything.] Incidentally, when you write to me, please use my "*NUMBER,*" which is 83908—and whose reality i reject—these folks get all upset otherwise. Or write directly to Mr. Palmquist, my boss. This, especially if you are sending material. His name & address can be on the outside and mine inside. As long as he gets it personally, I am a cinch to receive it. Okay?

La otra cosa que le iba pedir es que me mande unas fotos de usted y sus colaborantes; ya sea group shot o individual snaps. Hablando de retratos, ¿no retrató usted, por casualidad, la estatua de Don Ernesto, en su reciente visita a Chile? Me gustaría mucho obtener tal foto. También, si tiene un colega por Los Angeles, que pudiera mandarle algo (flix) sobre los "Watts Towers." [*The other thing that I was going to ask you is to send me some photos of you and your colleagues; either a group shot or individual snaps. Speaking of pictures, did you photograph, by chance, the statue of Don Ernesto [Guevara], during your recent visit to Chile? I would really like to have that picture. Also, if you have a colleague in Los Angeles, who could send you something (flix) of the "Watts Towers."*] They have fascinated me, always. In my younger days (en Soledad), i had a photo taken from the Sunday Times weekly section, pasted on my wall for a couple of years. ¡Qué maravilla dejó el Simon Rodia a la posteridad! Las conoce, usted? Tarjetas postales, etc. también serían esenciales. En otras palabras, los visual aids, hermano. [*What majesty Simon Rodia left for posterity. Do you know of them? Postcards, etc., also would be essential. In other words, the visual aids, brother.*] These walls get a might dull after a few calendars.

Comments and/or criticism on the material you sent, solo esto: Punto #3—show that literature tiene raíces populares, etc. Me puse a pensar de las canciones del *trafíque*, contrabando y folk heroes de las cantinas—"La Carga Blanca", "Cuatro Cargadores", "Contrabando d'El Paso", y las del "Güero Polvos": "Año del mil novecientos cuarenta y nueve al contado / mataron en San Antonio, al Güero Polvos mentado . . ." Otra omisión (taking into consideration that yours is not a definitive study) son las canciones "*tabiqueras*", o ya sea, jailhouse ballads. [*Comments and / or criticism on the material you sent, just this: Point #3—show that literature has popular roots, etc. I began to think about the drug trafficking songs, contraband and folk heroes of the cantinas,*—"La carga blanca," "Cuatro Car-gadores," "Contrabando d'El Paso," y las del "Güero Polvos": *"In the year nineteen forty nine to be exact / in San Antonio they killed the renowned Güero Polvos . . ." Another omission (taking into con-sideration that yours is not a definitive study) are the "tabiqueras" songs, or rather, jailhouse ballads.*] These are a unique—we think—form unto themselves. In Texas, it is an accepted way of life that 17 is that age when Chicano youths who have been to *la corre* [*the juvie*], become eligible (?) for la pinta [*the joint*], as others become eligible for the draft. In view of this sad fact, they hang out in the barrio street corners, drinking wine, sniffing & doing smoke, usually with only one guitar among them, to sing songs such as "mi jefe me lo decía, mi jefa con mas razón / hijito no andes robando, vas ir lo correción. Wow! ¡Qué viajes tan dolorosos, en los cuales me voy a veces, pero . . . , la nostalgia es saludable en estos lugares! [*What painful journeys I go on sometimes, but . . . , nostalgia is soothing in these places!*] No, en serio, Profe [*But in all seriousness, Prof*], there is a wealth of material out there among our people. An untapped reservoir. And it is best that people like yourselves try to preserve it, rather than have it ripped-off, otherwise. May we offer a tour by experienced guides? Estoy que no me aguanto [*I can hardly contain myself*].

By the way, i asked the following question of Luis Valdez and never got a reply—which is about normal—one way or the other. Are Chi-cano artists (poets/painters/musicians) actually being judged on their true merits, or are we just a hot commodity on MAD Ave. this season? i mean, like what's the going price for meskins? You know how *that* CHUMP is, all he does is say "buy Black" or "buy Brown," and you get poor unsuspecting dudes thinking they are really into something literary & artistic-wise. Then too, you get the fake jivers hitching rides and traveling in the same set as the dedicated, struggling, for-real peo-ple. And, as is usually the case, the public will go for the carbon-copy, rather than the original. Pero, ahí se va.

Incidentally, if it is not too late, and if you copped "Trip . . ." from La Raza magazine, there are a couple of typographical errors that need amending. On line 45, the word *responded* is mispelled. Then on line 8, following the grafitto, it should read "loud *funky* music," rather than "loud *negro* music. También el nombre del autor debería ir en minúsculas [*Also, the name of the author should be in small letters*], both en "Los Caudillos" y en el "Trip . . ." i think i've run my head long enough, and God (azteco) knows, i don't want to scare you off, as i have most of my past correspondents. So, gradually i am going to start tapering off.

There is one thing that i would like to mention; check the artwork of one, Ruben Estrella, whose piece & illustrations appear in the enclosed publications. This is the calibre of work some of the brothers here are creating. He is a very talented (self-taught) artist, 27 years of age, who is going to shake up the art world! His pieces are known in the Houston area, where he exhibited for the Raza Art Festival; in San Anto (his home) where Sunny & the Sunliners used one of his canvases to grace his latest record album; and in the Kansas City area, where he has donated, on behalf of C.O.R.A., innumerable paintings. He also does pen & ink work, though he is not *the* pen & ink man for our publications. His portrait of Tijerina in our last issue of *Aztlán*, has already been picked up by Papel Chicano of Houston. The portrait's (which is also) background should have been red, rather than pink, but someone got cold feet in the production end of the paper. Oh, yes, i'm proud to call him friend! He is also in the process of doing the cover for a proposed book of my poems which i intend to publish someday.

> Saludes de todos los Pintos
> Chicanos de C.O.R.A. /
> Aztlán / Leavenworth.
> yours in the struggle,
> raúlrsalinas

Please address all correspondence to:[3]
J.S. Palmquist
Asst. Supvr. Education
USP Leavenworth, KS 66048 (Ed, materials)
    or
Roy Salinas #83908
P.O. Box 1000
Leavenworth, Kansas 66048
(preferable letters only)

■ ■ ■

circa early December 1971

Americo Paredes, Director
Center for Mexican American Studies
University of Texas

Estimado Sr. Paredes:

   This is just to inform you that we have been receiving most of the CHISME newsletters and find them very stimulating and informative, from a Chicano educator's point of view. At the same time, we'd like to inquire as to whether your group is receiving our publication, *Aztlán*, as well as a few other inquiries pertinent to our cause.

   Speaking of our publication, when we first came into existence as a journalistic-artistic-literary voice for the Chicano recluses [*captives*] of Leavenworth, we sent it out to various prominent (and some not so prominent) Chicanos-Latinos throughout Aztlán. Being a native Austinite, i sent copies to several persons in the area. With the exception of yourself and Jorge Lara-Braud, we have received no acknowledgment to date. To George I. Sanchez, because we felt he *might* be interested in those social outcasts whom he has written so graphically about; some of these who now happen to be here; studying sociology, educational psych. & the liberal arts. Could it be that the view from Scenic Dr. towards the Highland Lakes/LBJ country obscures his vision of those *"wretched of the earth,"* whose study helps him publish rather than perish? To Jacinto Quirarte for what may have been accomplished between him and some of our *primitive*, naturally talented artists. Unfortunately, we did not prove exciting subjects. Even Leo Nieto responded, if only by the grace of god!

   The reason why you are catching all this ill-wind is because you *have* responded. No, but really, we've had some terrible experiences with MEXICAN-AMERICAN educators. Especially, the ones who have solicited us. Then, when we reply somewhat within their intellectual realms and question their dedication, it seems to turn them off. As if we destroy their image of what Pintos are. We aren't trying to be brusque, but the mere fact that we are Pintos doesn't give these people license to come in with their erudite asses and try to woo us out what is supposedly "de moda" ["*in style*"]. They must realize that LIBERA-TION is the key word in this new hour.

Por ejemplo: (queriendo decir que podemos preparar un estudio sobre [el] fenomeno educacional) the approach is ususally con su stationary muy de color "brown", toda clase de slogans en su busqueda de algo "por la causa." That's all well and good, si estuvieran sinceros. Ironically enough, todas las mujeres profesoras (especially the more militant) corren por surname gabacho. Interesting point for our Pinto Psych. students to go into, que no? [*For example: (assuming that one can prepare a study about this educational phenomenon) the approach is usually with their stationary which is conveniently "brown" in color, all manner of slogans in their desperate search for something "for the cause." That's all well and good, if they were sincere. Ironically enough, all the women professors (especially the more militant) sport gabacho surnames. Interesting point for our Pinto Psych. students to go into, don't you think?*]

The other points: is there some way you can put us in contact with austin's MAYO group, Teatro Chicano and a bookstore that might stock your book, "With His Pistol in His Hand"? Besides the bureacratic hassles we have to contend with in ordering material, when we do get our orders processed, the bookstores don't stock our particular wants. Un carnal aqui ya trato de conseguir ese libro de usted [*A brother here already tried to obtain that book of yours*] through Corky in Denver and La Causa Pubs. in Califas, to no avail. Both places list it in their price lists. Por favor déjenos saber si hay lugares en austin que la podran tener de seguro [*please let us know if there are places in Austin that can obtain them for sure*].

La U.T. siendo [*being*] the *bastion* of *arch-conservativism* we think it is, would it offer any aid for Pintos in the way of EOP, Grants, etc.? Whatever information you can convey to us concerning this matter would be muchly appreciated. Two final questions: Is Alma Canales "del valle" ["*from the valley*"] attending school there? Also what percentage of Chicano students are austinites; from east austin?

By the way, creo que'l Ballesteros y Rivera han contactado a nuestro Profe de historia cultural del Sudoeste, de Kansas City, con interés de venir a vistarnos, a según nos hace saber el patrocinador "external." He aquí mas ejemplares de Aztlán. Si en alguna manera les podamos ayudar, no dejen de escribir. [*By the way, I think that Balles-teros and Rivera have contacted our Southwest Cultural history Prof, from Kansas City, with the hope of coming to visit us, according to word from our "external" sponsor. Here are more copies of Aztlán. If in some way we can help you, don't hesitate to write.*] Alcabo los [*Anyhow the*] above-mentioned diatribes don't apply to *all* Chicano academicians—certainly not to you—only to a few.

Saludos de todos los Chicanos
Pintos de C.O.R.A./
Aztlán/Leavenworth
Atentamente,
raúlrsalinas
redactor

■ ■ ■

December 6, 1971

Sr. Raúl Salinas

Estimados carnales:

Many thanks for your letter, which I received Friday, and for the copies of *Aztlán* and *New Era*. We have received several copies of *Aztlán* to date; they all go to the reading room of our Center, where they are read by many Chicano students, as well as by ourselves. I am glad that you have been receiving *El Chisme*. You are on current mailing list, and we will be sending you anything we publish, though so far *El Chisme* is all we have put out. It is good to know that Jorge Lara-Braud has been in touch with you. In my opinion he is a good and sincere man. Some of the others you mention are good and sincere men in their own way, I suppose, but men exist within many varieties of "mind jails," to quote from a well-known poem. I was amused by the well-aimed descriptions of some individuals you did not name in your letter; I think I recognized them all. I agree with you that "studying" the Chicano "esta de moda." And there is little we can expect from the faddists.

Talking about the "mind jail," I sincerely think that Mr. Salinas' "A Trip through the Mind Jail" is one of the best poems that has come out of the movimiento. Apparently, there are many others who agree, because I have seen it reprinted a number of times.

On the question about "With His Pistol in His Hand," the University of Texas Press both prints and distributes the book, and you should write directly to them (Frank Wardlaw, Director) if you want to order copies for your bookstore. By separate mail I'm sending you a copy of the new paperback edition, dedicated to the Chicanos in Leavenworth.

En cuanto a los otros puntos en su carta, recibirán una carta en pocos días de Jose Limón, assistant director of the Center, quien es miembro de que especializa en "student affairs." He's going to check his information and then write you. Austin's M.A.Y.O. group, by the way, furnished us most of our Mexican-American Studies student body. We are also working closely with the local Teatro Chicano. Mr. Limón will give you the latest news of that, as well as on Chicano enrollment. He is going to check on whether Alma Canales in enrolled at UT now. I see her now and then but am not sure that she is enrolled now. If we get her present address we'll send it on to you.

On the question of aid for "veteranos de la Pinta." You are quite right about UT as a bastion of conservatism, but as the saying goes, *la lucha se hace*. We really can't know until we have tried something definite on them. I am asking Mr. Limón to pursue this matter in his letter.

Saludos a todos los Chicanos en Leavenworth C.O.R.A. We admire your dedication.

cordialmente,
Américo Paredes

■ ■ ■

December 7, 1971

Estimado Sr. Salinas:

Primeramente let me congratulate you on your excellent poem "Trip Through the Mind Jail" which usually takes up two to three days of study in our English 342—Life and Literature of the Southwest: The Chicano Experience. In my opinion it is the closest thing we have to an authentic Chicano epic poem surpassing (by far) Corky's poem which has never really impressed me that much.

Let me answer some of your questions to Dr. Paredes. We have approximately 1000 Chicano students on the campus generally from San Antonio and South Texas. Of these approximately 25 are from Austin. The M.A.Y.O group on campus is trying to do more in this respect by organizing a M.A.Y.O. barrio group in East Austin. I myself spend my Saturday mornings working with a group of high school kids de la Johnston. We hope that these efforts will improve East Austin representation on the campus. Dr. Paredes and I are also making plans to teach Chicano Studies night school courses in East Austin starting next fall.

Financial aid for pintos: We have a financial aid package available for any needy incoming University student. I am sending you the necessary application forms. A student with less that a $6,000 income should have no trouble getting an adequate amount of financial aid. Admission into the University may be a problem if a student with a low SAT (Scholastic Aptitude Test score) is trying to come in the fall semester. However, *any student regardless of his SAT score* can enroll in the summer. If he can pass four courses with a "C" average, he becomes a regular student. If any of the guys in Leavenworth want to try any of this, have them write me. I'll be happy to work with them on an individual basis. UT does continue to be a bastion of conservatism, but I think you will find una buena casa aqui. We have a good Chicano student body, an active M.A.Y.O. group, a sound, stimulating Chicano Studies program and a lot of plans for the future including further co-operation con los pintos de Leavenworth. Let's stay in close touch.

Alma Canales is not an official student although she audits one of our Chicano Studies courses. She is currently working in Raza Unida activities in Austin. Her address is . . .

In case you want to order standard Chicano books, you may write Rudy Saenz . . .

Rudy has built up an impressive Chicano reading shelf and should be able to help you.

I hope I have answered some of your questions. Please feel free to write if I can be of any further help.

Sincerely,
José E. Limón
Assistant to the Director

■ ■ ■

[circa early January 1972]

Sr. Mario Cantu Jr.
San Antonio

Ese Mario:

We received the package of goodies, along with your letter explaining the necessary details, just a few days before xmas. It goes without saying, we were well fixed. Gracias

We will comment on the material accordingly: we had an initial viewing of the slides while loading the cartridges, which only a small number of carnales were able to see, therefore we will have one viewing this evening Thursday since the Educ. Dept. is open again since the holidays. Then we will have a second viewing, possibly at our weekly juntas on Fridays, at which time we will return them to you.

The retras [photos] were placed in plastic document protectors and are getting a lot more play. These will also be sent very shortly. You were right in regards to the calendarios. We need more; if only to make the marking of time a bit easier to handle. Whatever you can spare. We are okay on the souvenir programs.

Los discos de los Mascarones . . . ¡que barbaros! [*The albums from the Mascarones . . . solid stuff!*] They are (in our estimation) the best thing that could have happened to the United States, to Texas, to La Raza, and to the Pintos Chicanos of Leavenworth Penitentiary. On xmas eve, about five carnales sat in the bare room of the Ed. Dept. and listened to the Mascarones' full message. They have been taped and played on the joint radio. Al Brava: No le hace que chingaos diga el culero del Bernal [*We did it our own way: it doesn't matter what the fuck that asshole Bernal says*]. Ha-ha! We couldn't resist that cap.

Concerning possible entries from here for the exhibits of Los Pintores de la Nueva Raza, se puede hacer, pero ya sabes como son estos bueyes [*it can be done, but you already know how these asses are*]. We will attempt to get clearance and at the same time select suitable material from the brothers. Tenemos unos pintores cabrones [*We have some badass artists*], Mario. We have two outtasite pen & ink artists, Tone Briones de Laredo y Carlos Becerra de San Anto. As you well know, we have a number of oil painters, the more advanced had their works displayed at a Raza Art Festival in Houston last year. Pero, sí hay manera [*But, if there is a way*]. We could stand some more information on the "Pintores," brochures, perhaps?

Since your letter arrived during the holidays when the school building is shut down or operating on a skeleton (no pun intended) crew we are not able to send you the requested cards. Especially, if you need them to send out to camaradas. However if you wanted them for display purposes or as "regalos" [*gifts*] from la pinta, we can still accommodate you. Enclosed you will find some of the cards made by our most dear hermanos de C.O.R.A. *Aztlán*. We will also include a few more copies of our paper.

While on that subject, we should go to press early next week. We have what we consider the best issue to date. Without a doubt, you will receive un chingo de copies. Expect in the mail very, very soon. Any thing else i can do for you, for the movimiento and for the well-being of nuestra gente, feel free to ask, con toda la confianza.

In conclusion, we'd like to express our sincerest gratitude for the trust and faith you placed on us, the Pinto Chicano, with your costly collection of slides and fotos. And, because you have shown this much humanness, we'll not betray that trust nor take advantage of your generosity. Tell society to put that in their pipe and choke on it.

Sin mas, recibe saludes de parts de todos los Pintos Chicanos del "11" [*Finally, accept our greetings on behalf of all the Chicano Convicts from "once" (Leavenworth)*]. On behalf of C.O.R.A. / *Aztlán* / Leavenworth, we remain

> Buscando liberación,
> raúlrsalinas

■ ■ ■

February 15, 1972

My Darling Nan:

This is in reply to your keen "shortie" letter of the 27th last. As usual, i was most pleased to hear from you again. Your stationary is freeky; i used to get into that type of thing quite a bit; you know, designing stationary. Of course, i had more time to spare then.

Christmas was just another day for me. No inspirational turn-on, whatsoever. Glad to hear that you got a black light for your room. Perhaps, i can find a way to send you some outtasite posters, later on. Although it seems that day-glo posters are getting more play than black light, these days; they are still readily available.

As for the album, "J.C. Superstar" is nice, but i'd hoped you might get either "El Chicano," or Santana's "Abraxas," which are heavier rock with latin influence. Have you dug on any of these?

Speaking of "El Chicano," our latest issue of *Aztlán*, which is about a week away from being completed, has them featured throughout. i'll send you copies of it as soon as we get the first run.

Incidentally, i became a professional writer this month. A check arrived in the mail for permission to use my lenghty narrative poem. You remember "A Trip Through The Mind Jail," don't you? Did you ever get to read it? It has received some pretty good response all over Aztlán and elsewhere. Anyway, the check didn't amount to a hill of beans, but it's a start, right? Both anthologies of Chicano Literature in which my poems will be included, are due out this Spring. In fact, one of them has already been advertised in Publisher's Weekly.

The weather has been cold, but i very seldom go out. Snows have been light but constant, this winter. Healthwise, i'm alright. "i may be dying inside, but i don't feel a thing." i do appreciate your concern, though.

About the Janis poem, i am enclosing it along with this letter. Like i said before, it's not the finished poem, because i feel there is more to be added. However, this is all i've been able to express thus far. i will be anticipating your comments. Okay?

A couple of weeks ago, there was a 3 hour Janis special on the local underground station. And guess what? i missed it! The following night there was a Jefferson Airplane show. It was alright, but Gracie Slick will never attain the stature of the late Miss Joplin. What do you think? If you get a chance, try to pick up on a couple of jams entitled "Malo" & "Garcia." They are excellent rock showcases.

Getting into a would-you-believe trip, i received your second letter while in the process of writing this one, between my little excursions to and from the print shop, where i have to check on the paper. Needless to say, i was immensely turned on by it, so i'll incorporate them both here.

While on the subject of school, i'm not doing too hot myself. At present i am carrying 12 credit hours, hoping to grease on by. Maybe, just maybe i'll get a A.A. degree (2 yrs.) Your school flik left me beaming with pride and i'm still flashing behind it. Very lovely woman / child. Yes, naturally bronze. Chicano Brown to be more specific. You are the future of our people of the sun. This is why you have to dig in and learn all about what's happening with La Raza. I am very heavy into Chicano History, Azetc Culture, and Mexico.

Incidentally, did a lecturer by name of Andrew Pulley speak at Travis? Listen, mi'ja, since i'm getting in tune with myself pretty good, and being that the lines of communication between me and your folks are not cool, i would like for you to write as often as you are able to. i want us to keep close contact with one another for the next few months. Say, i didn't know you were a thing-saver. i promise to send you things from time to time. Regards to everyone there. Anxiously awaiting your reply, i wish you

> Love & Contentment,
> "Dad"
> raúlrsalinas

■ ■ ■

[circa late February 1972]

Querido Carnal Tapón!

I received your cartita and was very happy to hear from you, I'm doing a toda madre, tu saves, me estan pegando en la pura "pata de palo" [*you know, little do they know that in trying to hurt me they're helping me*]. The only days that I do hard times is on Friday nights when you vatos are cutting it up at the grupo.

Yea! carnal I think it would be a good idea if you write the vatos at McNeil and see if they will send me another of them certificates. Thanks carnal, and give them my saludos, ok.

Say brother Tapon, are the carnales getting it together now? I mean are we going pa' delante with our cause or como la miras [*I mean are we going forward with our cause or how do you see it*]?

You know carnal, the way I see it every carnal, and I mean todos, are able to defend themselves, but few are willing, and that's no good!

We got to be able and willing. That's the whole concept. All of our lifes that's what's been preserving us and I don't think there's a whole lot of carnales that have been brainwashed and have a negative attitude toward freedom for our "pobre jente." Let me just tell you this, carnal, we have a tough job y esta cabron, but you know me brother, muerte o libertad por medio de la Revolución [*death or liberty by way of Revolution*]. You and I know carnal there's no other way, y no esperamos mirarla llegar pero nuestra gente sí [*and we don't expect to see it happen but our people will*]. Tu saves carnal [*you know brother*], Death is the price of revolution. I assumed that responsibility because I know the role I'm playing, Venceremos! Siempre!

Say carnal, mandame some papiros chicanos con el "charro negro" está bien? Orale pues carnal, saludame a mis "homeboys" el David y el güerito a todos y al carnal Chacón y al Manuel Lerma al comandante "meme" la mesa collectiva y todos los chicanos revolucionarios. [*Say brother, send me some Chicano publications with the "black robe," ok? Orale pues carnal, give my regards to my homeboys David and el güerito and all of them and to brother Chacon and Manuel Lerma, commandante "meme," the collective leadership and all the Chicano Revolutionaries.*]

Chairman Mao Tse Tung says,

"whatever the enemy supports, we oppose.
whatever the enemy opposes, we support"
"and power comes from the barrel of a gun!"
Brother Fidel says,
"those who are not Revolutionary fighters cannot be called
Communists." Hasta mas alla de la Victoria.

Beto Gudino
P.S. Saludos de todos los carnales en el "hoyo", y aganle el cale a poner musica chicana que este de aquellas hombre! estas pinches rolas que estan poniendo parece que están en un "velorio", se salen de amadre con la musica esos vatos hombre! Ese tapón, esta muy loco mi homie el David, que no? Ya hablaste con el? Tiene un chingo en la bola and he's ready.

Saludes de los vatos en la C.U.
[*P.S. Greetings from all the brothers in the "hole," and Hey man, try to*]

get them to play some righteous Chicano music man! The fucking tunes they're playing make it seem like they're at a funeral wake, those dudes are fucked up for playing that music. Hey Tapon, my homeboy David is real crazy, ain't that right? Have you talked to him? He's got a lot on the ball and he's ready.]

P.S.S.

Say Brother Tapon,

Also tell my comandante Meme that I received el mensaje [*the message*] and to keep up his work because he is doing a real good job and not to worry, it's a hard job and we got a long ways yet, siempre pa' delante [*always forward*], wherever I may be, I'm with you carnales. Viva La Revolución

■ ■ ■

[circa late February 1972]

Spirit in the Dark
c/o Guardian
Attn: Stephen Torgoff

Camarada Esteban:

Your prompt reply arrived yesterday. We will certainly appreciate the plug in your column. Thanx. Regretfully Guardian readers cannot subcribe to *Aztlán*; it being an extension of our Chicano Cultural Group here, with a limited circulation. We do, however, send it to concerned folks who we feel are interested in the Chicano cause as one means to the the total and complete freedom of the common people. Therefore we can spare a few copies, if contacted.

As to whether you can ask your readers to send us material, we would like nothing better. But, the fact remains that they've got us where we're not. There are still certain regulations we must abide by and limitations as to what comes in. And since we have no control over such matters we've been advised to inform you that permission cannot be granted.

On the other hand, our somewhat liberal sponsor—who feels that one should become aware and better informed in all areas—has agreed to our receiving a book or two (we prefer dog-eared, weather-beaten paper backs) from *you*. Our interests, at the moment, center around the role of the artist (poet, painter, musician) in a social movement in general, and in people's poets/poetry in particular. If you can avail us of something along these lines, we'd be muchly grateful. Also—when addressing mail to *Aztlán*, please be sure that the name not appear on the outside; this for matters of expediency and other things.

We have not, as yet, received the pamphlets you mentioned, but as soon as we do we'll surely inform you. Enclosed are a few more copies of *Aztlán*. We hope to have issue #4 off the press before the end of this month. Expect your copy(ies) shortly thereafter.

> Till the walls crumble, we
> remain
> Yours in the struggle,
> raúlrsalinas

■ ■ ■

February 29, 1972

Mario Cantu Jr.

Estimado Carnal:

Apenas en estos días se nos presenta la quebrada de escribirte unas cuantas lineas. Creo el Borrado to escribió ayer, no?

Bueno, hemos terminado con el *Aztlán*, y a pesar de unos errores, pensamos que salió bien. Espera un escante de copias en la semana entrante. O, si, quisieramos saber si es posible que tu le puedas mandar al *RIUS* su ejemplar? Todo lo que el cartoon significa, eso el lo que pensamos de sus caricaturas. Como van los planes respecto al Centro Cultural? [*It is only in these last few days that I have found the time to write you these lines. I think Borrado wrote you yesterday, right? Well, we have completed* Aztlán, *and despite a few errors, we think it came out fine. Expect a short stack of copies in the coming week. Oh, yes, we would like to know if you could send RIUS his copy? All that our cartoon represents, is how we feel about his caricatures. How are the plans going for the Cultural Center?*]

Incidentally, could you send more details concerning the letterhead? Los carnales ya estan en eso de "sketches", solo que manda mas detalles, si hay manera. También queremos saber que mas podemos hacer. Que clase de camello tienen donde puedamos donate our services? [*The brothers already are doing "sketches," so just send more details, if you can. We also want to know what more we can do. What kind of work do you have for us [so we can] donate our services?*]

Nos movió de establecer embajada Chicana en el Terre [*We were moved by the creation of a Chicano embassy in el Terre (Mexico)*]. Why not one in Chile? O en la isla del barbudo [*Or on the island of the bearded one*]? Argelia [*Algeria*]? We are glad that you got to meet our ex-alumnus Ramon Tijerina, he's a very dedicated brother. We have a lot of faith and confidence in the dude, es el primer soldado que C.O.R.A. ha producido [*he is the first warrior that C.O.R.A. has produced*]. We are quite proud of him (witness current issue of *Aztlán*).

Quiero que sepas que nos quedamos malias despues de haber leido los magazines *POR QUE*. No tienes algunas copias mas? Estamos al corriente de los sucesos en las sierras de Guerrero y la tragedia fatal del companero Genaro Vasquez. El material que mandaste sobre el, fue utilizado para un "lecture" en nuestra clase cultural.

Otro carnal que está para salir pronto, se ha ido para el "hospi" in Ft. Worth. Se llama Ramón Chacón y quisiera que le mandaras unas cuantas lineas. El sabe de tu correspondencia con nosotros, oyó los discos, leyo los materiales, etc. Es uno de los camaradas quien mas nos endoctrino en lo de la politica y *pensamiento progresivo*.

Ahi te va una copia personal de *Aztlán*. Esperamos tus comentarios sobre de él. Después te mandaremos mas. Saludes fraternales de todos los pintos Chicanos de C.O.R.A./*Aztlán*/Leavenworth. [*I want you to know that we were left longing for more after having read the POR QUE magazines. Do you have more copies? We are up to date on the events in the mountains of Guerrero and the fatal tragedy of brother Genaro Vasquez. The material about him that you sent was used for a "lecture" in our culture class.*

Another brother who is about to get out soon has gone to the "hospi" in Ft. Worth. His name is Ramon Chacon and I would like for you to send him a few lines. He knows of your correspondence with us, heard the records, read the materials, etc. He is one of the brothers who taught us the most about politics and progressive thought.

Here is a personal copy of Aztlán. We look forward to your com-

ments. Later we will send you more. Fraternal greetings from all the Chicano Convicts of C.O.R.A./Aztlán/Leavenworth.]

Hasta la liberación,
raúlrsalinas
Editor

■ ■ ■

March 2, 1972

Ms. Dorothy E. Harth
Onandaga Community College

Dear Ms. Harth:

i was asked, by our Chicano Culture Group's Correspondence Secretary to reply to your letter; give you a bit more information concerning our publication, *Aztlán*, and the contributors therein.

First off, thank you for your comments (and praise) on the content of our journalistic/literary/artistic endeavors. We are equally impressed. Especially, when we take into consideration that we are all amateurs. Issues 1 & 2 are somewhat scarce and difficult to find. In fact, the supply has, for all intents and purposes, been exhausted. However, we think we can come up with a copy of each. In the meantime we are sending our latest issue, we think you will appreciate it.

Concerning the proposed anthology you mentioned, is this intended for publication, or merely a personal compilation for classroom use? We think something can be arranged. Could you send us more details and information on this matter? We have a loose-knit group of poets who have been reprinted in various Chicano Press (periodicals & magazines) Publications throughout the Southwest. A couple have been featured in Chicano Anthologies due out this May and Summer. Prentice-Hall is one of the publishers, the other will be handled by Vintage Press. Among the more prolific poets are Juan Reyes, Alberto Mares & Carlos Becerra.

Poets, incidentally, are not all we have. There are some talented individuals in other areas. Jose Rubio is a writer of merit, as you can well determine by the past two issues of *Aztlán*. Our artists are also of a high-caliber. Ruben Estrella, who does mostly oils & acrylics, is a

2-time winner of the Penal Press Contest Awards. His work can be seen in the Kansas-Missouri area, New Mexico and Texas. An album cover by Sunny & the Sunliners, "Young, Gifted & Brown," was done by Estrella. Pablo Valdez is rapidly gaining stature in our confined art colony. Antonio Briones & Carlos Becerra are our pen & ink men. They produce, collectively and individually, some of the finer drawings we have seen. They also do oils. Our goals in C.O.R.A. are to produce these talents, or rather, help cultivate them, for the benefit of our people, and the world. We also have speakers, lecturers & scholars; all self-taught and prison-made.

Now, about "Journey II." It, along with several other poems, are at present being put into manuscript form, for possible publication at year's end. This is why we'd like more details regarding your project. Another poem, "A Trip Through The Mind Jail," has received an overwhelming response in the Chicano communities and elsewhere. It will be appearing in the two anthologies previously mentioned. One is being edited by Luis Valdez (Teatro Campesino) & Stan Steiner (La Raza); the other is being put together by Antonia Shular/Joseph Sommers/& Tomas Ybarra, all from the University of Washington at Seattle.

Your offer of textbooks is most generous. We can always use reading materials. Whatever you may care to send will be greatly appreciated, and utilized to the fullest. However, when you do send any educational material, please address to J. S. Palmquist, Asst. Supvr. Education, USP Leavenworth, KS 66048, rather than directly to *Aztlán*. You can mention us inside the contents, okay? Thanks.

In answer to your query posed: yes, all of the material in *Aztlán* is the work of Chicano prisoners at Leavenworth. Only on two occasions have we included an article by one of our outside sponsors. Our primary aims are to promote the talent among the brothers here.

If there is anyway we can be of more assistance to you or your project, please let us know. Receive warm regards from all the Chicano pintos of C.O.R.A/*Aztlán*/ Leavenworth.

> Hasta la liberación,
> raúlrsalinas
> editor

■ ■ ■

Mar 3, 1972

Decade of Struggle
Year of Unity
Time of Dragons

Bro Tap, Brothers of Aztlán,

"When the prison doors are open the real dragon will fly out." sd. Ho Chi Minh, the Grey Fox of the Jungle, he did 18 mos in a Chinese prison.

We got a whole lot of Dragons in the slammers across Babylon. What fire they'll breathe when they fly out!

What hell we all must live in till we fly out. It's hell inside. It's hell outside too. We could have heaven right here on Earth but for a few beasts and monsters. Those few potbellied, bald headed, cigar chompin' Institutional bandits called the ruling class. The world's all time con men running the killer con game of all time. The People's Enemy Number One! Armed robbers, murders, rapers, that's what they are. And they got the nerve to lock us up? If we're criminals what are they?

"Free Enterprise," that's the con they run on us, that's the bag they work out of. Competition that's their games, they want us to believe that to compete with each other is natural, to struggle against one another is the only way to survive.

There is enough on this planet for everybody, the problem arises when a few take more than they need and the many go without. When the few take more than they need then the rest of us, the majority, must compete with one another for the leftovers, the scraps.

"Free Enterprise," indeed! You and I are expected to compete with Rockerfeller, Ford, Howard Hughes, Du Pont? Ha! They got tax laws on their side, foundation loop-holes, Judges, Senators, Governors, the President. How are we suppose to compete with them? They got all the tools.

But when do we compete with them, when we use our own meager little tools, when we go into a bank with our little gun and compete for some cash, they call it bank robbery. When we use "Free Enterprise" and develop International Trade, they call it smuggling. When we get involved in Interstate Commerce, they call it car theft. When we use the mail like an Insurance company does, they call it mail fraud. When we use tax breaks, they call it Income Tax Evasion. When we refuse to join their gang of armed thugs, they call it draft evasion. Weird ain't it?

I got some ideas on what needs to be done, but I don't want to be accused of advocating the overthrow of the government, ya know what I mean?

I really dig this issue of Atzlan, I'm very honored to see my name in it, really, I know John and the rest of the Bros and Sisters at the A 2 Sun and the Rainbow People's Party are too.

Just came from a nightmare called Springfield, headin' for a bad dream called Terre Haute.

> Yours, In Struggle
> Dragon Power to the Human
> Flame Throwers
> Pun Plamandon
> RPP
> Revolution is the way to live
> Genie + RPP give their love
> and revolutionary embrace.

■ ■ ■

March 6, 1972

Kell Robertson
Desperado Press
San Francisco

Brother Kell:

Uptight like a most mutha'. But, guilt feelings began to creep their way into my being. Your letter fixed me good and i regret not having answered any sooner. Things happening throughout the country seem to have an effect on all the convicted masses. i'm glad you dug the Tijerina poster. Incidentally, in the process of going mad and gathering our marbles back up, we also managed to get another issue of *Aztlán* off the press. Minor discrepancies aside, we're quite proud of this one. Yours is enclosed; need more, sound us.

The goodies you sent were glommed up by compañeros and i, then back again. "Thunderlips Jones" is a gas. It would be nice to meet all you good folks. i'm winding this bit here, and should the fellers down yonder not press for my "corpus christi/corpus delicious," i am headed for the Pacific Northwest. A small contingent of Chicanos up there are trying to get me sprung. The common people in general and La Raza in particular, is what i'll be into, should liberation be granted me. The way the trend is moving, in regards to smoke and chemical laws i might just luck out. This could be my year. Otherwise, i'll be buried deep in the heart o' Tex-ass for another pair (or two) of calendars.

Have you by any chance read *Maximum Security*? It's a book of prison writings from Soledad & Folsom. If you have, let me know what you think. i read a review in the K.C. Star by an inmate who wants out BAD. It was a bad review. A righteous put-down man. i'm just through reading Sam Melville's "*Letters From Attica*," and it is really good. Of course, it can be torn apart from a literary point of view, or a revolutionary analysis (whatever that may be); nevertheless, i liked it because he was like so many of us in this nation's lock-ups; struggling, forcing ourselves to learn, and attempting heavy works of progressive thought.

Listen man, i'm going to come right out and hit on you for some very inexpensive literature from China Books on 24th Street. One is the Little Red Book which costs 60 cents, and the other is a set on the chairman's writings on the Cultural Revolution. Complete it sells for 1.75, but the two pamphlets i'm interested in are "On Literature & Art: Talks at Yenan" (.60) and "Five Documents on Literature & Art" (.20). Maybe these items won't be so frowned on and difficult to cop, now that Pricky has been to Asia. Oh, yes, i'll repay this gesture someway; drawings, poems, or in cash when i come through. And don't go for everything bad you hear about convicts. In reality, we are just people. A very tolerant people, i would say.

Just copped a new crew on board, and they're already getting down. Hopefully, there'll be a NEW ERA out by next month. One is a fat Chicano who writes a taste, and is bad, bad on the rapidograph. His warped sense of values clashes grindingly with mine (or my lack of). He is from San Antone, where else? The other is a freaky little dude from Detroit. He writes and rights and maintains the proper equilibrium necessary for the sanity of our temporal pad.

Will write more later. i promise not too take this long again. i wish you

> Euphoric contentment,
> Raúlrsalinas
> editor

■ ■ ■

April 4, 1972

Director
Board of Pardons and Paroles
Austin

Dear Sir:

I am writing to inquire about the status of Mr. Roy Salinas of Austin, Texas, who at present is a prisoner in the Federal Penitentiary at Leavenworth, Kansas. His number in 83908-132.

Mr. Salinas first came to my attention because of his creative writing. I have since received several personal letters from him, in which he discussed his problems, his plans for the future, and his aspirations. I am not certain of his present circumstances. There seems to have been a detainer placed against him for violation of parole, but I do not have the specific facts in this matter.

The motivation for this letter of inquiry lies in the strong possibility that he might be eligible not only for admission, but also for an academic scholarship to the University of Washington. Several of my colleagues who have read his published material and his letters share my high estimate of his personal and his academic potential. We feel that the stated change in life goals is actually a sincere, internalized one. Further, and of great importance, there now is an ongoing program, with support services, designed to integrate a select number on ex-convicts into academic careers at this university. This program includes part-time employment, housing, and personal counseling.

As you can see, the question of the status of Mr. Salinas is an important one. In fact, it may determine his future. I will appreciate any concrete information which you may be able to make available, as well as any advice which you may be able to offer in this regard.

With best personal wishes, I remain,

Sincerely yours,
Joseph Sommers
Professor, Latin American
Literature

■ ■ ■

April 7, 1972

Professor Joseph Sommers
University of Washington
RE: SALINAS, Roy

Dear Sir:

Your letter of April 4, 1972, has been received, reviewed, and referred to this office for reply.

We have requested the official at the Federal Institution, Leavenworth, Kansas, to advise this office sixty (60) days prior to his release from the institution. Once this notice has been received, Mr. Salinas' file will again be reviewed by the Texas Board of Pardons and Paroles, and a final decision reached.

One of two decision can be made at the time of review. The Board can decide to let revocation stand, and Mr. Salinas be returned to the Texas Department of Corrections for service on the remainder of his sentence. Another decision that can be made is to reinstate parole to an available plan. Prior to the last decision being made, the Board would have to be certain that such a plan exists and parole authorities from the State in which the plan exists would be requested to verify this plan.

We greatly appreciate your interest in this situation, and feel that interest of persons of your stature will greatly contribute to Mr. Salinas' overall rehabilitation. We are making your letter a part of Mr. Salinas' permanent file.

Yours very truly,
J. Berger, Director
Division of Parole Supervision
George Young
Parole Staff Supervisor

■ ■ ■

April 13, 1972

Carnal Raúl:

I have what I feel is good news. Our first "thrust" to the Texas Parole Board in regard to your detainer was received quite well. Tomas y Joe Sommers y otro Ph.D. in Linguistics por nombre de Sol Soporta, Elda, Rene (haciendo pedo como siempre) y yo, tuvimos un "war session" sobre el contento de la repuesta de Tejas.

It was the general opinion that the reply, though guarded and uncommittal as was expected, offered us a very clear avenue of attack to achieve our goal. We have made definite plans which hinge on "timing" as the key factor. We must prepare a full comprehensive plan for your out-of-state parole and present it at the time their letter suggests. There will, of course, be continued communication with them so as to keep them aware of our desires.

A big part of the "package" we must prepare is getting you admitted to school. From there follows, housing, employment and what I feel shouldn't be too much trouble obtaining because of a few persons I know, acceptance of you by the parole authorities of this State. If you indicate your proposed field of study we feel we can obtain added support for you from the appropriate department.

Tomas Ybarra has recently returned from a conference in Indiana University where he presented a paper. He renewed an acquaintance with Tomas Rivera (*y no se lo trago la tierra*) and interested him in our efforts to bring you here. Being that Tomas Rivera is from Texas he will undoubtedly be able to help tremendously.

Bueno, ya tienes una idea por donde vamos, any suggestions? In considering "timing" we have to know your MR [mandatory release] date. También manda la applicacion que te mande.

Hasta las otras,
Tu Carnal
Armando Mendoza

■ ■ ■

IN MAGAZINE

Iowa City, Iowa
June 8, 1972

Raúl R. Salinas

Oh, Ye of Little Faith:

Who the hell are you to squat there in your little self-woven womb of characterless disbelief of your fellow man and talk to me of the best-laid plans of mice and men?

I do agree with you about not waiting around for busses that never come. What you do is you raise your lackluster ass from the curb and propel your shuffling, shucking feet to a place where the busses do run. And if you have to walk a couple of blocks out of your way because a fence or two is in your way, you do that too. But what you don't do, Tap, is you don't sit there in your own puke and spit your frustration out at the passerby's legs who is trying to get where he must be in order to get to where he wants to be. Because all you'll hit is his feet, Tap; and that hurts no one but you.

Since I've been out I've written you nine (9) letters. I got you a scholarship to Famous Writers. When I first went to Texas, I talked to one of the best defense lawyers in South Texas about your detainer. I wrote you and asked you for more information; no answer. But where you and I differ is that I assumed my letters weren't getting through to you. I made the stupid mistake of thinking that you would know that was the case. Understand this: I have not been able to get letters into Leavenworth. I was turned away from the doors of Marion a month ago when I tried to visit Greek and Vern. I didn't know you were there because the last issue of *Aztlán* led me to believe you were still in Leavenworth. I can't get in touch with Ruben and I've lost all contact with Famous Schools because one of two things: either you two fuckers blew off those scholarships or little Mac & big Palm refused to allow you two the course. Which is it Tap? Communicate, damn you; it's the only way to get something done.

Your letter doesn't anger me because I understand what you're going through. Too many convicts do adhere to the "Of Mice and Men" syndrome, so I can see why you might believe that of all men.

But you are wrong this time and the first step you must take is to just once more forget your inbred skepticism and believe in the integrity of another's goals.

Cornfields don't spring up in the middle of the night. You plant one seed at a time on a one-to-one relationship. It takes preparation just as my obligations do. You make a few wrong starts, you don't quit; you keep going on.

My board of directors is made up of seven Iowa City businessmen. There are a cross-section of Republicans and Democrats, Liberals and Conservatives. Our corporation, Penology Publications, Inc., is so set up that as we get into the black John Ricardo and I can buy out their shares and make it an all-ex-convict run operation. We differ from PDI in that one, we pay salaries so that every person can live his own lifestyle; two, a person must be an ex-offender in order to work with IN or Penology Publications; and, three, we are trying to bring about change through *total* and *truthful* communication between the keeper and the kept. Sure, we're going to get doors slammed in our faces by both the keeper and the convict. But that won't stop us because there are just enough people on both sides who are willing to work for the goals we believe in. To give you an example of this, in two weeks we are holding a special meeting in order to sell fifty thousand dollars worth of stock. There will be forty-five people at that meeting and every one of them wants a piece of the action.

What it all means, Tap, is that IN and Penology Publications is going to be an answer to a talented convict's need of a outlet for his talents and motivations and the opportunity to be paid in this society's accepted method of recompensation; bread and recognition.

At this point, we're paying up to twenty-five bucks a piece for well-written and informative works from convicts, upon publication. Our first issue is due to hit the presses in the middle of August. It's a thirty-two page monthly printed on enameled stock and in two colors.

As you say, the place for action is wherever one happens to be.

Wes
Wesley Noble Graham

■　■　■

June 25, 1972

Charles W. Hoehne
Attorney-at-Law
Austin

Sir Charles:

It has been some time since our last exchange of correspondence. Many, many things have occurred to me, in the interim. i will try to relate some of them to you now; at least the ones i feel are more valid and which need airing before any more time elapses.

In looking back through some of your old correspondence, i notice where you ran some advice past me, about "the sad fact is that you still have to do that (Leavenworth) time. Take advantage of the opportunities which might arise. Study, learn a trade and we can utilize all this when we present your case to the Board of Pardons & Paroles." Or words to that effect. Well, four years have passed since that letter was sent, six since i last read your NY times! i did just as you advised. During my stay at Leavenworth, i became editor of *New Era*, which is the general prison publication. i instituted *Aztlán*, a Chicano publication, which has received acclaim from several sectors of the world. We set up an information center on Chicano and Third World data.

My poetry was published in the magazines *Con Safos* (L.A.), *La Raza* (L.A.) & *Entrelineas* (K.C., MO). The only two anthologies of Chicano Literature which have (to my knowledge) been published, includes four of my poems. They are, *Anthology of Chicano Literature* by Luis Valdez & Stan Steiner, and *Texto Y Contexto* by Antonia Castaneda Shular, Prof. Joseph Sommers & Prof. Tomas Ybarra, all of the U. of Washington-Seattle. In 1970, i won 1st. prize for Best Sports Story in the American Penal Press Contest (3 yr. scholarship to Famous—ugh!—Writers School.) Now, i've a thin volume of collected poems, and about five short, short stories, ready for publication. The people in Seattle are trying to get me in school up there. All this is well and good, but i still have that crude, "southern-style" sword of Damocles hanging over my head. So, with less than six months remaining in this bit, I don't know what's going to happen.

The other thing which i am heavily involved in—and which is the main reason for this letter being prompted—is Penal (again ugh!) Reform and/or Prisoners Rights. While in Leavenworth, i was involved directly and indirectly in three work stoppages (strikes?). The last one resulted in my new address. Here's what's *HAPNIN'*: experiments are being conducted at Marion Federal Prison, employing Americanised-Chinese Communist Brain-Washing techniques. Perhaps it sounds like a whole lotta' paranoia, but i can assure you it's for real! On July 5, 1972, a Report to the United Nations Economic and Social Council will be submitted by attorneys from the Center for the Constitutional Rights (Kunstler, et. al), The New York American Civil Liberties Union, and the NAACP Legal Defense. At the same time (hopefully!), other attorneys around the country will be doing likewise. Belli in S.F., John Thorne in San Jose, other in St. Louis, Seattle, Detroit & Washington, D.C will be calling press conferences.

To date, no one in our area (Austin, Dallas, Houston & San Antonio) has been contacted. Perhaps you could call a press conference and give out copies of the U.N. document, with direction that the report will be submitted simultaneously on July 5th, with our lawsuit and invitation to the Judiciary (House) Subcommittee No 3, asking them to get in here and listen to what we have to say.

Within the next few days i will be sending you all of what we have authored, compiled and stumbled upon. i guess you know me well enough to know that i would never resort to putting you in no *trick bag*, contrary to what police records may indicate. However, if you feel somewhat apprehensive as to the authenticity of our sources and labors, you can check out the *Corrective Psychiatry and Journal of Social Therapy* Vol. 8, no. 1–4, 1962. The brothers i am engaged in this project with are from the Pacific Coast and can be spoken of knowingly by authoress Jessica Mitford, Christina Ramer (administrative aide to U.S. Congressman Ron. V. Dellums), John Bell of the *Seattle Times*, and Ron Silliman of the San Rafael, California Committee for Prisoner Humanity and Justice. Their addresses can be found in some of the materials you will be receiving from me. Check out the veracity of some, if you find it necessary to do so.

Because of mail tampering, please acknowledge receipt of this letter and enclosure upon date of its arrival to your office. Also, on the face of any correspondence you direct to me, type or print "Attorney/

Client Mail: Open in presence of addressee." Anticipating a prompt reply from your office, we remain,

Yours for a better world,
Raúl R. Salinas #83908-132

■ ■ ■

Sunday Evening

25 June 1972
Raúl Salinas and Lanier Ramer

Allen Resler

Appeals and Law Reform Office
Kansas City

Hello Allen:

Some things have been happening up here in Marion that it is time to cut you in on.

The enclosed report of the Federal Prisoners' Coalition to the United Nations will tell you where it is at and what it is.

You'll notice on the last two pages the names of some prisoners at Leavenworth and Eduardo Castro listed as being in Springfield (we now hear that he is back in Leavenworth). We need for the guys to be notified of the Report and its content because they may get pushed-on by the prison staff when it comes out and not even know why. They could be sent copies under the attorney/client mail privilege if you will represent their 1st Amendment cause and rights for them to be part of uttering such a document.

In addition to the report to the U.N. we've asked the Committee on the Judiciary (House) Subcommittee No. 3 to get in here and listen to what we have to say.

What you can do with the U.N. document is call a press-conference and give out copies of it with directions that the report will be filed in New York on July 5th by attorneys from the Center for Constituional Rights (Kunstler et al), the New York American Civil Liberties Union, and the NAACP Legal Defense Attorneys. If you can get the press briefing done on Friday the 30th that will be best; for at the same time attorneys around the country will be doing the same thing. To make a big-bang for Kleindienst and Carslon for the 4th is the point.

While all the hoohraw about Prison Reform has been going on they've been doing their greased-pig number by quietly setting up brainwashing centers in each of their prisons using Marion as their model. It has been going on for 3-1/2 years, and has spread to about a dozen other places thus far. We don't know when they have Leavenworth scheduled to become part of that.

It is all supposed to be a big secret hidden behind an impenetrable shield of mumbo-jumbo terminology.

Did you get Joe Perez's letter with the censorship article and a statement from Professor Maruyama of Antioch College? If so acknowledge receipt of it, please. Professor Francisco Ruiz of Penn Valley Community College will be in touch with you for a copy of the U.N. Report. Run it down to him what it is about.

■ ■ ■

Mr. Whiteman, Cap'n, Bossman, Massa, Sir/

June 26, 1972
Wes Graham
Iowa City

Dear Sir:

i do know how to get a reaction, do i not? Do you really think you laid me down with your stenographically dictated tirade? No bet, mister. And I have not lost my faith in Humanity, not by a long shot, just calling them as i see them.

You must obviously (and erroneously) think the bus services have been curtailed in all areas, but you are absolutely wrong again. SOME busses *are* running. These are the ones i am now riding in. And as for my lackluster ass, it's been shining ever so brightly, in the past year and a half, since i am constantly moving. That rhetoric about going around and over fences (walls?) in spite of their barriers, is what i would advise to those whose perseverance and determination is somewhat lacking. To those liberal "spokesmen" and/or publications that would help.

All that we ever got from you was letter from a place called Big Rock Candy Mountain and a wedding invite from Mason City; neither with a return address. You say you wrote me/us 9 letters which went unacknowledged, due too (as you assumed) their not getting through. What about the legal dept. at Phase IV, could they not have interceded/visited? Where is the commitment to the nation's prisoners? But asides from all that, you could have contacted Carmen or Duji or Miz Hill or Prof. Ruiz or Divonna Lynn; if you'd *really* wanted to communicate that badly. No? You didn't, okay, that's solid. We just waited, *WITH MUCH FAITH!* And just what did you learn at the school you attended??

We received the initial copy of that other periodical, and that was the extent of it. John Henry wrote a beautiful letter to the staff, no acknowledgment. When Vern kited us from here, while setting up his publication (long since defunct), i hooked him up to you and the next thing we pick up on, is that Vern's letter has been printed. Said info coming from a transferee. O' Yea? That's cool. Then every swinging dick in the joint starts getting the periodical . . . except us (NE). We read on borrowed copies where you are running around with Rex Fletcher & JOHN SEVERSON WATSON!!! Wow! Watson still relying on his snake-in-the-grass journalism. By this time the Signet articles and drawings start appearing in your rag. Richard was still with us, so it was kicked around some. No defamation of character, mind you; just simple befuddled i-wonders. When we went to get the flats of CHE, for another run due to demand, it too was gone.

Talking about little faith, no, Ruben and I did not blow off our scholarships. When they arrived, naturally, we were profoundly grateful. Ruben, pissing in his pants with anxiety, wanted to scribble you a thank-you kite. i, the undaunted stoic, would wait, as per *instructions*. Finally, his impatience got to bugging me and i told him to write you. He sent a simple but very warm letter of gratitude & appreciation; no reply. Oooo! That messed with the dude's head.

My scholarship is still intact. The introductory correspondence was tampered with. So i never even got started. Ruben sent in two lessons and that's the last he heard from them. According to Montecalvo, who supposedly got it from McK., the Famous Schools went bankrupt. Who knows?

What followed was the scandal brought in by Art Rabel's people. It had to do with a coup you attempted on Joe and it backfired. To really put the icing on the cake, Art comes out listed as representative of the Big Top!⁴ Hey man, like, we're not beggars seeking alms, nor are we *that* hard-up for recognition, but that was cold! But so much for that.

i can see by your letter that you have gone up in this world. Yours should prove a profitable venture. Were i on the sts, making my own, i'd be tempted to buy some of your shares, to assure THE PEOPLE some means of publication. That is, provided shares were available to such as my kind. Another thing—about your format—the keeper has a tendency to lie more than the kept, these days. Besides, he's always had unlimited access to the media, to allow him IN is a cop out. He doesn't need any more. What are you doing about the concrete reality of Penal Reform to eradicate these zoos? Better yet, what are you doing so that we may all say "Wunce upon a time . . . "? i mean aside from literature and publications? Do you want to get involved?

The prisoner doesn't need anyone to be his spokesman. He needs help in removing the gag from his mouth, so he can speak for himself. As it stands, penal mags (outside ones) are stuffing the gag further down the prisoners' throats. In other words man, don't lobby, furnish the platform. i am very, very deep into the realm of Prisoner's Rights. For how long, I don't know. You should be receiving some interesting material from somewhere soon. It will give an idea of what's happening. If we were assured our labors wouldn't wind up in file 13, there could probably be a hook up made. And must you resort to such *stationary*? It ain't all that cool. U dig? The registered mail trip is what's happening. i only wish i could send all my outgoing mail that way.

Listen, like i don't know where your head is at anymore, but i could really hook you up with some good folks. You recall my correspondence with Len Fulton of Small Press Review? He's in the process of devoting an entire issue of SPR to prisoner and ex-prisoner publications. He asked me to help him out, but since i am IN-capacitated and there is no publication (yet) here, i thought maybe you'd be interested. Could you let me know what's going down at "Search For Tomorrow"—530 N. Clinton, there in your town? A sister from Onandaga Community College in New York, a Chicano Prof. from UT-El Paso, and Trends Magazine are handling some of my work. Jaimy Gordon, you remember her (creative writing instructor at the RI joint) don't you? Well, she wants to sponsor a thin volume of my poems which she'd get published by Hellcoal Pubs. (Brown Univ.). I did a review of a novel which one of her prisoner-students wrote and she really dug it. i think she likes me too. But i have not committed myself in anyway yet. A critique of "Trip . . ." by Prof. Glauco Cambon (U of Conn) appeared in *Anali di Ca' Foscari*, a literary journal from the Univ. of Venice Italy! The Steiner anthology is out already, as is the one from the Washington U clique. Things have been clicking for me, and it has all been unsolicited and i have received nor asked for any bread. But it's all bullshit! i leave for the Texas Penitentiary by year's end. i'm through here, and ready for the turnrows.

Ruben has also had his fair share of exposure. He did an album for Sunny & the Sunliners called "Young, Gifted & Brown." It's a righteous monster! The cat offered him 5 bills and Ruben only asked him to give a concert for the brothers. He's got an Agustin Lara miniature oil that some museum in Mexico is vying for. The last issue of Entrelineas was devoted to him. But, he's also still in prison. The name of the game is total and literal liberation, by any means necessary. i guess if you really cared, you could write to him; or to the Prof.

i showed your letter to a few of your old cronies. The bit about the 25 bucks lit their eyes up quick. No doubt you will get inundated by manuscripts (and those fellers can write) and pleas for helping handouts. Greek *informed you that i was here*. He's the one i copped your letter from.

This will suffice. The place for action is wherever one happens to be at, the time for action is now. With the pride and dignity of MAN, i remain

In the struggle for Liberation,
raúl r. salinas #83908-132

■ ■ ■

June 26, 1972

marion prison

[to Robert Chandler]

Hey, Loco! / What kno', what kno'? / yr gem came thru & laid me! / it was sho' packin' some "feel-good" waves / So much so, that it tugged at the ol' sentimentalist-sometime poetickly-tick-tocking pump, something fiercely / dee-lited to kno' U and yr sax-o-phone effectively reconciled / i kno' the separation was carryin' U thru some weird changes / Do Lil' Mike catch yr open-air sessions? / Sister Mayme (shades of Lateef!) is doin' U worlds of good, too; huh? / She run a game on me in her last scribe, tho' / Hitched a ride with yrs, attached a 4-line note, wid promises of a lengthy, getting'-into-it thang, later. / U just go 'head & blow, like yr free-form frazees & i'll catch them from the 1st. row / Okay? / Yeah, agreed; during off-season, kite flyin' ain't always kool / Say Man, U came down hard on the ol' Parson's haid, too. Ha-ha! / Cold man, Chan. / But U figgered right, it would've been *ruts*, instead o grooves! / The re-routing of yr bus wasn't almost kool / But i kno' U layin' in the cut for the next go 'round / Well, now dig *Dis Heah*: *where* will *we* carve the bird? / Hunnh? / Of course, that's provided the I Ching coins fell right & Tarot cards read truth instead on un . . . / Put that in yr tom sawyer-huck finn corn-cob pipe & puff on it. / At least til we get the turkey *and* the straw / Ha-ha! / Toe-knee cut in / Good lookin' out Cuz—i'm hip / The prof. will lay the lesson down. / Like, it really fixes me to kno' U dug the scribblins from my psyche / The few dudes who read it also dug / He say: Taps, U could not have described freedom (liberation) any better than U did in the lines "to squeeze de mud between de toes" / It carried him back to his toe-jammin' days & he sd that's the freest time of his life. / He's got feelins, so i let him read yrs / & he say he could dig yr appreciation of the pome / He sd you sound like a beautiful dude / My reply was: he only sounds (zounds!) that way, he's really a nut / Yea, there were some thangs in it that were gassy / What about the cat we left standin' on the corner wid his screechin' paper in his hand? / Ha-ha, too much! Wow! Ooooweee! & a ring-a-ding-ding! / Was he upset? / And, of course, the last day i saw yr "good vibes" ebony mug, is also recorded. / i'm glad U liked it, Chan / It does my soul much good / The little Aztec Princess, she of the bronze hue / Is eagerly anxious to climb aboard the freedom train wid Pops / She's real, a solid-stepper / Did Sister Mayme run down what i laid? / Or did she just send U the pome / ? i wanted yr sis to cop me some prints of yr session flix / O' yea, tell the Bros. i shall always respect their feelings toward me / How's Lil' Mike? / i've got to hook it up wid 'im some way / i really-actually-leavin' all shuck aside, miss you guys / You were all wonderful to me /

Especially U, Ol' Third. / Dug Herbie doin' a thang called *"You'll Know When You Get There"* / i b'lieve the album is called *"Mondoshi"* or somethin' like that / Also dug a version of his *"Maiden Voyage"* by Odell Brown & the Organizers / Joe Farrell does one called *Circle in the Square*, on soprano that's nice / And Bro. Yusef did a number called *"Down in Atlanta,"* that killed me / So, what's wid yr little bro. Fulton? / Is he straight? / The verse preceeding the article on *the* artist was not seen by folks due to my temporary state of insanity at the time of its creation / Lil' Mike was about the only one who suffered thru *that* ordeal / tell john henry to behave & that i need the lady lawyer's address in Houston. / Later for U / U bad-mad, JZ musician-note physician, hoo (doo) man bein'-brother-friend / With love, mutual respect, & a whole lotta' admiration. / i remain forever

Your Brother,
"Taps"

■ ■ ■

June 28, 1972

Walter Quintero
Committee for Prisoner Humanity & Justice

Estimado Hermano:

Enclosed you will find a copy of the U.N. Report, which was authored for the Federal Prisoners' coalition, by Lanier A. Ramer and associates, here at Marion Prison.

As you can well deduce, upon reading same, this *psychic oppression* is being waged upon Blacks, poor Whites, as well as upon Chicanos. All of them caged in the Bureau of Prison's numerous prisons.

What we had intended, as a result of this contact, was for you to have said Report published verbatim, with perhaps an introduction of yourself, in as many of the Chicano Press Association's publications, as possible.

One reason why we are unable to make the necessary moves to re-establish contact with these papers is because of our present situation. Most of us working on this project arrived at Marion Prison due to *Punitive Transfers.*

Ramer, Sing Louie, Leano & Gudino were active on the Pacific Northwest, whereas the rest of the Chicano contingent were based in the Leavenworth-Kansas City area.

Perhaps you may find it necessary to check the veracity of this document, enclosures & letter. If so, Ron Silliman of your same Committee for Prisoner Humanity & Justice, can verify for some of the signators of this letter. The rest of us are somewhat new at this manner of articulating our collective and frightening situation; however, we are equally concerned.

We feel that not enough concern has been expressed on our behalf by the Chicano press and of organizations; as has been done by the Black and Anglo groups. Aside from *Basta Ya* (S.F.) & *Grito del Norte* (Espanola, NM), the Chicano Press seems reluctant to do so. We are hoping that you can hook this up for us.

A copy of the U.N. Report has been sent to *El Grito del Norte*, but they have no idea what to do with it. Maybe, once you receive the complete run down from Ron, you could relay all the information to them.

The subjects of the brainwashing techniques described in the document, have already begun to move in on some of our people here, quite subtly. Perhaps this can be dismissed as paranoia on our part, though we can assure you, it is well justified. This is just to give you an advance notification that our act of exposure will not go unretaliated by the administration.

Because of mail tampering, please acknowledge receipt of this letter as soon as it reaches your office. On any correspondence directed to me/us, type this on the envelope: Attorney/Client Mail: Open *only* in presence of addressee.

> Sin mas, me subscribo
> atentamente,
> Hasta la liberación,
> Raúl R. Salinas

■ ■ ■

July 6, 1972

Allen Ressler, Attorney

Brother Allen:

We received yours of the 29th, along with the complaint. Thank you for being there.

On the censorship article, you could send it to PDI, if you would, with the instructions to use it if they find it suitable. The author of same is Gil Leano. All you have to tell Richard Tanner is that it comes from "TAP." To my knowledge, the Prisoner's Rights Newsletter does not come in at this jail. PDI only sporadically, although i received word from a sister there, that if they ever establish contact with me, they'll gladly send it. The Prison Law Reporter has been coming in, up to the past two months. But we will make every attempt to receive them.

At the present time, there are only two people whom i would like for you to send copies of the report to. They are:

Genie Plamondon
Michigan Committee for Prisoners' Rights
Ann Arbor, Michigan
   and,
Manuel Cermeno
Austin, TX

Again, just tell them that Tap asked you to forward the report to them. Thanx.

As of today, things are beginning to get a bit sticky around here. The heat was placed on the Supvr. of Education by alleging that the mimeo was made on his machine. We produced a letter from a local attorney stating that 200 copies of the report were enclosed, which got the old dude here off the hook. The reactionary forces have not been put into play yet, but we are getting a few leers n' sneers. Who knows where we'll be writing you from next? How is Red's (Lanier Ramer) wife faring out at the Big Top? Is she having any success? Fill us in to all of the details on the "go-down"/Please inform José Rubio and the rest of the brothers (brown, white, black, and green) that we have not had a moment's rest, but are determined to voice our treatment, loud and long, whatever the cost.

yours for a better world,
raúlrsalinas

■ ■ ■

Legal Aid and Defender Society of Greater Kansas City, Missouri

Kansas City, Missouri 64106

Dear Brother Raúl:

July 12, 1972

This is to acknowledge your letter dated July 6, 1972.

On the statement, I appeared on the CBS affiliated station in Kansas City concerning the United Nation's statement. The station gave me ample time to explain the allegations in the statement. None of the other television stations responded to our request for coverage. However, I think the CBS coverage was good. I forwarded a copy of the statement to all the brothers at Leavenworth and am forwarding a copy to Genie Plamondon and to Manuel Cermeno.

Red's wife, Chris Ramer, was here on July 5, 6, and 7. The prison authorities at Leavenworth denied her permission to interview any of the prisoners. Dellums was out of town and could not be reached, and it was impossible for us to get them to change their minds.

Power to the prisoner,
Allen M. Ressler

■ ■ ■

July 24, 1972

Professor Joseph Sommers

Estimado Compañero:

There is nothing I would like better then to correspond with you in Spanish. However, my freedom is of the utmost importance; so in the interest of expediency, i will restrict myself to English. Besides as brother G. J. used to say in his many letters: "Things ain't right tonight."

Okay i owe you a reply; you were the last to write. Every bit of correspondence from you—which has not been answered—will be dealt with here. From your letter on Behavioral Science Center stationary to the pair of memoranda, and your mini-letter of yesterday. One reason (excuse) why our exchange of correspondence has been so shaky up to this point, is my being constantly on the move. There might still be yet another move; i hope it's up your way. ¿Quien sabe?

Incidentally have you Antonia's address in Mexico, or did she go at all? Upon arriving here, i received a letter of hers from San Diego. When i mentioned that i was allowed an occasional phone call, she sent me two numbers (school & home). Well, not able to contain my excitement of speaking with someone over the phone after all these years, i called and never made contact in three days! ¡Que triste! As i understand, she won't return from "las tierras indias" until the end of August. Is this correct? i have a gift for her which i am having difficulty sending, simply because of our both moving around so. At the moment i have it in Kansas City with Prof. Ruiz. by the way, did you receive his latest issue of Entrelineas? There is a biographical piece on Estrella, which i wrote.

I've not read Alurista's book, though i saw the ad from UCLA. It, like Ricardo Sanchez' volume, is somewhat expensive; i'll wait until i raise before reading them. i made some observations about Alurista which i related to Antonia, and which she has never commented on. He is "asi, asi." Speaking of traditional poetry, i find his work exceedingly traditional. His references to Aztec mythology and Mexican folklore are consistent with his knowledge of literature. Muchly academic then, he is no street-corner poet. i prefer him in either Spanish or English; su bilingue, ¡nomas no! Sanchez, on the other hand, though cruder and less scholarly (whatever that means), is more spontaneously natural, singing "la cancion del alma atormentada." His (Ricardo's) work is appropriately suited to your remarkable statement of being endowed with that "fresh quality of having recently left the furnace of experience and the sufferings of the people." Wow! What a beautiful expression. Small wonder a Puerto Rican counselor at Leavenworth said when i mailed a letter to you, "Do you mean *The* Joseph Sommers?" To which i so stupidly replied "i don't know," i gather you are (pardon the expression) un gran chingon in Latin American Literature. i shall soon know. i don't know either Alurista nor Sanchez, but i hope to meet them someday. Or are they above meeting folks the likes of me?

Okay, now el estudio for which you were awarded by the PCCLAS, is the text available or was it published? i would like to read it. Your address to them really laid me. It's going to be the experience of my life (fun) sitting down to rap with you. i become more frantic each day that goes by. The cards you sent were nice. My two comrades (Estrella el pintor & Stephen, both of whom nursed me back to sanity through the years) shared them with me. i kept the one that reads "La Poesía Esta En La Calle," which i can relate to easier; in all of its implications, i think. i also received the advance brochure on the anthology. Listen, did you ever send Flaco's critique on antitraditional poetics? If you did, i never got it. Of Flaco's work, i've only read two pieces that appeared in the UW daily. They were fair. i hope that you don't misconstrue my comments as being elitist. You must realize that my opinion stems from my limited knowledge of poetics, literature, and education. What little i do know, i've had to Bogart and rip it off. ¡A la Brava! Which doesn't mean, truthfully speaking, either; but out-front, raw-jaw, indiscreetness! 'Tona did send me Omar Salinas' "Crazy Gypsy," and i really liked him. He's so different . . . fresh . . . weird!

As for *OUR* anthology, i have yet to receive a copy. in fact, i didn't even know Garcia-Giron was supposed to send one until Prof. Ruiz wrote, informing me about it. Days after, i got Garcia-Giron's letter, which i've already answered. A copy of it is enclosed with this letter. No book yet, though.

Oh! And do send me copies of all your correspondence with the texas authorities, for my files. Okay? Yes, October is definitely *IT*. Provided i get a handful of days which i am now haggling over. Otherwise, it will be the middle part of November. i am getting very uptight as the days proceed on into Fall. My skepticism is increasing because, contrary to the claim that theirs is one of the best (?) prison systems in the country—Texans are very inhumane and backward in the area of penology. That coupled with overt bigotry and blatant racism, is more than i care to contend with.

i have analyzed the situation as objectively as possible, and i don't see how they can justify keeping me imprisoned much longer. Aside from the fact that they can do so, merely because i owe it to them, and they're the law; my accomplishments towards becoming a better man far outweigh any justification for the sole purpose of punishment. It is my contention, that the major transformation which i have undergone, in spite of insurmountable odds—and which is so obvious to those who i come in contact with—should be most carefully considered. If i am forced to continue living like an animal, soon—very soon—i will be reacting like one. The consequences will no doubt be fatal, but the debt has been paid in full; there's no more for them to collect. They've had 5 years of my life for $5 worth of grass; 15 years is preposterous!

i understand their grass laws are finally up for revision, after constant pressure from the government and other states. State Senator Kennard (Ft. Worth) led a fact-finding committee, which naturally, came up with some good results. Now he has introduced a bill to the legislature for decreased penalties. However, the legislature is not in session and i think Preston Smith is going to shift the weight on the incoming governor. Have you contacted him regarding a "time-served" pardon, taking these past 6 years into consideration? Of course, he would most likely still have to consult with the parole board, regardless of whatever.

How do you feel about the response from down there, so far? Do you really think they'll give up any action? Prof. Ruiz, and the people in Austin (Dr. Paredes and Lara-Braud) will furnish you with supportive letters of reference, if you wish. As will Glauco Cambon. Do you think that would be necessary? My case worker here is also supposed to write Texas concerning my retainer, next week. See, if any affirmative reply came through before i am released, i could be transferred to McNeil Island. By the way, did you know Palmquist was on the Isla? He would come up with a solid report if you asked him. He is the one person whom i have worked with the most, throughout my incarceration. Therefore, he'd be qualified to give an evaluation of me. ¿Que no?

Have you heard from Prof. Jean Franco lately? Where is she now? In regards to your comment of movement cooptation, i can just imagine the mass absorption taking place. That's why it's so vital that we study and learn the devious nature of el monstruo, in all aspects of society: Politics, the Arts, Education, and Progressive Thought must be delved into with much seriousness and dedication. Otherwise, how can we even hope for liberation; or at least, self-determination?

Hasta la próxima, saludos a Mando (a letter with postcards from Mexico from him, arrived the same day as yours), Elda, and, of course, Antonia. Oh! and the reference to "friends of Sommers" in Garcia-Giron's letter, was intentional. Sort of a smoke-screen, since i didn't know how you felt about having the proposed plans divulged to everyone. If you should send materials other than letters, please address them to Mr. Hendrickson, Supvr. of Education here. An enclosed note, letting him know who is to receive them, will suffice. Any reviews on the anthology you may happen to run across, please send them in.

Sin más,
su atento compañero de lucha,
raúlrsalinas (preso)

■ ■ ■

USP—Marion, Illinois

7/28/72
Segregation Committee
SALINAS, Roy, 83908-132

Salinas appeared before the committee because of two reports indicating agitating the work strike in intimidating other inmates, and a memorandum indicative of his attitude in his original quarters. Salinas denies that he agitated at all although he does admit that he has very negative feelings about the handling of the inmate grievances.

He was informed that as he had asked, his record will be carefully researched, that he will receive weekly reviews while in segregation, and that a decision will be reached in the near future whether to eventually return him to regular population status, or to place him a special housing unit for control programming.

■ ■ ■

August 7, 1972

Dear Dorothy:

Your refreshing letter (forwarded from Leavenworth) could not have arrived with much better timing, today. It reached me in Segregation, where i have been (along with 150 others) since July 25, and where correspondence from the world is of the utmost importance. Thank you for affording me the opportunity to communicate with you, once more.

Before proceeding further, i will offer some background into my present situation and how i arrived here. Then i will deal with the particulars of your letter. During the last week of March, an incident occurred, involving the entire Leavenworth population. Whereas, I was not a direct participant, i was subjected to a punitive transfer because of my involvement in the Chicano movement and my outspoken views on Prisoners' Rights. Which is all that i have done, besides some college work, since my arrival here, on April 8. An incident similar to that of Kansas took place on July 15. Again i was picked up, as an assumed leader of the Chicano faction, and have been locked up since. The first 10 days in my own cell under general lock-up and thereafter in Segregation (Special Control Unit). i don't know what your personal position is in regards to this, Dorothy. But i can assure you that the main reason why i am locked up is because i am a man who refuses to be broken. For too many years have i have been victimized by the penal system of this country. i too, was once a young, naive, student experimenting with grass. However, the misfortune of not being from the affluent society (and since political power is non-existent in the barrios of the Southwest) led to my imprisonment early in life. Now when i have learned to deal with what i've been, and these infernal monsters which contain me, i will not be deterred from my dedication to the convicted masses and oppressed peoples of the world. i feel that i have much to contribute and quite a number of years to make up for. But so much for my problems.

It was with immense pleasure that i received the news about your book finally becoming a reality. And yes, you have my permission to use "Journey II." The only comments are that you make sure the passage about Josie reads "Confederate Cemetery." The "Confederate" was mistakenly left out in one printing. Since i don't have my personal property here, i can't think of anything else that may need checking. O' yea, my name should be all lowercase, run together. Okay? The bit about "Anglo rip-off" was unnecessary. i trust your sincerity. i am muchly curious to know who else will be included in "Voices of Aztlán," and how you happened to make the selections. Who will be doing the introduction and/or preface? Could you, perhaps, send me a Xeroxed copy of these, plus table of contents?

i am in complete and total agreement with your desire to publish an inexpensive paperback edition, where it will be made available to the target group of readers. i'd like to know how you arrived at the two organizations mentioned as recipients of any royalties. The reason for this question is because, personally, i feel that there are much worthier organizations than these. The Chicano Movement has undergone many stages of development. We (C.O.R.A.) were fortunate to be isolated from the heart of Aztlán. For not only did we keep feeling the pulse of Movement happenings across the nations and abroad, but we established an extensive resource center at Leavenworth, expanding our political consciousness, in the process. It is with this experience that i make the following party-line criticisms.

The M.A.S.H. organization resorts to a means of soliciting funds to which we are diametrically opposed. We feel that (from each according to his ability) these are able-bodied, talented brothers, who can find more productive ways to obtain funds than just "send us some money." This may sound harsh, but i can assure you that i am merely criticizing their methods of operations, which are more detrimental, than beneficial, to our cause. Our course of study has led us to a point of observation wherefrom we view the Chicano Movement as only *one phase* of the overall struggle; the working class struggle. Thus, with a well-grounded nationalistic awareness, were we able to broaden our social scope to encompass the poor workers of the world.

As for Chavez, he has brought our people a long way, and his wooing of the democratic camp was understandably a strategic necessity; to hopefully secure better labor laws. We can't help but feel that he obstructed the work of La Raza Unida Party; which is to offer the people a political education. One of the basic and most fundamental goals of La Raza Unida is self-determination. The right to determine our own destiny, whereby we can acquire political and economic power to eradicate conditions such as you witnessed at Tierra Amarilla. Conditions which are also prevalent in South Texas, Southern Colorado, and other parts of Aztlán. The party could've gained much-needed strength by his endorsement. As it stands, if he ventures much further into *that* other area, he along with the masses of farm workers will soon be dictated to by giant corporations. Therefore i would ask that you re-evaluate your choices. It would please me very much if some part, or all, of the royalties went to La Raza Unida party of Crystal City, Texas and "El Grito del Norte" newspaper of Española, NM. Maybe a minor contribution in my name even. i can provide you with as much information on them as you may want.

i'm glad you were able to break away from your Aspen vacation to see life in the raw around Tierra Amarilla. That's an education! It's good for the soul, it allows one to see and realize that the voices of dissent aren't always without justification. We weren't around when your books arrived. Thanx anyway. We're sure some of the brothers left behind put them to good use. Hasta la liberacion! — Tu amigo, raúlrsalinas.

■ ■ ■

August 12, 1972

Dear Dorothy,

Hello again! Your second letter arrived (lucky me!) on the heels of my reply to your first one, which should be there by now.

I'm sorry to hear that your books were returned unacknowledged; they probably reached Leavenworth during the siege. Perhaps, later on we can make other arrangements for their worthy disposal. Incidentally, Mr. Palmquist is no longer there. He is now Supervisor of Education at McNeil Island in Washington State. He's one of two (out of all the individuals i've come in contact with during the past 6 years) for whom i have a great deal of respect for; who treated me like a human being.

Since you should have received my letter already, there's no need in commenting further on the permission to use the poem. At this point, i'd like to express my gratitude for your comments concerning my literary effort "Journey II." You are most generous. It must have had a positive effect upon you. Do you realize that you are, in fact the only person aside from my captive brothers who's shown any interest in it. Really! Have you ever read my other long narrative poem "A Trip Though the Mind Jail"? That received such a tremendous response that it tended to overshadow this one. It (Trip) has appeared in 1 general prison magazine and 2 Chicano prison papers; in 3 national Chicano magazines, 2 anthologies and 1 Chicano Press newspaper. It was also the subject of a critique in a literary quarterly from Venice, Italy and now plans are underway to film a 20 min. documentary around its recitation. Complete with artwork and music. Whereas "Journey II" has only been in *Aztlán* & *New Era* from Leavenworth, until you came along. Thanx. Personally, i feel stronger about "Trip"; like a firstborn *"consentido."* Perhaps it's due to the nostalgic "rememorings" being more painful to re-create. Most of Journey's (the second child), on the other hand, are pleasant. However, i still get some good flashes from it too. There are other pieces which i could send for your perusal. At the moment, though, that's entirely out of the question. i also have about 6 short, short stories which i eventually want to air out, but they are still rough drafts.

By the way, i received copies of both anthologies this week, and they look beautiful. I found duplications of several pieces, so you may want to check them out against yours, to prevent more of same. One is "Literatura Chicana: Texto Y Contexto"—Prentice/Hall paperback. The other is "*Aztlán*: Anthology of Chicano Literature"—Vintage Paperback. i have retained all authors' rights, only because of a proposed collection of poems, to be published upon my release.

Okay, now i'd like to know more about you. Who are you, where did you matriculate at and how did you happen upon your course of study? Have you lived in New York State always? O' listen, since i'm still in lock up, staring at bare walls, with limited personals, could you possibly send me some snapshots of yourself and the Syracuse area? Even picture postcards would suffice. If i get out soon, i'll send you some photos of myself and some brothers. There's a really good photo project here, that's handled by the (ugh!) Jaycees.

Well, Dorothy, i have about 3 or 4 months remaining on this sentence and i am really getting jittery. Of course i still have an unexpired term pending over me in Texas, although the editors of the "Texto / Contexto Anthology" are working towards getting me re-instated. If they succeed, i will be living in Seattle and attending the University of Washington. So wish me luck, i'll certainly need it. Should this plan materialize, i'll go up to visit you early next year, if you wish. Wow! It sounds good just writing about it. i've never been back East, because of the cold weather. i prefer the desert or tropical climates. But you should know that. They tell me that Washington State is always damp. Please pardon my using a pencil (3" stub), but we're not allowed ball-point pens; plus i have to write on the floor!

> Hasta la liberación!—tu
> amigo—raúl r. salinas

■ ■ ■

September 5, 1972

Ese Compa: [Armando Mendoza]

When your letter arrived during the third week of July, things here were pretty much at a standstill. Ahora, as of July, 25, i am enca-rruchado. Such are the hazards of prison.

Well, i am becoming increasingly uptight about my pending release. Thus far, no definite commitment from either end. Was my application finally processed? i fear the deviousness of the Texas authorities. The days i expected to earn did not come through prior to my bust. Therefore, it will be the first part of November when i raise. Do you think i should solicit a few letters from some of the other educators/publishers with whom i've worked, so as to strengthen our case?

The Mexican postcards you sent me were quite picturesque. i marvel at the grandeur of our ancestors' works. Of particular interest to me was the one of the mural. Did you check out the original? If i ever get my personal property, i'll share the cards with the carnales up here. i was sorta expecting some flix, pero te aventaste!

Listen Bro, i am grieved to learn about your rift with María Elda. ¡Que aguite! Like there's not much i can say man, but i sure do know how you feel. Some changes on my last outing. i'm a stone chip, tu saves, promiscuous de amadre. Well, when i raised from "La Tejana," my woman of a dozen years, and sprouts, were laying for me at the crib. Our reunion lasted 4 months and i joined with some widow. i called myself playing on her purse, but she carried me off into such an emotional trip / trap that i blew my family completely. That was rank. i really felt guilty too. Because in all my years of carrying on affairs, one-night stands and running gals, i never left my family. Recently i learned that my two oldest sprouts are not too excited about whether i come home or not. My ruca wants to make another attempt at reconciliation and my youngest boy writes positive kites, but so much time has elapsed. No se. Wow! Se me fue la onda. But i do hope that by the time this reaches you, the kinks in your marriage will have been ironed out. At least for Rene's sake and the bienestar of you and Elda. Both of you come on like righteous people, pero que saliste muy sabres de volada.

Incidentally, while reading the Austin paper, i ran across an article on Cons Unlimited and the Resident Release Project. The writer, Charles Barouh (Associated Press) ran down the whole program with comments by Vivian, Ron Jarrett and others. Of course you were mentioned throughout, also. But i'm sure you've read it ¿Que no?

¡Oye! ¿Y que razon me das de La Toni? She seems to have drifted away from my world somewhere enroute "al terre." Her letters, as you well know, were my sustenance during some of my doggie days. ¿A la mejor ya se achanto? If she shows in that area, give her my warmest regards. Betin and our Boricua brother estan de neighbors; te saludan. O' yea, El Boricua: *"tell him his dedication does not surprise me. I knew he possessed good Chicano material, even when many of our people still hadn't realized who we were and what it was we were struggling for. Through the years, i have spoken well of him. We were once good joint-mates and today i'm sure, partners in the struggle. What became of Pelon Gomez, give him regards if you ever see him. Pa'lante, carnal, we have much work to do."*[5]

Prof. Sommers wrote to me before i landed in Seg. and at that point, things still hadn't really jelled. Now, all i can do is sweat out "los pinches rinches."

By the way, did you check *the* book out? Salio maton de amadre. Huh? El retra of Toni on the back cover is identical to the one she sent me, only smaller. And it's also the one from which the oil painting was made. ¿Se ve cuerita, que no?

There was another thing I wanted to mention. Did you or anyone in your sindicato attend La Raza Unida Conference in El Chico? Try to cop as much material / info on it as you can and send it. Okay? Like, i'm completely cut-off from movement happenings.

So much for now. Writing with a 3" pencil stub on the floor is a bitch! Maybe Monday i'll get sprung from jail. Ya me sueño en Seattle! Regards to Sommers and the rest. You, Elda & Rene receive my best—raúl.

■ ■ ■

September 10, 72

Brother Richard [Tanner]:

This is not an answer to the beautiful scribes full of freedom vibes, which i received from you and sister Becky; and which were confiscated in the "go-down."

Moreso, it is a last minute, desperate attempt at . . . something . . . anything! I am getting uptight, and it sure ain't alright. It has to do with my P.V. detainer and the neglect of the Marion official to notify Texas that i'm sixty (60) days (less than that, now.) shy of release. This is all Texas is waiting on, to proceed negotiations with Seattle. i ran it down to Ms. Jane; you can fill her in on the zoo's regulations and manner of doing things. Do you know what procedures are taken when release is due, going to a detainer? Is a report sent in, or do they just specify date of release? i think they'll try to get their digs in.

Did you ever get the copy of our U.N. report i sent with who knows who? How about the run-down on this present beef? A lawyer from downtown asked me to write an account of it. He had it typed up and distributed to the brothers. i asked him to send you a copy. The reason why i didn't elaborate more and just dealt with specifics, is twofold: i wanted to get it out immediately and, writing on the floor with a 3" pencil stub is a drag! Do with it what you will. Work it up into an article, use it for your own personal information, or shit-can it. No sweat. i have the second part almost complete, too. i can also furnish you with Red Ramer's account of what was transpiring on the compound. He played it like i did during the March thing in Leavenworth. Which was to grease around and stay out as long as possible, doing people's work. Everyone is confident of his involvement to the cause. He has authored a beautiful affidavit in support of our litigation, so i understand. Did he notify you of my inactive status? He read yours and Becky's letters a day before the "go down." I had him jot down your address. He's a good brother from the West Coast. A very concerned dude who stays busy.

Today i was informed that our case will go to court tomorrow (9-11-72), and the following week we start going out to testify. Can PDI make it down? The class action reads "Eddie Adams, Dillard Morrison, Vern Thogmartin, Raúl Salinas, et. al. -vs- Carlson/Fenton/Pickett/ Buzard."

O'Yeah, i got all the back issues of PDI. Beautiful! Trying to drum up some trade for you, here in seg. Bro. Leon Bates got his 1st issue when i received the latest edition. The "mad stripper" of the old print shoppe cracked up with your Rasputin beard. Too much! Brother. We are trying to convince those who (like ourselves) had downed PDI during a bad period. Two brothers, Parker and Alwardt have already sent their $6. You remember Freddie Holstein from Houston, who worked in the computers? He had his woman-partner send PDI a dime, which she said she did, and he still hasn't heard from ya'll. He figured mama might be jiving, so he explained exactly what PDI was, and had her re-submit. i'm getting on the pump as much as possible. O' yes, Red Odum, downstairs just came back with "*all of it*" over an icing at Lewisburg. He's supposed to order a subscription.

Further comments on PDI: excellent photography by Levicoff at the Attica scene. Very expressive and certainly commendable. Some heated discussions regarding the Anti-Heroin boycott. And listen, we have no one to ordain us, if we are to enter the Realm of Eclat. Jay Lewis is the only minister and he's in H-unit with a cracked head. Incidentally, "Hawaiian Al" got whipped and gassed after being on Valium for days. He went completely out of it and is now in Springfield.

i still don't dig what i've read about the Leavenworth affair. The news item in February was sort of rank, to be from a brother. That type of report tends to show separatism, leaning towards the right. The Lewis article at least pulled the cover off Mad-Dog Malley. i'd still like to write up a more accurate rundown, but by the time i do, it probably won't matter to anyone. Man, i had seen the creations section before i got locked up, and i had collected some poems and drawings to submit, but . . .

Well, brother, do keep in touch and write. We know you are busy, but a word from you lets our more disillusioned brothers know someone cares. If i make it out to Seattle, i'll come crash with you as often as possible, to help out with the workload. Everybody you know is locked up. About 140 of us. Regards from Albert, Miranda, José Perez, Red Odum, Jack Callison, Chester James, Bobby Anderson, Freddie Holstien, Bono, Delraine, all the K.C. & St. Louis mobs, and a host of beautiful, hanging-tough, getting-down brothers, who won't let concerned folks down, under any circumstances.

> In unyielding solidarity, i
> remain
> Your Brother,
> "TAP"
> Pride to the people!

P.S. Leroy Peckham died of hepatitis in Springfield. That's all we know.

■ ■ ■

September 12, 1972

Honorable Don Edwards
U.S. House of Representatives

Dear Sir:

This is to verify the comments and remarks made by Alberto Mares, in his recent reports to your office. There are, today, responsible prisoners who are willing and able to articulate their grievances, at the risk of retaliatory measures taken upon them. Men who are sincerely concerned with bringing about constructive change.

i too am locked up as a result of the July 17 work-stoppage, which was effected as a peaceful demonstration in protest of an arbitrary attack by a guard upon a prisoner.

Now, i am due for release from this prison within the next sixty (60) days, however, there is a parole violation detainer lodged against me from the State of Texas. A group of educators from the Washington-Seattle, are attempting to secure my re-instatement to a suitable educational and employment plan in that state. i would assist them in a para-professional capacity on drug-abuse programs, edit the Resident Release Project's newsletter, and attend classes towards a B.A. degree in Journalism. With this in mind, and on the basis of the enclosed information, i'd like to ask you for a letter to the Texas Board of Pardons and Paroles, recommending that such a re-instatement be instituted.

From 1949 to 1952, i was a resident of San Jose, Santa Clara County, California. i attended the old San Jose High School for a year and worked the fruit harvest the rest of the time. Some of my relatives settled there are now tax-paying members of their community.

Should you care for additional information regarding Mares' account of the situation here, i'd be glad to furnish you with pertinent facts in further support to his statements.

In conclusion, i'd like to say that your vote of assent for the passage for bills HR 13118 & HR 10843, would be most beneficial to, and certainly appreciated by the nation's prisoners. One last item which has me somewhat ill-at-ease: it is common procedure for the proper authorities to notify a state with detainer warrant, when a man is sixty (60) days due for release. In the negotiations between Texas and Seattle, this notification is what Texas is awaiting before making a final decision. Due to a recent changeover in caseworkers, and because of my segregated status, this has not been done. Could you perhaps check this out? Thank you for your attention and cooperation. i remain yours for a better world.

Respectfully Submitted,
Raúl R. Salinas—#83908-132

■ ■ ■

Sept 15, 1972

Dear Brother Raúl,

It was far out rapping with you last week. Once again I am reminded that this country's most articulate and compassionate people are locked in cages. As you may have heard from Arnie our day in court wasn't entirely successful, however to some extent I feel we have taken the offensive and because we have filed the suit and because of the press coverage the prison is clearly uptight.

We have a hearing set for the beginning of October and hopefully we can expose to some people the true nature of American penology. It's possible that we even may be able to get the legal and personal papers of the brothers back. I have received several packets of valuable information from Ramer. He also asked me to convey to you his wife's address: 2490 Channing Way—Room 202, Berkeley, Calif 94704.

Arnie talked to Tippy and he said he was going to talk to you—Has he done that? There is much work to be done to prepare for the hearing to expose these people and what they are about.

Please convey my revolutionary solidarity to all the brothers in I unit and tell them we will most definitely win cause truth, justice and humanity is on our side.

Michael Deutsch—Attorney

■　■　■

September 15, 1972

Board of Pardons and Paroles, Parole Supervision
ATTN: Mr. George Young

Dear Sir:

Accept this as a personal plea on my own behalf for consideration towards the re-instatement of my Texas parole, prior to my release from this institution within the ensuing 60 days.

When i leave here, i will be under Federal supervision for about 2 years. As soon as a decision is arrived at, by your office, we will know whether to proceed with the establishing of such supervision in Seattle, where i plan to reside.

From copies made available to me, of your correspondence with Professor Sommers, et. al., i am safely assured that you are familiar with my proposed plan.

Since my incarceration in April of 1967, i have made some major and constructive accomplishments, which i feel should be seriously considered, when my case is reviewed. So as not to bog you down with any lengthy ramblings, which would take up valuable time, prolonging your decision, i will simply list said accomplishments on a separate information sheet.

During this time, and due to my activities, i established contact with several publishers, educators, and clergymen throughout the country. As a result of these contacts, many opportunities were afforded me towards a successfully future in society. The most immediate and significant of these being the offer from Professor Sommers, and Armando Mendoza of Resident Release Project, both at the University of Washington in Seattle.

To further express my concern, and emphasize the importance, in a favorable decision regarding my reinstatement, i will make the following comments. These will be supported by statements from leading authorities in the fields of corrections and/or penology, as they relate to my situation.

i will not attempt to offer empty testimony to my obvious transformation, nor will i try to deceive you by expounding on the virtues of my rehabilitative potential. Instead, i will deal with records and concrete facts which can be substantiated by the people with whom i have worked.

In spite of my past incarcerations, i have managed to salvage my life, by preparing myself academically towards a degree in Journalism & Mass Communication. As of now, i qualify to serve Resident Release Project as a paraprofessional in publications and lecturing.

comment: " . . . a prisoner eligible for release is entitled to consideration of more than just his criminal record." Fifth Circuit Judge Elbert P. Tuttle—Parole Ruling

-AND-

" . . . provide satisfactory emphasis on the development of community-oriented programs for assistance to parolees— assurance that states include the following elements:

(a). employment of ex-offenders in such professional or para-professional position as may appear appropriate to their particular expertise and knowledge"—Omnibus Crime Control, Safe Streets act 1968—Title III Grants to States Plan— H.R. 1311B Introduced February 9, 1972

At 38 years of age, with numerous opportunities available to me in the above and below mentioned areas, i sincerely feel that further imprisonment would be detrimental to the development of my promising aspirations and goals, towards being a contributing member of a free society.

> comment: ". . . when doing time stretches into so many years, it becomes self-defeating."—Roscoe Pound American Trial Lawyers Foundation Conference—June 1972

-AND-

> ". . . the rehabilitation process must convince the offender that there is hope in the free world . . . the offender must come to know there are people who care about his plight and that such individuals have the power to do something to help him. It is in this area that the punishment process exerts it's most malignant influence."—Seymour L. Halleck, Professor of Psychiatry Before Judiciary Subcommittee—#3—Nov. 23, 1971

Furthermore, i feel that in the event my parole is reinstated, that i can make a successful adjustment. Today, i speak as a middle-aged man; adequately prepared, somewhat educated, and fully aware of my capabilities; with a strong determination to succeed in my chosen field.

Whatever your final decision may be, i wish to thank you for your attention and consideration.

Respectfully submitted,
raúlrsalinas
Raúl R. Salinas—#83908-132
Roy Salinas TDC #165336

INFORMATION SHEET

- Incarcerated: 5 years, 8 months—no credit toward detainer
- College credits: 45 hours (give or take 4, due to transfer)
- • Editor of *Aztlán*—Leavenworth Chicano Paper 1970–1972
- • Co-editor of *New Era*—Leavenworth Penal Magazine 1970–1972
- 1st Prize-—"Best Sports Story"—American Penal Press Contest—1970
- Scholarship—Famous Writer's School—·3 year course 1971

Published: La Raza Magazine—Los Angeles, Calif—1969
Con Safos Magazine—Los Angeles—1970
Entrelineas Magazine—Kansas City, MO, 1970–1972
Penal Digest International—Iowa City, Iowa 1970–1972

- "Chicano Literature: Text & Context"—Prentice / Hall 1972 (To be used in high school & colleges) eds. Shular / Sommers / Ybarra
- Aztlán: Anthology of Mexican-American Literature—Vintage Press (To be used in high schools & colleges) eds. Steiner / Valdez— 1972
- Epic Poem—subject of critique in literary journal—Venice, Italy—1971
- same, used in English 342: "Literature of the Southwest:—University of Texas
- Same to be filmed as 20 min Documentary—1973
- 1 book poems, 1 book short stories ready for publication— 1973

THE ABOVE CAN BE VERIFIED BY THE FOLLOWING:

- J. S. Palmquist—Supervisor Education—Steilacoom, Washington
- Prof. Francisco H. Ruiz, Penn Valley Community College— Kansas City, MO
- Stan Steiner—Author/Novelist—Santa Fe, NM
- Armando Mendoza—Director, Resident Release Project—UW Seattle
- Profs. Antonia Shular/Tomas Ybarra/Joseph Sommers— Univ. Washington
- Richard Tanner, Director Prisoner-Affairs—Penal Digest Int.— Iowa City, IA
- Prof. Glauco Cambon—Italian Literature—University Connecticut
- Dr. Dorothy Harth—Onandaga Community College
- Dr. Americo Paredes—University of Texas

■ ■ ■

Sept. 20 [1972]

Estimada Nita [Gonzalez]:

After your maginificent performance at Leavenworth, we contacted a couple of members from the teatro troupe only to learn of your sudden departure from Colegio Jacinto Treviño.

There were some excellent action photos taken, which we hoped to send to you. However, after your appearance there, things became somewhat uncool. In March, a "go-down" was effected and a large Raza contingent were sent here. In July, after being here for 3 months, another incident was kicked off and we were picked up indiscriminately and placed in lockup, where we've been since July 17.

Such being the case, we are completely cut off from any news of Aztlán. i was wondering if you could, perhaps, furnish us with some information regarding the recent Raza Unida conference held in El Paso. Do you know if Prisoner Rights were discussed?

Of course, we'd like to know how you are doing, what you are into these days. Equally important is the progress of the Crusade for Justice. How is Corky? Listen, is El Gallo still being published? Some carnal ordered from here and never received acknowledgement nor newspaper. Let us know if it's been discontinued or is our problem a local one on this end. Write to Leavenworth in the meantime to recover some of the photos we have for you.

My release date is due this year, in the next few months i intend to go study in the Pacific Northwest. That is, providing Texas doesn't decide otherwise (P.V. detainer). I will definitely be coming up to Denver to visit with you good people, and to help out in whatever way possible.

You will probably receive some information concerning our present situation soon. What type of material does El Gallo need? Or is it accepting Pintos writing at all? Do you think you could send me some pictures from La Cruzada, or some Martinez murals, maybe?

> Recebe en el espíritu Aztlán—
> un fuerte abrazo de
> carnalismo.
> Atentatmente
> "Tap"
> raúlrsalinas

■ ■ ■

September 22, 1972

Pathfinder Press

Dear People:

Recently a young Socialist correspondent of ours, asked us to write you concerning free reading material. Throughout these past six years i've never taken undue advantage of the "free or ? price to prisoners" offers. Instead, i've managed to spread my nickels and dimes among the alternate culture publications and periodicals of progressive thought.

Now, my funds have been exhausted and i wish to obtain the below-listed books. i have less than 6 months remaining on my sentence. Therefore, upon release i would immediately remit $10 to $20, sufficient for payment of said books, plus ordering more literature for the brothers here.

My plans are to enter Journalism School on the West Coast, doing free lance work for such papers as The Militant, Penal Digest International, and El Grito del Norte. There is a small political education group here whom I plan to supply with literature from Pathfinder Press, Monthly Review Press and others. At present, we have most of your pamphlets, including Che Speaks and Cuba for beginners. Thank you for your attention.

Yours in the Struggle
raúl r. salinas 83908-132

The books desired:
Black Voices From Prison—Etheridge Knight
Black Nationalism and The Revolution in Music—Frank Kofsky
Trotsky on Literature and Art

■ ■ ■

[to Arlene Dewberry]

Ndada Washire / Bro. Lucius say / lay some rap / Tap / on Sister Arlene / Poetick-ly speakin' / you is seekin' / O'Tender, yng. African

Princess / in monstrous-modern motown jungle / yo' Blkness self /

Beware / Take care / longfellow? / he jus' ain't mellow / an' poe? / he ain't no mo' / Don't be so col' / Dig Mister Langston / he gots whole lotta' soul / Check out Miz Nikki / for yo quickie / lesson / in down-home poet-tix! /

Pursue yo' muse / who ain't from Greece / He bees a Bantu Warrior / or Swahili Prince / or even clean hip dude / struttin' down D-troit Sts./

Poet wid de world / Sis-ter / blow yo' tender tunes / til they become / Bad-Boss-Blues / jagged-Jazz-Riffs / if you must / just blow yo' / Blk / Brown / Rainbow-hued experiences / yo Blkness self /

Cast yo' gifts / to de winds of Liberation / sing the Human-sounds / of Freedom / in a world gone mad / bad / sad chant yo' choruses of the New Society / of thangs to come /

Nobody luvs a Poet (-ess) / folks jus' needs them / B-kause dey feels widout touching / & sees widout lookin' / kause dey bees cookin' / on de righteous skillet! /

Joy / Peaceness / & / Contentment,

> Bro. Tap
> Occupation: *poet-soldier*
> segregation unit
> 9-24-1972

■ ■ ■

Septiembre 29, 1972

Mario G. Obledo
San Francisco

Estimado Sr. Obledo:

Your invitational letter (plus Tentative Agenda and Statement of Purpose) to the *National Conference on the Administration of Justice and the Mexican-American*, reached me at a time when i could not render a prompt reply.

For obvious reasons, which i will state below, it would have been impossible for me to attend. However, i am muchly interested in such an undertaking, and would like to make some comments, and pose a few questions. If i may.

First of all, i wish to inform you that i am a *prisoner. The Federal Prisoners for Freedom of Expression Committee*, is only one of several committees within the *larger Federal Prisoners' Coalition Intra-National*. Said organization exists throughout the federal system. It is a close-knit, unsanctioned / unofficial group, which is recognized by *some* prisoners and *no* officials. The group and its various committees are composed of members who are concerned, responsible individuals seeking constructive change within the nation's prisons with not too much success!

When your letter arrived, i along with 149 prisoners was in segregation as a result of a peaceful demonstration protesting the beating of a Chicano prisoner by a known, overly aggressive guard. We have been here since July 25. Prior to then, the entire prison (600) population had been under general lock-up for a week. The first nine days in Seg., we were held somewhat incommunicado, without writing materials. Therefore, I was unable to contact you any sooner.

Due to our limited sources of information, we are not cognizant to the extent of MALDEF's activities. We do know it has been involved with the civil rights cases, but not in Pinto rights actions. There was a group from the Bay Area which was attempting a couple of years ago, to file a class action suit against prisons, regarding Chicano Press publications. Was this your firm and was it ever accomplished? The problem still exists in federal prisons.

In the past, when situations have arisen within our confines, the groups which always lend their assistance and / or support, have been the NAACP & ACLU. The general consensus is that, were MALDEF to do likewise, it would strengthen what most times are legitimate causes.

Though your agenda was considered a tentative one, we noticed a grave omission of Pinto speakers, panel discussion on prisoner's rights, and sessions on narcotics drugs. We sincerely hope that your agenda was amended to this effect, before the Conference goes underway. In fact, the only mention of (ex) Pintos was in the Statement of Purpose staff section, under the heading of Rehabilitation.

You are aware, i'm sure that there are at this time many able and competent Pinto Chicanos who can serve in professional and para-professional capacities. A few known to me are: Armando Mendoza, formerly of Seattle, now of Oakland, who is an eloquent speaker/lecturer on the Chicano Movement, Drug Abuse, and prisoner's rights; José Rubio of Brownsville, who will be released to Los Angeles (or Chicago) with a B.A. in Sociology; and Fred Cruz, an expert research & appeals lawyer, writer, and president of Texas Prisoner's Coalitions, formerly of San Antonio, now residing—we understand—in Houston. This last gentleman i don't know personally, although we have been in the same prison at the same time; i am familiar with his work. These are men who, without a doubt, can be valuable assets to your (or any other) organization.

The Statement of Purpose seemed to us, somewhat vague. Therefore, we are curious to know where funding will come from. Also, the administration of justice will be in the interest of whom? Let me clarify this last question by stating that the problem is not solved by, merely the "Chicanoization" of the law. This does not in itself constitute progress, nor will it guarantee positive change.

From experience, we can say that the few Mexican-Americans now in judicial and law enforcement positions, resort to extremes in carrying out their duties. Their concern seems more in appearing impartial in the eyes of their masters, than they are in the application of justice. The Mex or Spanish judge metes out a stiffer sentence to the tecato, who supports his habit by serving as middleman in nickel 'n dime drug transactions, than he does to the international narcotics courier, usually of a different ethnic origin. The attorney hired by a low-income family to represent some relative, will take their meager savings in return for a cop-out. The guard is, by far, the worst of the lot. He actually *thinks* he is *supposed* to harass *only* those of his own racial kind. Before any effective policies can be instituted, this camouflage has to be done away with. We feel it would be detrimental to Pintos, simply because it is a carbon copy of the typical, middle-class American mentality. The same mentality which believes that the best means of dealing with prisoners is to lock them up and throw the key away.

As was stated before, our comments and inquiries are merely prompted by our interest, and lack of information. If in some places our observations come through as criticisms, please understand that they are honest and sincere criticisms.

In the area of police-community relations, we have experienced that in Model Cities and Urban Renewal (read barrios & colonias), store front police offices are set up and, aside from issuing bicycle registration tags & police dept. pamphlets, they do more harassing than protecting of Raza neighborhoods. We've all read, as you have too, the lengthy & detailed reports by the Commission on Civil Rights. Fact-finding committees get underway with much fanfare, the findings are reported in serious tones; then, after scant distribution of said reports, the remainder are boxed up and stacked in Washington warehouses to gather dust. The proposed projects lost in bureaucratic oblivion.

Because of these subtle ploys, empty promises and lip service paid to the lower socioeconomic minority groups, we are hoping that the *Chicano Institute on Law and Justice* fares better in its quest. Prisons are big business and, as such, an interest of the ruling class. As in all their endeavors, the rulers of society must depend on poor masses of working people to keep these businesses functioning. Consequently, to dispense with the concept of prisons as an American enterprise, will require more than moderate penological reforms. This will necessitate drastic measures toward effectual change. We will continue in our struggle to educate our convicted peers, study, and inform the public of prison conditions and the ineffectiveness of existing archaic methods of correction; until we can awaken prison administrators to the hard fact that as human beings, we are prepared to suffer whatever consequences, in securing human rights.

Prior to our arrival at Marion on April 8, we (a group of Chicanos, members of C.O.R.A. de Aztlán) were at Leavenworth, from where we came on *punitive transfer*, as a result of another work stoppage on March 31, 1972. This would indicate that we are some type of agitating/instigating rabble. Let me assure you, sir that more than this, we are—in the words of our keepers—"ACTIVISTS," dedicated to the proper implementation of prisoners/human rights, in the area of penal reform. At present, we have litigation filed against this prison, in Benton, Illinois. First proceedings should begin sometime during the week of Oct. 16.

Marion Prison—unlike Leavenworth, which is a decaying, antiquated hulk—is a clean, deceiving edifice. The outward appearance of the physical plant is antiseptically modern. Its contemporary architecture imposingly hunkers, monster-like, in the very heart of a wild game reserve, conveniently hidden from view. Its construction belies and hides the psychic oppression and coerced experimentations which prevail within.

In state prisons throughout the Southwest, which contain untold numbers of Raza, the oppression is of a more physical & brutal nature. However, this does not detract from the fact that Huntsville, Cañon, Santa Fe, Florence & San Quentin are in dire need of modification and/or amelioration.

Did you receive our report on Brainwashing Techniques used here, which was presented to the U.N. on July 5, 1972? Are you familiar with Penal Digest International? It is "THE" publication, representative of prisons throughout the country. The publisher and editor are ex-Leavenworth alumni; very perceptive and much aware of prison problems. The paper is published in Iowa City, where they support a halfway house. Prison Law Reporter, a newsletter from Seattle has been finding its informative way into us here. I've been asked to solicit your assistance in obtaining the addresses of Vickie Barron from Denver, and Fred or Francis T. Cruz from Houston.

In conclusion, i'd like to ask if it is possible for your office to make available to us, any information regarding the Conference? We'd appreciate proposals, resolutions, position papers and list of participants; or whatever you can afford to provide us with. Thank you in advance for your attention. We remain yours for a better world.

Respectablemente,
raúl r. salinas

■ ■ ■

[circa late October 1972]

Colegio Jacinto Trevino
Mercedes, Tex.

Tapón:

I want you to understand that we value you. Upon your release report to Colegio Jacinto Trevino. You have a job waiting with the teatro and you can have sole control of our newspaper. Also your tuition will be taken care of. We will see to it that you visit your parents or whoever you wish to see. Chacon is attending Colegio Jacinto Trevino. Forget about attending another college, we will see to it that you publish your work; we are in need, understand. *Sin Mas*

Hermelinda De La Cerda

■ ■ ■

28 de Octubre, 1972

Prisión de Marion
"Segregación"

Querida Madre:

Me enteré de que te habías presentado para un examen físico. Y me preocupé. ¿Fue algo grave, o nomás tu examinación anual? Me interesa saber.

También me dí cuenta de que el señor se había roto un pié, pero no supe los detalles. ¿Como sigue, mejora o es seria la cosa? ¿Pero que se siente? ¡Ní pa' cuando!

Ya hace días que traía esta carta en mente, pero no había tomado el tiempo para plasmarla. Esta mañana, al despertar de un sueño—o ya sea, una pesadilla—horrenda, me trastorné y decidí comunicarme contigo. Sabes que me retiré tarde y me eche un bocadito de potato chips y jugo de naranja antes de acostarme. Como había estado conversando con un compañero, sobre mis intenciones de reconstruír la estructura de mi famila cual dejé rompida atravéz de mi batalla en búsqueda del si mismo.

Se me gravaron mis hijos y esposa en mente. Pues, a quien sabe que hora, me eché un grito y desperté ahogandome con ansiedad. Una tragedia fatal envolvia a Leanor y al recibir estas malas noticias— Lorenzo se encontraba en manos del los cartes por otro caso—se me quebró el espíritu de alguna reconciliación con ellos. Al momento en que sentí el llanto salir de mis dentros apareciste tú a aconsejarmer locante a lo que debería hacer—irme lejos y dejar los sobrevivientes en paz. Allí es cuando abrí los ojos y desperté. Ví a Carmen y Ricardo también pero muy nebulosos. Tú fuiste la única que apareció.

Te mandaré más informes sobre este asunto, según yo los reciba. La única condición impuesta es de que no puedo ser de residente en Tejas por dos años. Pero en este tiempo, si todo sale bien, puedo reorganizar mi familia (si así lo desean) y cumplir mis estudios con un bachillerato de Artes en periodismo.

Mi muy estimada jefita, creo que por aquí me voy despidiendo, con la esperanza de saber pronto de ustedes . . . saludos a las familias Hill, Salians, y Samaniego. También a Doña Gabrielita y tía Nene. Tu recibe un caluroso abrazo y beso de tu hijo que te quiere muchisimo.

[I got word that you had gone for a physical exam. And I got worried. Was it anything serious, or just your annual physical? I would like to know.

I also heard that the old man had broken his foot, but I did not get any details. How is he; getting better or is it something serious. But to get him to sit down? That will never happen!

I have had this letter in mind for days, but I had not taken the time to put it down. This morning, upon awakening from a dream—or should I say, a horrible nightmare—I was shaken up and decided to write you. I had stayed up late and had a snack of potato chips and orange juice before going to sleep. I had been discussing with a friend about my intentions to rebuild my family structure, which I had destroyed in the process of struggling to find myself.

My wife and children are still engraved in my mind. Well, who knows what time it was when I let out a scream and awoke choking with anxiety. Leanor was involved in a fatal accident and upon receiving this bad news—Lorenzo was in the hands of the court on another case—I lost hope for a reconciliation with them. At the moment a howl of despair came from within me, you appeared and advised me on what I should do—go far away and leave the survivors in peace. That's when I opened my eyes and awoke. I saw Carmen and Ricardo also but they were only shadows. You were the only one who appeared.

On that other issue, I will send you more information as soon as I receive it. The only condition imposed is that I cannot be a resident of Texas for two years. Then at this time, if all goes well, I can rebuild my family (if they wish) and finish my studies with a B.A. in journalism.

My very beloved mother, I think that I'll be saying good bye, with the hope of hearing from all of you soon. Greetings to the Hill, Salinas and Samaniego families. Also to Doña Gabrielita and Tía Nene. You receive a warm embrace and kiss from your son who loves you tremendously.]

con cariño y respeto,
raúlrsalinas

P.D. oyeme, ¿mandáste pedir el libro? Es necesario que ya lo tenga aquí antes de salir. Pues quiero que sea firmado por el autor. ¿Me entiendes?

Gracias

(O y a la tía Pepa, también su halo. En fin, a toda la parentela ¡Ja!)
[*P.S. by the way, did you order the book? It is necessary that I receive it here before I get out. It's that I want it signed by the author. Do you know what I mean?*

Thanks

Oh, and also a "hello" for tía Pepa. In fact, for all the family, Ha!]

■ ■ ■

November 6, 1972

Janet Barbour
Probation & Parole Officer II
Seattle

Dear Ms. Barbour:

Your letter arrived today. It helped relieve—somewhat—the anxiety of these last few days, which is akin to sleeping on a bed of porcupine needles! And, my nerves will continue to misbehave until i am certain that the "cowboys" have called off their "posse."

True, i have met some wonderful people (through correspondence) in the latter 3 of these 6 years imprisonment, who have expressed a genuine interest in helping me. Not only in Seattle, but in New England & the Midwest & the West Coast as well. These prospects all rest with educators relating to my writings. Of course, i've had to nurture my small talents; develop my capabilities despite almost insurmountable odds. i've undergone a complete spiritual and mental transformation in the process. From all indications, i have emerged triumphant. i can honestly say this has been the most rewarding period of my life.

i am a prison-educated, poet-of-sorts. Nothing much. i have been published widely & extensively, though all of it does not amount to a hill of beans. There are a volume of poems & some fragmented disorganized short stories in my coffers, and an established market for freelance, straight journalism articles.

In regards to my financial status, there are three checks totaling $75.00 which can be collected upon signing a permission slip to have my poems published in future anthologies. Prof. Francisco H. Ruiz of Kansas City has been working on rendering a 20 minute documentary film on one of my long narrative poems. According to his calculations, this project should bring in a few dollars. i am also aware of the University aid, since i receive copies of all correspondence that goes back & forth & around. If necessary, i think i can obtain a small loan from relatives, to tide me over the month of December. That about sums it up.

As for living quarters, i am grateful for Mr. Cardinas' offer, i will accept it should nothing else result. However, Prof. Sommers and colleagues (Ms. Castaneda & Prof. Ybarra) are also seeking out possible lodging with friends of theirs. i'm not too particular, so that even a service closet (environmental conditioning!) would suffice.

Viewing my situation realistically, do you think Texas will relinquish me to Seattle? i fear that if they turn me down, this opportunity will never present itself to me again. At this point, I've been given 3 versions of my release date: Nov. 24—27—28. Do you know for sure? Please keep me informed for further developments. Thank you for writing. I, too, am very much looking forward to making your acquaintance within the next 20 days.

Sincerely / Raúl Salinas

■ ■ ■

November 13, 1972

Hon. Ron V. Dellums
U.S. House of Representatives
Attn: Frank Callahan

Dear Frank:

In view of the fact that you will be coming back to Marion soon, Ramer & Ben asked me to contact you. It is quite possible that i may be able to provide sufficient information on several aspects of our present situation.

As you undoubtedly know, we had our day in court on Nov. 2nd & 3rd. From all indications, it looks good. However, it would be difficult to predict the judge's decision, if at all. The brothers, armed with "Truth," fared out extremely well. Our beloved "head keeper," on the other hand, did not give a good account of himself on the witness-stand. Removed from his natural milieu; the farcical adjustment committee, over which he reigns supreme, he appeared to be composed of a gelatinous substance.

We are still in Seg. and, contrary to what Fenton & Co. say, *no one* related with the July 17 incident has been released. There are some subtle ruses to get recruits into the *"START* Program" going on in Springfield, and inviting proposition of release in exchange for entering the Askelepeion (Groder's Guerillas) Society." Fortunately, they are not meeting with much success on our part. Incidentally, did you catch the lengthy article on "Butner" in the Nov. 5 Washington Star? Do so, it is *scary*! You should read some of Carlson's replys to queries on Butner, posed by Senators & Congressmen to whom we sent our U.N. Report on the Behavioral Research Center.

My release will be on Nov. 27, so i hope to get an opportunity to talk with you before then. If not, i will contact on reaching my destination. We are not seeking to gain anything from out lawsuit, but a chance to inform the public. For all the imprisoned masses, i remain

Yours for a better world,
raúl r. Salinas

Sustained Correspondence with Select Individuals

Glauco Cambon: The University of Connecticut

January 6, 1971

Dear Sir:

May I thank you and your organization once again for putting me on "New Era's" mailing list. I had missed it during the abeyance period, and I am very pleased to see it make this wonderful new start. I am interested both in the overall nature of the editorial effort (because of its educational meaning in the special circumstances) and in the variety and seriousness of contributions. Some of the contributions impress me; notably, in this issue, the photos taken by Mr. Wagner and the long poem by Mr. Raúl Salinas, "A Trip through the Mind Jail." These are achievements that would take their rightful place in any good professional magazine. Please tell Mr. Salinas that I find his poem strong and moving. Talking from a purely literary point of view, I think that he could make it even stronger if he cut out from the last stanza but one the following words: ". . . identity . . . a sense of belonging . . . so essential to adult days etc . . . ." It seems to me that these are mere explanations of what is actually contained in the loaded lines:

> "La Loma—Austin—Mi Barrio
>   i bear you no grudge
> i needed you then
> i need you now."

I am not trying to play academic uncle to a man who obviously knows how to master his singular experience verbally—and *what* an experience it is! —but to advise a fellow writer.

I also suggest you place Mr. John Seelye of our English Department on your mailing list.

With best wishes to all,
Glauco Cambon

■ ■ ■

April 29, 1971

Glauco Cambon

Dear Sir:

We received your most impressive letter of January 6. Unfortunately, we were not able to reply as promptly as desired. Local problems, you know! Nevertheless, we finally managed to catch up with our work long enough to acknowledge your praise of our literary and artistic efforts.

We too, felt the same way about our photographer, who will not be here for our second issue (A.D.) In fact, we have also lost our editor who did such a magnificent job in reviving New Era. They shall both be missed.

In regards to my poem, "A Trip . . ." I am grateful to know that you found it worthy of your complete attention. And, as for playing academic uncle, wail on, mister! My poetic efforts have long been orphaned, without a relative to claim them. What you say regarding the explosive nature of the lines that tend to imply rather than explain, is true. And, with such generous comments offered by people of your stature, i may someday evolve into the complete poet. Don't quit now!

Incidentally, while browsing through one of our many dreambooks (catalogs, brochures, price listings) i came upon one entitled "Dante's Craft." Since this is the area in which we are most needy (materialistically), could you / would you spare a dog-eared (paperback, perhaps) copy of same for a worthy cause? Thanx.

Stan Steiner and Luis Valdez are collaborating on an anthology of Chicano literature and have asked to include *the* poem. The handball article in New Era placed "best sports story" in the American Penal Press Contest, which resulted in a three year scholarship to Famous Writers School. Mr. John Seelye has been placed on our permanent mailing lists, as per your request.

For the staff
PEACE
Raúlrsalinas
Assoc.ed.

■ ■ ■

May 4, 1971

Dear Mr. Salinas,

Thank you for the good news—meaning, of course, that your poem is going to be included in Steiner's and Valdez's anthology of Mexican-American poetry. I look forward to seeing it in that context when it does appear, and I also anticipate the pleasure of reading comparable work by other writers who share you crucial ethnic experience. Even more, I look forward to seeing your next poem, and poems (or prose). It seems to me that you have something to say especially because you paid very dearly for it—in advance. But it wouldn't matter unless you also had a way of saying it, which you have, and on which you can work (ars longa, vita brevis).

For a related reason I am glad that you came across a reference to my book on Dante. (I shall have it shipped to you by the publisher, because I have no spare copy left, and as for the paperback edition, it hasn't materialized yet.) You probably are among the few people who have read Dante, and if so, I do not have to tell you how *he* paid in advance for his privileged poetical experience. Does your library have a copy of the *Divine Comedy*? Do let me know; for I shall send you one if it is needed. There are good bilingual editions available by now. May I add a fanciful remark, prompted by your letter? I have been lecturing on Dante's *Purgatorio*, and I see a strange connection between your mention of the "New Era" colleagues who have left or are about to leave, and the *Purgatorio* episodes of souls that are departing because they have fulfilled their otherworldly penance . . . Is there a sense in which the experience of Fort Leavenworth can be viewed (or felt) *purgatorially*?

Keep it up, and never give up. My best to the staff.

Yours, very sincerely,
Glauco Cambon

■ ■ ■

June 27, 1971

Dear Mr. Salinas

Enclosed please find the carbon copy of an article I have just written on your "Trip through the Mind Jail" for an Italian academic magazine. The journal is "Annali de Ca' Foscari" (Ca' Foscari being the venerable building that houses the Department of Modern Languages of Venice University). The editor, who is Professor of English & American Literature at that university (his book on Fitzgerald has been very well received in this country), has asked me to contribute a piece on American Literature to the 1971 decennial issue of his journal, and I thought that your poem, along with an appropriate mention of "New Era" & background, would provide an interesting and unusual subject for my fellow scholars there. I had a very close deadline—the end of June— and I have been moving around a bit since the end of classes at the U. of Connecticut (I'm now teaching a summer course on the theme of innocence in American & European Fiction at the U. of Wyoming). But for that I could have added a full translation of your work—which would have necessitated some consultation by letter. But the readers of "Annali" are all conversant with English anyway.

I hope you won't have too much trouble deciphering my Italian since Spanish is your original language—at least I found that whenever I met Spanish-speaking colleagues, we understood each other pretty well, I on the basis of my Italian and they on the basis of their Spanish. I never studied Spanish formally, but I can read it with the help of a dictionary.

(I apologise for continuing this letter in my hand—the typewriter ribbon just gave out and it's Sunday; we live in a rented house out of town, with no other typewriter in sight.) Did you receive my Dante book? I intend to mail other books whenever possible for the common benefit of you people who are trying to make the best use of your time out there. Since writing you last, I read with interest some further pieces in *New Era*—for instance, Mr. Soric's lively "baseball" piece.

One further thing: when I say "ingenero ingenuita" it means *naive, naivete*. But I relate that to F. Schiller's use of the term with regard to the "whole, spontaneous, naive poetry"—and I use quotation marks to stress this. Only in one case—toward the end—do I use the term in its common sense—but with qualifications you can't miss.

I would appreciate seeing some more of your work. Please share this letter with your fellow staff members and keep up the good work.

Sincerely,
Glauco Cambon

p.s. The content of my article makes it superfluous to ask you and the *New Era* management for permission to reprint parts of your poem, but I would like to have that permission anyway.

■ ■ ■

[circa July 1971]

Dear Sir:

2 letters to answer, wow! How . . . ? Knee-deep in copy; written & typed in 3 different languages and 5 dialects, not to mention the signs and symbols, at this time. Immediate (devious) thoughts were to write you an entire letter in Chicano street vernacular. Then again, you'd probably blow my whole trip by coming through like a champ translator.

First off, thank you muchly for the copy of *Dante's Craft*, which has literally turned my head around! Due to some "hectic days" around the old place, i've not completed it, yet. Thus far, it is a bit difficult for me to comprehend in its entirety. Perhaps, in time. And here, i might explain some questions which have no doubt arisen since the start of this correspondence exchange. Hoping not to conjure up vision of ogres and monsters in your mind, I'm a 37-year-old, thrice convicted narcotics offender. That does sound like some kind of nasty, no? But I'm a human being above all. What little learning i have acquired has been through self-study. Therefore, i'm not too swift, really. All of my confined days/months/years have been spent going to school, which isn't saying too much for the country's penitentiaries' educational facilities. However, in the solace of my cell, i have managed to take on some of the tougher scribes, bards, free-thinkers and revolutionary minds. It hasn't been an easy task, and i don't claim to have understood fully, what they're *all* about, nevertheless, it keeps the *bogey-man* away.

Regarding the study you did on "Trip . . . ," i want to thank you for even considering it worth your time; i am deeply honored. Now, a minor anecdote: upon receiving your paper "Nuova Voce . . . ," i sat down with a 75 cents Italian/English dictionary from the commissary, labored for three days and finally came up with four pages of crudely and literally translated material. By making this effort, i expected to better understand the paper, rather than have a misinterpretation of it, run by me. In fact, one paisan said "that's too heavy for me, man." Needless to say, i myself had to put it down also. Thus my reasons of initially wanting to retaliate in my native (?) tongue, out of payback. So, I got a Puerto Rican patriot of some 20 years servitude, to translate it into Spanish; which is equally difficult for me to grasp, being a C•H•I•C•A•N•O, a hybrid mixture of, rather than spaniard or mexican. At any rate, he did a beautiful job. Oh, incidentally, permission granted for the use of *the* poem. Will it be possible to obtain a copy of *that* particular issue of "Annali de Ca' Foscari"?

Guess what? No *Divine Comedy* in the library. As a matter of fact, no library! Making way for . . . a new "learning center," whatever that means. The other books were well received, and rest assured *that they* will be read! Personally, i have gotten so hung up into the business end of this publication(s), that my neglect towards the Muse actually brings on pangs of guilt. Some of the brothers here are into Comp & Lit., College English, & Elements of Fiction Writing, so this will be good outside reading. i have put aside Faulkner & the portable Twain for my own reading, whenever that opportunity presents itself. i really haven't the time (absurd!), i laid out this semester to get my writings in order, do my own pleasure (and otherwise) reading, and prepare my being for the trip back to Texas, for commitments which are yet unexpired. With 14 months remaining, perhaps i can make enough noise in that short a time, to get myself liberated and on the streets.

As for wanting to see more of my writings, you asked for it. Here is

SIGNET, a one-time job we handled for the jaycees in the absence of their editor. Truthfully speaking, we took on the challenge to sort of get our feet wet, in preparation for the resurgence on NEW ERA into the Penal Press. My only contribution in SIGNET, aside from the work of putting the magazine together, is the poem "In Memoriam: Riche," on page 24, In the first issue of NE that you received, my works consist of: poem on page 1 from what i refer to as "Early Poems-Huntsville, Texas '64"; essay on (editorial rather) pages 4 & 5; essay of page 25; "Defiant Grafito" accompanying illustration of poet in jail on page 32; Handball article on pages 42–45, which by the way won 1st. place "Best Sports Story" in the American Penal Press Contest on 1970; and of course, "Trip . . . ." At the same time, i am enclosing copies of *Aztlán*, our Chicano Culture paper of which i am editor. To date, we have published three issues and are (right now, again) in the last stages of putting out #4. Don't expect to have much in that one, other than work. In issue #1, the English editorial is mine, as are the artist's biog. on page 2, and the supplement. In issue 2, two poems (Los Caudillos & Ciego/Sordo/Mudo) on page 3. In issue 3, "Journey II" on pages 4 & 5. On page 7 of the same issue, the second photo was taken while we were actually in the process of putting out our paper. The only one wearing glasses is me. I also have all my poetic efforts compiled in one volume for possible publication someday. The cover would be done by our staff artist, the introduction by one of the most self-educated brothers in this prison. Other than the intro, preface (perhaps by some competent (sympathetic) academician), tables of contents and dedication page, i have broken it up into three sections, titled simple: Soldedad 1956–59; Huntsville 1961–65; and Leavenworth 1967. There is still much work to be done on it, however, i would like to do as much of it as possible between myself and the common people. My short stories (times is of the essence) lay scattered out, all over the prison; one of these days. So much for my writing, because i can go on and on, and for the moment, i've not produced a thing. On to other topics.

Listen, don't get the impression that we are *that* "heavy" and that *much* into Dante. Personally, the last reading i gave to Mr. Alighieri's works was in the Texas penitentiary. A group of four convicts used to sit in the Catholic Chaplain's office and read (in spanish) aloud from the Commedia, then we would try to analyze it, but really we just used it as therapy against craziness. i still can't remember what the fate of

Beatrice finally was. There have been other attempts at getting into Dante, but the lack of discipline and other things have prevented me from doing so. As much as i respect John Ciardi (and his snide ass) as a poet, i have yet to read his version. i think i also saw in my book list a certain T. G. Bergin's *The Diversity of Dante*, but know absolutely nothing of him. Do you? What about Dino Campana? Who is he? And you? More about yourself in future letters, okay? Last week i read about an Italian "lifer," Alfredo Bonazzi, who is doing time in Milan; he just won 1st prize in the Castelforte poetry contest. Could you/would you please, try to get me some more information on him? Here is the newspaper clipping.

Oh! yes, in regards to your fanciful remark about whether the Leavenworth (the fort is a separate jail down the road; military) experience could be viewed in purgatorial sense; if anything, it would be closer to an infernal sense! Ha-Ha! i would assume our penance has been fulfilled!

Naïve & naivete? Very much so, no doubt. But was it necessary for you to bombard me with all that Schillerian/Auerbachian artillery. Sorry, but i have no idea what they were all about. Maybe later on you can school me some, ok?

Do keep in touch, you are my only outlet for expression and one of the few breezes of liberation that reach my asphyxiating cave. Until we exchange words again, i remain, yours
In the struggle,

raúlrsalinas
assoc. ed

■ ■ ■

October 28, 1971

Dear Sir:

i've sought you out, high and low, and have met with no success. where are, you, dammit! No, seriously, Teach, when i finally found myself clear to respond to your letters, which i had neglected for so long, i learned that you were no longer where you were.

A package of our publications were sent to you at your University of Wyoming address and it was returned, marked "addressee unknown." This really sent me into a panic! You happen to be one of the only correspondents left me.

If this letter reaches you, please answer immediately, so that i can send you the package and accompanying letter, which was previously sent you. In said letter i attempted to answer some of your questions and made comments in regards to your paper on "Trip . . . ."

Anticipating to hear from you sooner than soon, i remain

Respectfully,
raúlrsalinas

■　■　■

November 3, 1971

Dear Mr. Salinas,

Your October 28 letter is welcome. Perhaps I forgot to tell you in my summer correspondence from the University of Wyoming that this was only a temporary address, the University of Connecticut being my permanent one. I taught a summer session course for the Department of English at the U. of Wyo., with great relish, though I could have used some rest from my teaching activities. At the end of the session I sent to the staff of "New Era" whatever spare copies I had of the textbooks used for that class, and I trust they arrived. I know what books may mean to people in your situation.

My article on your remarkable poem has been duly accepted for publication in the *Annali di Ca' Foscari*, the Venice University journal I mentioned before, and if they don't send you a copy of the issue when it appears, I shall. Just let me know. I see, meanwhile, that you had little or no trouble at all with my Italian. I thought you wouldn't have problems reading it, of course. I never formally studied Spanish myself, but I understand it, even orally. By the way, I forget if I told you that I gave a reading of your poem at Brown University last Spring, with much student response. It was a good chance to advertise the serious effort of you boys and the enlightened assistance and supervision of your prison management. But my main reason for introducing the poem to an academic group was the quality of the poem itself.

Did you ever receive the copy of my *Dante's Craft* which I ordered for you?

All the best, as ever,
Glauco Cambon

■ ■ ■

November 19, 1971

Dear Mr Salinas,

Thank you for the delayed folder. I cannot for the life of me understand why the English Dept. staff of Wyo., who know me very well and have always been utterly kind and helpful, sent it back to you instead of forwarding it here. (And you, Sir, should have remembered that I had referred to Wyoming as a temporary job, without any implication of my leaving Connecticut yet.) Well, I'm mighty glad I got the whole thing finally, and meanwhile I've also heard from Joseph Sommers, who promised me (or I asked him to) a copy of the Chicano poetry anthology when it does appear. Thank you so much for putting me in touch with this worthwhile colleague: we need more like him around.

I enclose a few pictures of myself and part (a small part) of my family; there are no very recent ones, and I haven't changed anyway. I'll see if I have others with my wife in them. I gather you have kids too; congratulations and best wishes. And I am very happy to hear that your prison term is about to end—in scarcely more than a year, is it? No, Mr. Salinas, I had not truculent ideas about you, but thank you for letting me know something of your personal history. I am no arch moralist anyway, and I suspect that something of my Catholic upbringing has stayed with me when it comes to "judging" people. The story about the mote in other people's eyes, you know. What counts for me is the way you have obviously transformed your difficult experience into an enhancement of consciousness. Remember, please, that this is the basis of Dante's poem—his being lost in the *selva oscura* or Dark Wood makes his journey to the lower depths and to the subsequent loftier heights possible. I'll see to it that you get a copy of the *Divine Comedy*, if possible a bilingual edition; there are good ones. And nevermind the incidental difficulties; it's rewarding to read, and one does go back to it through the years, as I have done. You are no doubt aware that the strongest poets in our time (I mean those writing in English to begin with) have taken to Dante. Pound, Eliot, Tate, Lowell and others. Louis Zukofsky for instance, a member of the old guard of modernist verse, has lectured here for two months and he keeps quoting or paraphrasing Dante right and left. Most engaging guy (Kukofsky, not Dante, who was cantankerous, atrabilious, solemn, if gifted). Please forgive me for inflicting some technical prose on you & friends; I hope that some of it was at least digestible. About Schiller: he was a great German playwright and thinker of the late 18th century, friend of Goethe, and committed to the libertarian cause of his day; philosophically, he was interested in the educational power of poetry, and he also made the point that the greatest kind of poetry was the "naïve" kind. By "naïve" he meant chiefly spontaneous, which are the correlates of wholeness and immediacy; and he identified this kind of poetry with the pre-Christian culture of Greece and Rome and with any kind of old poetry. The essay where he defines the question is one of the classics of criticism, and it is called "On Naïve and sentimental poetry." Sentimental poetry, according to Schiller, is the poetry possible to modern, disabused times, when the human mind is split between past and present and tries vainly to recapture its lost innocence (naivete). He does not mean "sentimental" in our usual sense. As to Auerbach, he is a contemporary critic; he died not so long ago in this country, where he had taught for many years after leaving his native Germany under racist (Nazi) duress. In his book *Nimesis* he also talks of Dante, and he elaborates on the idea of the simpler syntax used by primitive poets. This is what I have in mind when I refer to him in your case, because "A Trip . . ." is paratactically conceived— i.e., the phrases are aligned in syntactical simplicity, one after the other, instead of being enmeshed into complicated sentence structures and "primitive" or "naïve" is obviously not a derogatory definition, quite the contrary. It denotes immediacy and power; it doesn't even exclude technical sophistication. I hope these explanations will help rather than bore you.

But one thing you have to keep in mind is that I did not write my article for you; I wrote it for an academic audience (and there's the trouble, of course!). So I sympathize with your bafflement. My Italian should not be too much of a puzzle in itself; it's the technical terms and references that make for harder reading. But if Literature is an art, why should it not have its technical terms and concepts, like any other art—music and architecture, for instance. You, to be sure, would rather see it as the direct communication-expression of felt ideas. But what concerns you is the act of writing. It does not dispose of critical analysis as a way to understand that art more carefully—that's all. For instance, if you like music you will say: "Oh, I love this Vivaldi concerto! or this Bach fugue! or this Dylan song!" That does not exclude the possibility of studying the structure, the style of each composer for further appreciation. OK? I elaborate on criticism because I do not want you to think of critics as the natural enemies of poets. Sometimes they are one and the same thing; Schiller is a case in point, so was Dante (who wrote very technically about his craft), and in our time, Eliot and Pound. But of course at times we can overdo it, and there is a plethora of criticism in our time. Ah me.

I am interested in your loyalty to the Chicano cause, and I am gradually reading *Aztlán*. Of course you would be entirely justified in testing my linguistic abilities with some street Chicano! By the way, did you every come across Walt Whitman's essay on slang? A great piece of writing. He loves slang and makes it the original form of language. So much for my (blatant) inadequacies, and for the many things that I am sure I can learn from you. Your other autobiographical poem has strong moments, but it is less taut than *A trip*. It makes me wonder whether you would be inclined to prose fiction; the narative bent is there. And—compliments on your autodidactic career! I wish many of your students could profit by their training the way you did by yours. I mean it. If you had told me that you had attended college, I should not have been surprised. More power to you. (Not that a college education is the prerequisite of literary respectability, of course). Well, congratulations on your bilingual aptitude, and many many wishes for your future, both IN and OUT!

saluti cordiali,
Glauco Cambon

Jaimy Gordon

17 June 1971

New Era
United States Penitentiary Leavenworth

Dear Editors:

I am starting a creative writing group at the Adult Correctional Institution at Howard, Rhode Island. Most of my writers are beginners.

Would you be so kind as to send me some recent issues of *New Era*? I would also be grateful for a certain back issue from 1970—spring perhaps?—that contained a long, almost an epic biographical poem by one Raúl Salinas, that I heard read by a professor at Brown University.

My workshop and I both would benefit from some comparative reading. Also, I personally would be interested in subscribing or getting Brown to subscribe to *New Era*, if you will tell me how to go about it.

Thank you for helping.
Yours truly,
(Miss) Jaimy Gordon

■ ■ ■

June 21, 1971

Dear Miss Gordon:

First off, we wish you well in the task which you are undertaking. There is no doubt in our minds that it will bear some fruit; as most projects of this nature—conducted by the right people—do.

Now then, a run-down on our staff members and contributors: much like your groups, we too, are mostly beginners. We think of ourselves as amateurs laboring for professionalism. Most of us are self-taught and self-motivated. In our striving for professionalism, we have discovered some interesting results.

Your request for our publication has been granted. Enclosed is *New Era* I (publication was suspended from Summer '68 to Fall '70, due to the relocation of our industrial printing plant); *Signet*, we put together for the Jaycees in the absence of their editor; and *Aztlán*, the voice of the Chicano (Mexican-American) Culture group. Since the publication of our Fall '70 issue, we have lost some talented beings: editor, photographer, & poets. Nevertheless, we continue trying to promote the convict by providing an outlet for their creativity and the expression of critical issues concerning penal reform. We hope you and your class will find these publications of some value to your group's progress. Our incentive will be your indulgence; our reward will be your understanding.

The poem you spoke of has received some very good response from out there . . . the free-world, that is. It is in the process of being published by Knopf Pubs. through Stan Steiner & Luis Valdez, in an anthology of Chicano literature, which will be out sometime later on in the year. We would appreciate more information about the professor who read it at Brown U. Who he is, how the poem came to his attention, and the possibility of corresponding with him. Can you assist us in this matter?

About yourself, may we inquire a taste? We are interested in knowing more about your academic background; where did you study, what did you major in? How you arrived at the Rhode Island joint, what methods of teaching or texts you intend to employ; if you have been published; in short, what you are into. Can you avail us of this information without considering us too inquisitive? Our clean-up is that we are interested in sure-enough PEOPLE; and contact/communication with same is almost non-existent. With this in mind, please pardon our desperation and thanx.

In regards to subscriptions, there is no charge; *New Era* is a humanitarian effort, not a commercial venture. We operate out of a limited budget, which allows us approximately 3500 copies. After we distribute about 2500 among the convicts here, the remainder we send to folks who express an interest in our sequestered existence, as well as our artistic/literary/journalistic endeavors. Therefore, you personally, Jaimy Gordon, are on our permanent mailing list as of this date. Again, success in your intended project. You have our moral support, and if in any minor way, we can be of some help, don't hesitate to ask. Do keep in touch. TILL THE WALLS CRUMBLE, RIGHT ON & WRITE ON!!

For the staff
PEACE,
raúlrsalinas

■ ■ ■

8 May 1972

Dear Raúl,

I see it's been almost 11 months, I might as well say a year, since I got a letter from you in response to mine asking you for copies of the Fall 1970 & other issues of *New Era*—maybe you remember, I was starting a creative writing group in the Rhode Island can, which I will tell you is considered among New England prisons to be almost a summer camp in such areas as free movement of prisoners inside the institution. The amount of writing-up that goes on, flow of dope, contact with the outside world and so on. You must realize that Rhode Island is a tiny state and the state prison (there is only one) is right down the road from the (not too) big city so the families and girlfriends are always in and out—it's almost, as a matter of fact it *is*, part of the welfare system, so it's all one big unhappy family. In the Massachusetts institutions on the other hand a man could get killed, I don't mean by the hacks. Not that there is no violence in A.C.I. (Rhode Island) but the levels of paranoia between the joints fed by Boston and its ghettoes, and Rhode Island's one institution simply can't be compared. I'm telling you this long spiel for a reason, having much to do with the enclosed novel by John McGrath. But let me backtrack briefly.

I'm a bad correspondent when under pressure of time, and besides teaching creative writing at Brown I was working on a novel of my own which I finally finished a few weeks ago. Since then I've written about 12 letters to neglected friends some of whom hadn't heard from me in 3 or 4 years. Your letter was far from the oldest in the pile. I regret to say I'm also sending a long poem of my own that just got published though I wrote it in 1967. I think it's a little bit repellently obscure now; a lot more air and light and the sound of real voices find their way into your poems, which I admit move me to my something altogether different if I go back to writing poetry again. But I'm sending it so you'll see at least something of mine, because it's illustrated by a great friend of mine (at least it has pictures I mean) & because both it and the McGrath novel are Hellcoal publications, and there's a very good chance that they might do a little volume of your work next year if you are interested and didn't have a "major" (pardon the word) publisher on your tail.

I hope you'll look at the novel by McGrath, which is set in a (now closed-down I think) detention center in Massachusetts; They also call them "diagnostic centers" but it's all the same, as you probably know. I'd like your opinion on the book (which I edited from an almost unpunctuated manuscript) because it's weird in a way, being all in dialogue, but not a play, John using what limited skills he had as far as they would stretch, I think they stretched pretty far.

I met him at A.C.I. when I went to "teach" this summer, held a workshop really—what happened in the end was what usually happens in the can; there were about three guys working very hard at their own writing but most of them 8 or 10 gradually lost interest as the novelty of the young female teacher wore off. So I got to work more closely with the others. McGrath had just transferred down here from the Mass. system, where, as I said, there is a great amount of tension in maximum, unlike here. Rhode Island & Mass have an agreement on transferring prisoners. I'm not sure whether McGrath came down here in June 71 of his own accord or not—I know that they sent him back to Walpole in August *not* of his own accord (though he was bored, he admits, in this place) after he started standing up on Ping-Pong tables and making speeches after Attica. His reputation is that of an activist.

Among other dubious attractions the Mass. Correctional Institutions have a "unit" at the Bridgewater State Hospital for the Criminally Insane—it was in segregation there, to keep himself from going really crazy, that McGrath started this book. The second half, but for about the last 20 pages, he did in Rhode Island. The end he wrote a few weeks ago at Walpole after getting out of another hitch at Bridgewater, this time "30 days observation" but I won't go into that. He's doing 12 years, I think, for armed robbery, and he's been in for 6, though I'm not sure where the present sentence starts. But his book will tell you where he began if you're interested. He's a crazy guy in a way because his imagination always fills in all the holes where other people say, "I don't figure" or "I don't know." But he cares a lot and he isn't lazy. I'm working with some other friends of his on a parole package for him but frankly it's a battle to keep him out of Bridgewater right now, nevermind getting him on the street. But this book might help if it gets any attention.

So I'm very curious for your opinion, though Boston—Roxbury—Dorchester Irish may be far from your experience, I know you also care; I know McGrath will be interested in you.

You asked me about myself. I'm 27, I went to Antioch and graduated (contrary to the protestations of some) in absentia in 1966. I never really wanted to do anything for a "profession" except write, which was in my mind, either in front or back at different times from age 6. I've held all kinds of jobs and been very broke and (as will happen if you're poor and not mentally broken or dead) been in a little trouble here and there. I was fired from a job in a very tight prison in a very red-neck county of Western Maryland (no black guards at all, black/white population between 4 & 5 to one, mostly inner city from Baltimore) as much because of "dubious associates" and my strange appearance in that county, where I lived alone on a mountain with my dog & bird working on a book, as because they unearthed my record. But I learned a lot while I was there, and I was proud to be fired; I guess that was when the guys I worked with knew I was really all right. But that was in 1968. In Sept. 1970 I came to Brown because they offered me a tiny income plus this half-time teaching job to go with the masters and now the doctoral program in creative writing. Creative writing degrees are the dumbest thing in the world but, frankly, it's a living, I like being poor in a way and here the school protects you whereas in South Los Angeles the police want to know why you don't have a job, a real job, nevermind the poetry. Besides, I'm more or less homeless.

A lot of writers take refuge in the universities now, since so few, especially poets, make any money from writing (I mean even from publishing). In my case I had been on the racetrack for a couple of years and I hadn't been writing. I was in a very bad personal situation with a horseman and it was time to go, so I took the chance when it came. This isn't a bad town if you can stay away from the university! This is the kind of school where (as today) the sun is newly shining, the trees springing new green, a band whaling on the green and maybe 300 people just sit there on their butts and listen, no one gets up for sheer joy and exuberance and dances. I can't understand it, it's not me. True, I'm feeling particularly good since I finished the book I'd started so long ago and had to put away for years in between. [I think it will get published eventually, I don't think I'll make any money for it, but it was more than anything the matter of finishing the things, doing my perfectionist best and then being FREE of it finally.] But on the other hand, without music, dancing and other people dancing life would seem to me like a mistake, or at least missing some main part, an arm or leg. I don't seem to grow out of this either, it's been going right on for 10 years, and getting worse [or better] in the last 2 than ever.

After I was 19 I always had an old jalopy or pick up truck until last Thanksgiving—my VW bus, inherited from racetrack days, threw a rod. Now I go by bicycle, anywhere, any weather. My lazy dog runs beside me if it's under a couple of miles. I have a bird Jesse James a half moon parrot (what the books say) about the size of a robin. He doesn't live in a cage, he doesn't even have one. He's on my shoulder snoring right now.

That covers the essentials of me. I should say my family was middle class Baltimore but fucked-up, and I was early set on my own and only now, about 10 years later, have I retained enough superficial (i.e. tell-your-friends) respectability, under the aegis again of this Ivy League Citadel of boredom and complacency, to be invited back to my father's household. My mother's OK, but somewhat loose. I have 4 sisters & brothers.

I am interested in reading any of your poetry that you care to send. I can read Spanish. I have held your letter all this time, I hope you'll pardon my incredible procrastinations, and will answer—supposing this letter can still reach you, that is. I do hope so!

I just remembered you wanted to know how I first came to hear "A Trip Through The Mind Jail."

It makes me happy to tell you! A distinguished but, moreso, a lively, funny, kind, rebellious, joyous, frank and wise Italian scholar, poet and critic named Glauco Cambon taught a course here last year in American Poetry since 1900. Somebody told me he was good, I would enjoy him. And it was enough just to smell his good cigar when he came in to lecture, beaming. He was full of good feelings, he also suggested burning all works of criticism 10 years after they were written, including his own. He has a book in paperback, *The Inclusive*

Flame and another little thing I'll send you. He usually teaches at the University of Connecticut at Storrs, Conn. if you want to write him. I have somehow managed not to run into him this entire year or I would certainly have told him I had a letter from you. But the very last thing he did in his class, after teaching Pound, Eliot, Cummings, Williams, etc., was read a poem, author unannounced, that every one listened to and was moved by, but no one could identify, and the poem was your "A Trip . . ." (somebody had mailed him *New Era*—I got your address from his copy). He demonstrated that poetry is still not only alive but also fresh and young, with that poem, and believe me, no one could be a better judge of those qualities or a more exacting and yet unsnobbish critic. So much for that, but I hope you feel good; you should. Peace.

Jaimy Gordon

■　■　■

marion prison

2:05 A.M.
June 13, 1972

Dearest Jaimy:

Greetings from, i know not where. Your very warm & human-ness filled letter,—plus things—found its way in (luckily!) to me, here. It was a most beautiful gesture on your part. i feel you. The effect was such, that i could not contain my desire to share you with my equally caged comrades. Needless to say, they were also moved.

Yes, i care muchly. About John, about Jaimy, about Tap, about Humanity. Would you believe, these jails have brought it all out front, for me. The novel is good. It conveys/evokes the exact mood of those state-owned, child incubators most of us were weaned in. From the little rip-offs to the futile runs through the woods, and the vivid description of the perennially incompetent caseworkers; it was all there. Throughout the book, i kept trippin' back to Brendan Behan's "Borstal Boy." Did you ever read that? John's dialogue is a bit unusual, but as i said before, it does put one *there*. His dedication page simply laid me out! Dig, my last Leavenworth poem is entitled "News From San Quentin (August 21, 1971)." i'd say brother John and i are tuned in pretty much into one another's wavelength. i really felt his desperation to express himself; an illness which prevails in these joints.

Incidentally, his experiences and mine have nothing to do with New England-Boston-Roxbury-Dorchester Irish, nor Southwest-East L.A.—San Antonio-Albuquerque-Phoenix Chicano. i mean they do, but it goes deeper than that. Like, the suffering-of-humans-in-bondage experience thing. Therefore, i care and am very much interested. Hell-coal Publications also interests me. Send more details. Stan Steiner & Luis Valdez did an anthology which should be out already, which included "Trip." Sommers/Castaneda/ & Ybarra of UW-Seattle also used *the* poem and "Los Caudillos" in a thing called "Literatura Chicana: Texto y Contexto" (bi-lingual) which was released last month; though i haven't seen it. i have a manuscript in progress of my collected poems, with intro, preface, illustrations & cover design to be done by convicts. Perhaps you could add a breath of freedom air to the project. But more about that later. O'yea, a parole package is also in the offing for me, out of Seattle. i've come to the end of my 8 years and this bit is just about to expire. However, the Texas Rangers are still interested in my "pound of flesh." Things are cooking to undo that bummer. Should things work out, i'll come up to see you, if you wish. i am very, *very*, short! Pre-release jitters beginning to set in.

Now then, Antioch (a very expensive school) as i've always thought, is in Yellow Springs, Ohio, right? Since your letter, though, i saw an Antioch advertised with campuses in Maryland, Columbia (?), and some other place. Are they one and the same? Tuition is higher there than at Harvard, no? About your booting from the slams in Western Maryland; well, you know that the "scarlet-collar" mentality doesn't allow strange women to live alone in the mountains, especially with a dog, and a bird named Jesse James. Wow! Where has *that* CHUMP carried people off into?

It's a wonder you weren't harmed under the guise of lawnorderpatriotizmkleanupthekommunity bullshit you know. I can certainly dig it, in regards to your parents. i've been waging battle with mine, for the longest. Did you check out brother George's frustrations (in his Soledad Letters) in his attempts to pull Georgia B. & Lester from the slave mentality thing? Too much! Say, you mean you are actually working towards your Ph.D.? That's far out. Like, can i tell my friends i know you? What's it like to have all that schooling behind you? All i've got is a lousy 28 semester hours and 3 quarter hours. As for the ponies, i never got caught into that vice, among my many others. i used to have a good grass customer out in Inglewood, Ca, who frequented the Hollywood Park racetrack. On any given day he would be living in a fine pad, then back to the trailer courts. His wheels would be in the mercury-pontiac range one day, the next he'd be in jeep. The dude was jam-up people, though. Still, i never let him hook me up to the nags.

About Cambon, you give me the impression that you sort of dig the guy. Well i do too. In the year of your silence, he has been corresponding with me; sending choice tidbits from his Dantean world. He even did a critique (?) on "A Trip . . ." for an Italian literary journal in Venice, Italy! At present, our lines of communication are down. i'll kite him soon. Do you know that i am having to go through a readjustment period? After 5 ? yrs. in Kansas, my head's been boggled anew. i don't enjoy the same facility of communicating with the world, as i once did. However, it may be better this way, with our revised correspondence rules, we are able to correspond with people on a more personal basis. NO typing (except for rare occasions such as this—not all caseworkers fit the stereotype, i must admit), though, and that's a drag. Because in my 3 allotted pages, i can't run my head enough, not even if i write on both sides. It's not letters that i write anymore, but something like novellas, ha-ha! There is no publication here, so you know where that leaves me, huh? Incidentally, what was the last issue of *Aztlán* you received? And how many had i previously sent? *New Eras*? i was quite pleased with the last issue of *Aztlán* before the "go-down." So let me know how you stand, because i'd like for you to have them. O'yea, write Prof. Francisco H. Ruiz at Penn Valley Community College, 560 Westport Road, Kansas City, MO 64111 for a copy of the latest issue of his *Entrelineas*. There is an article i wrote on an artist brother from the other joint. i'd appreciate your comments.

i am a resident of this place as a result of a McGrath-ping-pong-table type scene. For being a concerned individual, really. The Bridge-water trip is so very close to being *the* thing of the future as far as "corrections" go; all around the country's zoos. A most sophisticated (in true Orwellian fashion) and spooky place, this one.

And Poxdown, wow! Poxdown. You come on with mythologia out of erotica by way of the nostalgic down-home "rememorings" and like, you lost me. i mean, like you said, it's somewhat obscure. But that's no reflection on you, my stuff ain't that together to handle it. At times i felt like i was a triangle with Galanthis in the role of bum-kicker, but then i got other things from it. Un-ravel the mystery, could it have been the experience with the horseman?

Hey, do you know what's happening with the Teacher Drop-out Center in Amherst, Mass? Have you checked it out? Another thing, have you seen the movie "Fritz the Cat"? How is it? There are so many things i want to do, see, EXPERIENCE! It won't be long now, and as i said, i'll be up in that part of the country visiting, if all goes well.

Along with this letter i am enclosing a review of John's novel & notes to you by another brother poet, a Janis poem by me, and a flik of ourselves. In it appear myself, Don, Mao & a London-born/Chicago-bred/Prison-raised thug, which we have adopted. From you, i would like nothing better than a lengthy & prompter reply, along with some photos of yourself & maybe of Jesse James & your dog. Hope you can grant me this small request. Until we exchange thoughts again, i wish you

Love/Peace/ & Contentment
"TAP"—(Prisoner)
Raúl r. salinas #83908-132

■ ■ ■

31 October 72 Halloween Eve—Late

Hello Raúl, or did you mean I should call you Tap—

Long time no write, but I feel a little less embarrassed when I remember that I apologized in advance, or at least owned up that I have a fault in this area as unfigured out and unfinished as the San Andreas . . . I must have written you last in May? Months after your first to me. Anyway I've done it again. Nothing is ever resolved in this life, and yet what I catch myself doing, what I seem to be doing, is waiting until I know what's going on before I can write a "personal" letter. I know what this unreliability feels like to someone in the can: all the personal forgetfulness and negligences are cardinal not venal if the pope is doing 12 years . . . In short I don't even have ignorance for my excuse. But you may be reassured for the future at least; I can't be sloppy about answering anymore, since business is at hand and I do do what I duly agree I will do. I'm now representing Hellcoal Press, the official stationery makes me smile, I hope it does you too . . . but real books come out of it and that after all is the point; little books in small editions but books that get to strategically located libraries and big or art bookstores around the country (and even, hot dog! couple in Paris and I think even 1 in London)—Hellcoal is a "little press" committed to going, inevitably, bankrupt, but nobly, and having donated as many pages to unknown or insufficiently known poets, etc., as will surely paper its way to paradise as it goes. We want to do a book of your poems in, say, 6 weeks or 2 months from now; as your editor I have a probable limit of about 45 pages of print of line drawings (that is, straight black & white without half-tones, whatever the style) and I might be able to get the money for a couple of half-tones—I mention the graphics because you indicated in your last to me that you had an illustrator in mind, also in jail, and I like that kind of book, but above all in your position I liked sharing the trip (and it's not ONLY an ego trip) with someone whose work I admired and who seemed to understand my work and, in general in life, to see the same sights.

Let me roll back a little—in your letter, I hope you can remember back to the Pleistocene when it was written (apologies again) you talked about John McGrath's novel which just came out. Since there's slim chance that Hellcoal will ever make you a dime, never having made one themselves, I want you to know what benefits might come to you from our publishing a volume of your work besides the simple but undeniable job of having a book published (your grandmother kisses it and puts it on her night-table! your academic oppressors smile wanly and tell the next sofa in the faculty lounge that they knew you had it in you if only you had some self-discipline! a little sense of responsibility!) Anyway, when last I wrote you no one seemed farther from the unwalled light of day than John; before this year in fact in Massachusetts he wouldn't have been eligible for parole until '74 (I think) but even with the 2/3rds law repealed, specific pressure had to be applied to get him an early parole hearing 24 October, and as of now he should be on the street on November 22; he just has to come up with a job, any old job for now; no problem. Now, even though there's been only the scantiest publicity as yet for his book (but we have a reading with press coverage etc. planned—the problem last year was that all the Hellcoal publications were released at once, & almost within days of the end of the academic year) the fact that he had a published book to his credit and letters of praise and warm acknowledgment of his potential from various writers and teacher of the N.E area seemed to have the greatest weight in his parole package. You probably know all this—in fact, you already have significant national publication behind you and perhaps have found a major publisher for a larger edition (collection? selection?) of your poems. But New England is not a bad place to get some more concentrated attention in any case; & nobody can have too many books published, and if a "collection" is superfluous because some established publishing house has got there first (and so much the better if they have, and the quicker to freedom perhaps) we would still like to do a little book (45 pages ain't much in any case maybe less cramped, more amply and handsomely designed, of only a few of the longer poems; I hope "Trip" can be one of them whatever happens, just so everyone I know will get to know it!

As a business letter this may leave something to be desired . . . I look up at the letterhead, take a yoga-complete-breath and proceed to the next paragraph, confident you're getting the point.

Not only did I disappoint your appeal for a prompter reply in the last lines of your June letter; I also failed to acknowledge the notes on "Poxdown," the greetings and the very good review of John's book by your friend Don Schwartz. I did give John my copy of *New Era* (And by the way the only issue I ever owned was the one, that one, with "Trip" in it) but I forgot to send John Don's review before I went away this summer and by the time I saw him again I'm ashamed to say it had slipped my mind, so that I didn't do anything with it until I took out your letter this week. If I know John he'll respond to it himself, unless maybe he's too high with getting out, but he'll come around. I hope he writes some plays! I doubt if a sequestered university could hold him very long even in a "writing program" but I don't think he's capable of wasting his time either.

As for "Poxdown" I won't say much right now, not that I in the least mind answering any and all questions about "deeper" meanings, life-to-work-and-back, whatever, but just that its congestion embarrasses me; its farfetched vocabulary, it's flighty mythology are traits

I'm trying to get control of in my writing. The survival of poetry is not in that forbidding verbal surface, overwrought in the direction of either intellect or introversion, what difference does it make—it's too hard to read, to see and to live. It was my late-adolescent sexual auto-biography and it was meant to be funny . . . until sometime when we have more time, let's get back to (your) "business."

You wanted to know more about Hellcoal. It's university-supported but its precise position on the great chain of being is up a little from the college literary mag syndrome and yet down a little (in high seriousness, that is, thank god) from the real university press, and its heavyweight excursions into, oh, Biologically Structured Microfields and Stochastic Memory Models. It really is a "little press," it will be even more characteristically one if it can get some grant money from outside the mother school if for no other reason than to hire someone who knows how to market or even intelligently give away high quality but low volume volumes from obscure and often transitory coalitions of lovers-of-the-art in some dirty basement office . . . Hellcoal is rich compared to a college lit mag partly because of an accident of timing—it swung in on the fancy gift wrap-ribbon of the concessions made to students after the strikes of 69–70; a lot of money for student-based but not proscribed or strictly college-oriented publications. The press, like the graduate writing program at Brown, has been infiltrated by some older quasi-students like me who have returned after more or less sustained ventures, immersions, maybe near-drownings, in The Great World, to the university to sub-due paranoia and mitigate their vulnerability and impotence while penniless, plain old poor. Anyway because they have tended to be older and to have had a significant part of their experience away from the university, the Hellcoal editors of the last few years have deliber-ately avoided the local literary magazine, so inevitable a grab-bag of mediocrity that anything good kind of gets lost in it. And anyway col-lege anthologies are never read off campus, and hardly there.

The last chief editor was an undergraduate pushing 30 because of a 2 or 3 year bit in state mental hospitals—he had published a small vol-ume though (some beautiful poems too) and was well-acquainted, somehow, with well-known poets in New York, New England and all around the country, and he managed to put out two "Hellcoal Annu-als" that sell themselves and all of us nobodies with them because they're full of names, so they are in libraries & stores all around or so I'm told—anyway I'll send you copies. The editor was Jon Klimo; what he didn't know, he would find out, and there aren't many like him; but the energy he put out will survive his mere physical presence for at least a year or two; and then if Hellcoal gets grant money from various sources, it won't need that much pure heartsblood.

What we tried to do (and let me tell you at once I was no wheel, just a belligerent partisan of this general philosophy and of Jon Klimo's selflessness and know-how, who had an idea for on a pamphlet, namely McGrath's novel, and who was the poet of somebody else's idea for a pamphlet—i.e. "Poxdown," excited by this year's editor-in-chief, Bruce McPherson)—what we tried to do was, simply, to do the most possible with our money by doing small, cheap editions, "Pamphlets" or "First Edition Series" of about 350 copies each, mixing well-known with largely unpublished writers, distributing editorships of these small volumes according to the interest of the person's idea and the quality of the material it seemed likely to attract. For instance this year someone's doing a pamphlet of short fiction with the theme Women—if they can't get good stories by or about women, though, they'll settle for fiction simply . . . somebody else is editing 20th century French poetry, bilingual, with new translations . . . somebody else is doing parodies . . . last year there was a prose poetry pamphlet. This year and last year I got an editorship they call "prison writing," but all that means is that I was able to make a timely and eloquent bid where two of my abiding interests converged—last year I knew someone writing a worthwhile book, in prison, on prisons more or less, and along came a chance to see it published. This year again I know you, you are in prison and someone who is writing good, rich, living poetry that may include the prison scene but surely doesn't stop there . . . again I have the chance to edit a book that SHOULD be read and so, what do you think? No this isn't Random House or Doubleday giving you your break, far from it, but on the other hand it's a publication, it's your poetry in highly distributable, portable and reachable form, it's a beginning or (if we do only a few poems) a showcase, and all the rights are your own; the copyright is in your name, and you'll get plenty of copies if not money. I'd be shocked if we made money, frankly, so you shouldn't expect to . . . for one thing (and I'm one of the loudest supporters of this) we price everything dirt cheap; if I had my way, 50 cents would be the limit. I like the idea that if anybody at all had the impulse to buy a book by an unknown writer he could reach in his pocket, throw out his change and walk out with it before he had a chance to come to his senses.

I guess I should assure you as well that an edition this small and by such a minor operation would scarcely prejudice an "establishment" publishing house against doing a full-scale book of yours; and (Jon Klimo used to say so anyway) to lay a neat little "art press" edition of your work on some editor's desk might in fact be more inviting to his eye than to leave a ream of typescript. Admittedly, I'm no expert. Ask around if you have good advisors—I'd be interested to know what they say.

You said you were working up a manuscript with preface, intro, etc. by convicts. If you publish with Hellcoal your space is limited—however, the amount of direct attention you wish to give to the cause apart from the poems themselves (the cause or causes, prison, La Raza, human life) is pretty much up to you. I know the feeling of celebrating and propagating your own commitment by sharing it . . . but, to me, the cause, all of it, is there in your poetry, and no amount of propagandizing could persuade more efficiently than poetry that lives, as yours does. So if we do a book together, don't cut yourself short, but on the other hand make any inclusions (graphics, preface, etc.) that seem appropriate to you and I will, we will, do our best to put out the book as you conceive it.

Please include "Trip"!—in spite of its other publications, it's the best introduction to your work and a more feeling, living poem for the cause (not the political; the human, the living cause) could hardly be imagined. I have the Steiner/Valdez anthology, it's full of interesting things but nothing more actually informative (yes; teaching) than your poem. You asked what *Aztlán* issues I have—9 March 71 (with "Journey II") & 26 July 70 with "Los Caudillos" & Ciego/Sordo/Mudo"—I like them all; "Journey" again though comes so close to a life, it's just that. I like the Joplin poem less than the others because I'm already addicted to a personal, narrative quality in your work that I miss there. But I know why it had to be written.

Write back as soon as you can, send ms.—you'll have prompt replies, answers to all questions, and the greatest & tenderest care for whatever you submit. Let me have your ideas.

You asked for a photograph—somehow, cameras and I rarely cross paths but I do have a Polaroid thing of McGrath, me and Bruce McPherson (the Hellcoal Editor) taken in the yard at Walpole. I promised Bruce a copy so I'll make one for you too. It's about the most recent, come to think of it . . . I should get someone to take pictures of Jesse James & The Moor but, alas, such processes take organization. I promise to try.

> I hope we can do a book!
> Yours,
> Jaimy Gordon

It's 4 in the morning—I just wasn't thinking when I wrote out my whole name—so –

> as ever—
> Jaimy

■ ■ ■

6 July 1973

Hiya Raúl,
The last time you called, as you seemed to pick up, I was facing a guy I'm still in love with, whatever that is, wondering if I had a shot of making it downstairs, with or without him, without getting hit in the face. Not a joyful situation. My friend as you can infer from his flipped out condition isn't benefiting too much from my company either, after a year and a half. And the scene is basically a repeat, since we're the 2 people we are, but eventually something serious is going to happen, somebody getting hurt and or somebody going to jail. So best get out of town I keep telling myself, I know it, because as long as I stay in Providence he's in my mind. I'm hung up on this guy. It's a new experience. I don't really mind having my emotions all occupied by someone else, as long as they still flow, but as far as the world of acts goes it's plain that for him as much as for me nothing but pain comes out of our combination. And since I know somewhere I've given up, I ought to give up and go, and I do, only as long as I stay in Providence I always reach back for one little touch. But the only souvenir of this

attachment is the attachment. Every other sign of life has stopped or plays dead. We don't trust each other AT ALL. I feel for him, I can see he's got it just like me . . . I'm getting it together gradually though . . . I got an old pick up truck that should cover a distance of ground. And it's red. It should be ready to go in about a week. Nothing's the matter with it, it just has to be screwed tight here and there and it's missing this and that, like a choke cable. But fundamentally it's in the ON position.

And I made it to the Hellcoal office today (I wasn't even coming over to this side of town for a few days, because it didn't sit right with me to have to worry about blowing my toes off with a sleazy little automatic stuck in my shorts) . . . So anyway I finally mailed out of this absurd life 175 copies of *Viaje/Trip* to our distributor. You should refer orders to these people up to that number of copies—

RPM Distributors
Rockville, Maryland 20852

Then if you see other orders materializing, as for instance happened to me today when I was taking your book around to the 3 bookstores on college hill—someone teaching a class here next year thinks she could use it—let me know at once and somehow we'll scrape up the bread for another printing. Because once those 175 copies go, you're already out of print—out of 300 copies—(but the printer seems to have shorted us a few)—

175 to RPM

30 to you (sent today—to 4005 15th Avenue NE and if you've moved I hope you can still get a hold of them—I don't have an address for you at the university. Anyway that's where they're headed.)

5 to Cambon—no doubt he should get more and I'll tell him what the situation is, and promise him out of the next printing whatever he thinks he needs.

21 to the 3 shops I mentioned, 7 each.

5 to me

30 review copies already in envelopes for mailing

5 for the Hellcoal office

15 still undesignated but they'll go to potential sales outlets, speak-

ers, committees and so on, so we try to get you here in the fall, as well as insure you fame on the East Coast for the 21st century.

That accounts for 291 copies. Bruce says we never had a full 300, but also a couple of copies were left along the way, one to the typesetters who gave us such a break (and they do very good work, for whatever money) one to this or that dean who can help us get money, whom Bruce saw in the last few days he was here, etc.

He was assuming he had seen his last of this little city but the Admissions office offered him a job that will give him a year at a comforting salary without too much weight on the brain. So he is flying back in—as a matter of fact, he'll be back tonight—and he goes to work Monday. We're always cooking up schemes to keep some sort of little press going for us and if we can't make Hellcoal we'll try the next vineyard. Anyway if we are both in town for another 300 days at least, something will surely come of it. I WANT TO SEE WHAT YOU'RE WRITING NOW. What chance?

As far as my plans for the summer go, my brother Raúl, once again—I should go, I want to go, and very soon, I'll be able to go. Will I make it all the way west? I don't know. My writing is all in pieces, I haven't looked at the main things I'm working on in weeks because of the latest scenes with my friend, and if I want to take off in the right state of mind, calm and free, I've got to do what I've got to do first. I might stop at my sister's for a few weeks, in the county near Chicago, look after their horses while she and her husband look for a new house in Michigan. If I were sure she wasn't going to be there I'd go at once, because the labor is nothing to me, pleasurable in fact; but she herself is irritable, garrulous and bitchy and even though (unlike my other sister & brothers) I don't love her enough to be laid out by her onslaughts, they would do something to my concentration. You could visit there (or anywhere for that matter).

> Whatever I do, I'll let you know
> where I am.
> Love and light
> -sun on water -
> Jaimy

José Angel Gutiérrez

Septiembre 9, 1972

Estimado Hermano: [José Angel Gutiérrez]

Since my arrival here from Leavenworth, where i was editor of the Chicano paper *Aztlán*, i've had no access to CPA Publications, and am therefore oblivious to happenings around the Southwest.

Such being the case, i'd like to know if it's possible that you can provide me with information regarding the Raza Unida Conference held at El Paso. Whatever is available will be appreciated: transcripts of panel discussions, informational literature, names and addresses of participants, and proposals.

I am muchly interested in whether a position was taken concerning penal reform & prisoners rights. This area has, in the past, been grossly neglected by Raza groups. Whenever some situation breaks out in prison, the Chicano must seek assistance from Black or Gavacho Civil Liberties groups. Which, in a way, is good viewed from a Third World perspective, the solidarity is necessary. However, the support is sorely needed for a more concentrated pressure toward constructive change.

At present i am in Bartolina where i have been since July 25, along with 150 brothers. Causa de una manifestación de protesta. My transfer from Leavenworth was due to a peaceful work-stoppage, but mainly because of my involvement in Chicano activities and my work with several prisoners rights groups.

I am due for release in about 60 days, though Texas has a parole detainer lodged against me. However, the authors (editors) of "*Literatura Chicana: Texto Y Contexto*" are attempting to get me reinstated to a school program in Seattle. Should things turn out favorably, i'd like to meet you and, perhaps, work with La Raza Unida Party. i could serve in a communications capacity, write, lecture, type, organize, sweep floors, run errands, etc.

O'Yeah, some profesora in New York is using some of my writings in an another anthology. She informed me that all royalties would go to Chavez, the Pintos of McNeil Island. i explained how we (Cora / *Aztlán* / Leavenworth) felt about the methods employed by the M.A.S.H group to solicit funds. Also, what Chavez' endorsement of

La Raza Unida party would have meant for us. i went on to suggest the bread go instead to Crystal City's R.U.P & El Grito, so that axed that. i think i've convinced her about Raza Unida, though.

What happened to Alma Canales? She wrote me a very moving letter (toda en chicano) sometime in January although, i was swooped up before i could answer. i dropped her a card and heard no more. By the way, have you met the carnales Chacon & Tijerina? They're both ex-Leavenworth alumnus, y muy activos. Word from you would serve as a morale booster aquí en el pozo. Pardon my printing, but the pencil stubs are too short and the floor is hard. Do keep in touch, saludes de todos los Latinos, sin mas, me subscribo.

Atentamente,
raúl r. salinas—#83908-132

■ ■ ■

September 29, 1972

Hermano Raúl:

Me dió mucho gusto recibir tú carta. Te tengo mucha admiración por tú talento artistico. Fué una lástima que no se pudo traerte a Austin en la primavera.

Tan pronto como tengamos los documentos de la convención en orden te los mando. No creo que los pintos recibieron mucha atención.

Te pído disculpas por Alma Canales que no te volvió a escribir, pero la pobre está corriendo para Teniente Governadora bajo el Partido en Texas y se encuentra bastante ocupada. Le digo de tu carta.

Si antes de salir necesitas algo de mí como Presidente del Board of Education de Crystal City, avísame cuanto antes.

[*I was very pleased to receive your letter. I have always admired your artistic talent. It was unfortunate that we could not bring you to Austin in the Spring.*

As soon as we have the documents from the convention in order, I will send them to you. I don't think that pintos received much attention.

I apologize on behalf of Alma Canales, who was unable to write you again, because the poor woman is running for Attorney General with the Party in Texas and she is very busy. I'll tell her about your letter.

Before your release if you need anything from me as President of the Crystal City Board of Education, let me know as soon as possible.]

Saludos
venceremos en '72
José Angel Gutiérrez

■ ■ ■

October 1, 1972

Estimado José:

Your letter of Sept. 29 arrived a few hours ago and, though it was brief, it helped break up the monotony of the day. As with most mail that relates to raza or Pintos, it was put on the route as "People's Mail."

Needless to say, the gusto received from the exchange of correspondence, is mutual. It would please me no end to comunicarme contigo en Chicano. However, for the sake of my censors (who still do . . . bureaucratic myths notwithstanding), I will limit myself to lacing the English rap with an occasional phrase in our golden tongue. "Speaking (and writing) Spanish is a talent." But you know that already. (¡Ja!)

As for your comment regarding my artistic talent, thanx. Let me assure you i am only a pachuquito, no miento; a viejo pelado, really. At any rate, just a street corner poet. (¡Ja!) i'm no young sprout, carnal. Which is one reason i feel it's imperative that i gain my freedom. There is a burning anxiety within me to make a lasting contribution to our poeple before it's too late. They must have unrestricted access to whatever abilities i may possess.

And, listen, i had no idea you were responsible (in part, or otherwise) for trying to get me down to the University of Texas during the Spring. When it became obvious that i'd not be able to make the trip, we prepared a beautiful program which was also curtailed, due to our transfer. Our intention was to send you some video-tape, which according to our script would have run thusly: narrator opens with brief intro of what tape consists of. Introduction of C.O.R.A. steering committee members, ending with editor. i would run down the history of our newspaper *Aztlán*. Following this, a carnal would explain our Political Education class. Again narrator on a few other group activities and accomplishments. Finally, i would render a reading of "A Trip

. . ." throughout the tape, a solo guitar would provide background rhythms, with block scenes of brother Estrella's canvasses. This, along with the material we did send, was to have been our contribution from the pintos of Leavenworth. Hubiera quedado a toda madre. Too bad it didn't materialize.

Yes, i knew about Alma's candidacy through the Denver Post and Austin Statesman we get sporadic bits of information on the Partido's progress. Most of the better articles, however, come from the Camejos[6] and other socialistas. The press tried to blow the issue regarding the difference of philosophies betwen you and Corky. ¿Que no? Al Baldivia sent us a better account. También el Rudy García. He had a very good analysis in the Sept. 25 editorial page of the Denver Post, about the conferéncia.

There were two other interesting articles (for different reasons) in the Austin paper. One was on the rally where Muniz showered down hard on the Republican & Democratic candidates. That was righteous gettin' down! The other was an account of the "deplorable" conditions in Cristal, by AP writer Richard Beene. It put me in mind of the struggle on the "Isla del Caiman." As if i were reading of events shortly after the descent from La Sierra Maestra, complete with the mass migration of the middle-class. Aún así, our people still fear the severing of apron strings which have been strangling us all these years. ¡Que lástima!

By the way, you ask if there is anything you can do concerning my release. Well, what i desperately need is someone to appear personally on my behalf, before the Parole Board and / or Governor, to intercede and assure a definite liberation. But, i'm sure you are not the most popular guy around the state offices, ¿Verdad? Therefore, a letter of recommendation to support the educational plan which Prof. Sommers & colleagues have presented to them already, would suffice. My release date here is Nov. 27 and i am getting uptight! If my Texas parole is not reinstated, i guess that, as we say here, se me acabó el corrido. though i don't intend to leave prison a broken man, it is highly probable that i will be of no immediate use to anyone, should further incarceration be imposed on me. This can get morbid. Change of subject.

Our lawsuit will be heard on Oct. 2nd in Benton, Illinois. Sure hope things get straightened out then. One of the issues i would like to contest upon release, is the unconstitutionality of prisoners' loss of voting rights. Do you know if anyone has looked into that? MALDEF, perhaps? Bueno, carnal, son las 2 de la mañana, and i want to catch a few hours sleep. ¡Hasta la liberación!

raúl

■ ■ ■

Dear Mr. Salinas:

Your talent is recognized and admired by our Chicano students in Cristal. Realizing the limitations on your activities, could you video-tape a 30 minute or 60 minute show of your art work? Our students want to see "the" Raúl Salinas, a lot of his work, and the other Chicanos. We are able to defray part of that cost, if you can tell us how much it would be.

In your recent letter two questions were raised: 1) voting rights for Pintos. Our partido is on that one—suits are coming after November 7; 2) "the difference of philosophies between you and Corky." Hermano, there is no "difference of philosophy" only difference in style. Corky is more of a thinker, ideologue, poet, and idealist. Su servidor es un organizador y me aviento pa eso, carnal. Por eso le gané al Corky en El Paso.

My best regards. Enclosed is a copy of La Verdad, the local county paper. Please advise if you want more issues.

Venceremos,
José Angel Gutiérrez
President
Board of Education

■ ■ ■

December 29, 1972

Hermano Raúl:

Just a brief note to wish you a good year. I hope your release is upcoming. If I or anyone else en el Partido can be of assistance, do call on us. I want to repeat my offer to employ you and aid in any fashion your release.

In a conversation today with the new County Sheriff and County Attorney, the subject of assisting pintos, especially nuestros carnales through the county, city and school officials was accepted as a project for 1973. If the elected officials of Zavala County can help an inmate, let us know.

Un fuerte abrazo.

> Venceremos,
> José Angel Gutiérrez
> President, Board of Education

Antonia Castañeda

November 17, 1971

Querida 'Toña:

Recibí tu carta unos días después de haber recibido la del Profe [*I received your letter some days after having received the one from the Prof*]. And i must say that you people have a facility for vivid descriptions that just lays me! A knack for details that moves me to an emotional high.

Your commentary on the Mexican countryside was simply beautiful! At the moment—when my correspondence list has all but been depleted—this is exactly the type of communication i need. solo que déjate venir [*so let me have it*].

¿Con que te diste una quemadita con los indios del terre, eh? Pues, como dice el dicho, "No es lo mismo a lo mesmo". No, en serio, yo también he experienciado un escantito de eso. México, lo conozco un poco diferente que tú, solamente en sentido de negocio. Mi único viaje que se diga "pleasure trip," fue a Guadalajara vía Laredo, Monterrey, San Luis Potosí, y San Juan de los Lagos. [*So you were burned a little in your experience with the Indians of the homeland, huh? Well, as the saying goes, "no two things are the same." No, in all seriousness, I, too, have experienced a bit of that. Mexico, I know a little differently than you, just in terms of business. My only travel that can be called a "pleasure trip," was to Guadalajara vía Laredo, Monterrey, San Luis Potosí, and San Juan de los Lagos.*] The most memorable part was the ride—en autobus, 2nd. clase—from San Luis to San Juan, and San Juan itself. i was particularly fascinated by the quaintness of the villages. En la carretera vi los sacrificios que hace la gente en el nombre del cristianismo. Unas señoras caminando de rodillas por los pedregales; señores y chavalones cargando cruces gigantescas de Madera, o con pencas de nopal hechas escapulario. [*On the road I saw the sacrifices that the people make in the name of christianity. Some elderly women walking on their knees over the cobblestones; elderly men and boys carrying giant wooden crosses, or with cactus palms made into scapular necklaces.*] Too much! The partying in Guadalajara was nice too. That's really all that i know about México, aparte de las fronteras desde Tejas a Califas, y los químicos [*aside from the border from Texas to* Califas, *and the "chemists."*]

Tocante a la crítica o comentarios sobre su labor literaria, no hay mucho que puedo decir [*In regards to a critique or commentary about your literary work, there is not much that I can say*], except that it appears to be an essential work por/para nuestra gente [*by/for our people*]. Since your conclusion as to the unavailability of Chicano material is offered merely as a "*working hypothesis,*" i will add my 2 cents. ¿No estaremos tratando de quitarnos la muleta cuando decimos que un [*Aren't we trying to shift blame when we say*] "exclusionist & intolerant american society is responsible for the lack of material"? Even in my rare moments of extreme racism, i can't quite digest that premise. He aquí mi cuchara: ¿si la literatura Chicana, Mexicana, Latina, o qué sé yo, ha existido por diez siglos sin publicarse, no será por falta de [*Here is my two cents worth: If the literature by Chicanos, Mexicanos, Latinos or whatever has existed for ten decades without being published, is it not due to our failure of*] compiling/collecting/anthologizing? And since it hasn't, doesn't this indicate a lack of interest on the part of Mexican-American educators? This lack of interest—making ours a sort of closet literature, could it not have been due to the fact that "*BROWN*" wasn't fashionable? ¿Porque no estaba de moda eso de lo Chicano? Supongamos que esta teoría loca tenga algún mérito, ¿de quién es la culpa? Tú sabes, esta poca vacilona, para mí, la cosa. Pero ya nomás estoy corriendo mi cabeza sin ningún rumbo. [*Or, that Chicano stuff wasn't in style? Let's suppose that this crazy theory has some merit, who's to blame? You know, for me this thing is fascinating. But I'm just running my head with no clear direction.*]

By the way, how comes no Gregorio Cortés? ¡Se salen! Este era uno de nuestros héroes cuando chavalos. [*That ain't right! He was one of our heroes when we were kids.*] But you should know that, being from Cristal, and all. Why the ommision? Speaking of Cristal i read in the first copy of "El Grito" to penetrate this massive cage, un ensayo titulado "Crónica de Cristal" [*an essay entitled "Crystal City Chronicles"*] by one Irene Castañeda. Anyone you know? ¿Parienta [*a relative*]? Se describe la experienca del éxodo campesino del Sur de Tejas a los trabajos en el estado de Washington [*It describes the farmworker odyssey from south Texas to the fields of Washington State*], which is very similar to your childhood experience, as you related in your letter.

O' sí, tambíen está un chavo en El Paso, Ricardo Sánchez. Tambíen creo que es un ex-convicto. [*O yea, there's also a guy in El Paso, Ricardo Sánchez. I think that he's also an ex-convict.*] Anyway, las poesías que he léido de él [*the poems that I've read by him*], are so similar in tone, feeling and structure to mine, that i actually experienced "*in-tuneness*" with this dude. Do you know him (of him)? Ahora tiene [*He currently runs*] Mictla Publications, whom we have neglected to contact, thus far. No fue seleccionado para tu antología, ¿porque? Escribío un poema épico "Barrio Child" that even had an identical line (or two) as "Trip . . . ," pero, quién sabe. Otro camarada *bravo* es el Rafael Miranda, Portorro que estos días se encuentra en la pinta federal de Marion, Illinois. Es uno de los commandos del caso del congreso en 1954. Este camarada grita su protesta Boricua con aquel fervor que llega hasta el fondo del alma. [*He was not selected for your anthology, why? He wrote an epic poem "Barrio Child" that even had an identical line (or two) as "Trip . . . ," but, who knows. Another solid comrade is Rafael Miranda, a Puerto Rican who currently is locked up in the federal joint at Marion, Illinois. He is one of the commandos from the case [of the assault] on congress in 1954. This comrade shouts his Boricua protest with a fervor that reaches the depths of the soul.*] You should check him out for future publishing ventures.

Un carnalito Hawaiiano me regaló una subscripcíon a los back issues de "El Grito", que has mandado traer, consistiendo de los volúmenes 1 y 2. [*A Hawaiian brother gave me a subscription to the back issues of "El Grito," that I ordered, consisting of volumes 1 and 2.*] Le escribí a Quinto sol, explicando que hiciera process la orden [*I wrote to Quinto Sol, asking them to process the order*] in spite of the hassles (bureaucratic) that publishing firms are put through in order to obtain some books. Quizás después pueda conseguir todos los números del volumen 3 [*Perhaps later I'll be able to obtain all the issues from volume 3*]. I understand there are now three copies of vol. 4 in here, including the one i read.

No creas que me quiero dar paquete [*Don't think that I'm just bragging*] that i am a down poet, pero la verdad es que los poetas CHICANOS [*but the truth is that CHICANO poets*] (as opposed to POETAS Chicanos) aren't really saying that much. One time around y total [*and that's it*]. Tú sabes, esa escuela de pensamiento "ethnocéntrico" puede resultar en [*You know, that "ethnocentric" school of thought can result in*] non-creativeness. it is my warped assumption that this can be a hang-up in the development of the poetic spirit. Por ejemplo: el Yevtushenko es un chingón, como lo es el Mao y lo eran García Lorca y el Tío Ho. No creo que el poeta se puede limitar en su expresíon from within, tratando de comunicar con solamente una iota del universo. [*For example: that Yevtushenko is fucking bad, as is Mao, and so were García Lorca and Uncle Ho. I don't think that the poet can limit his expression from* within, *trying to communicate with only one iota of the universe.*] But you know something, mi querida hermana [*my beloved sister*]? i may be all wet. Fíjate, estaba leyendo al Víctor Hernández Cruz, poeta portorro (of SNAPS fame) y dice que el oye ritmos de Cha-cha-cha cuando escribe o recita sus poemas. Me cayó vacilón, porque yo, on the other hand, llevo ritmos del jazz en la chompa cuando escribo o recito. [*Check this out, I was reading Victor Hernández Cruz, a Puerto Rican poet* (of SNAPS fame) *and he says that he hears rhythms of Cha-cha-cha when he writes or recites his poems. I found this amusing, because I, on the other hand, carry Jazz rhythms in my head when I write or recite.*]

Nos dejan saber, a través de cartas, los pintos de la Isla, que el Ybarra anda desparramando alambres (positive) de mí, por allá. That's cool, pero que de perdida se deje venir con unas cuantas líneas. Si lo hubiera puesto en mi mailing list, como sugirio, way back then, quizás me hubiera dejao cai de amadre y me hubiera quedado bien malías.

De lo que me informaste sobre el Mando y Sra., que de pronto seran jefitos, ¡que de aquellas! Déjame saber de volada, tan pronto que se realice este milgrito de la naturaleza, porque les quiero mandar una tarjeta in "Raza Idiom", que se aventó uno de los dibujantes nuestros. Hablando de tarjetas, no sabes si algún lugar donde podamos mandar traer xmas cards con Chicano motif? El grupo de C.O.R.A. quiere adquirir para que podamos mandar a los papiros y gentes con quien correspondemos.

[*We are informed, by way of letters from pintos on the Island, that Ybarra is spreading the word through the grapevine (positive) about me, over there. That's cool, but at least he should send a few lines my way. If I had added him to my* mailing list, *like he suggested way back then, perhaps he would have let me down and I would have been upset.*

Regarding what you told me about Mando and the Mrs., that they will soon be parents, that's right on! Let me know as soon as this little miracle of nature happens, because I want to send them a card in the "Raza Idiom" that one of our graphic artists puts out. Speaking of cards, do you know of a place where we can order Christmas cards with a Chicano motif? The C.O.R.A. group wants to get some so we can send them to the newspapers and people with whom we correspond.]

Toña, me cure muy de aquellitas con el quotation in the beginning of your letter regarding "el préstamo de unos a los otros", a según el poeta Azteco. Estos cantones gachos ya nomás no. Cada día parece qu me vuelvo un poquito más loco. Ya necesito un arreglo con los aires de liberación. [*Toña, I got a real good feeling from the quotation in the beginning of your letter regarding "us being on loan to each other," according to the Aztec Poet. These brutal cages are just too much. Every day I think I get a little more crazy. I now need a taste of liberated air.*]

Aquí te envío nuestras publicaciones. Ya al Sommers le he mandado las del. Tambíen le mandé un papel sobre "Trip . . . " que escribío un profe de Connecticut para una revista literaria de Venice, Italy. [*Enclosed are some of our publications. I've already sent Sommers his. I also sent him a paper on "Trip . . ." that a prof from Connecticut wrote for a journal from Venice, Italy.*] Has he laid in on you, yet? Incidentally, el Prof. Ruiz, que nos da la clase de Cultural History of the Southwest, está preparando unos planes para hacer film mi poema, aquí en Kansas City. [*Incidentally, Prof. Ruiz, who conducts the Cultural History of the Southwest course, is making plans to film my poem, here in Kansas City.*] Funny, everybody is interested in my writings, yet no one seems concerned in liberating me from the depths of this dungeon. Pero, "así es la vida" [*But, "that's life"*], to use a well-worked, down-home cliché. Unos retras o tarjetas postales serían muy agradecidos, mi carnalita. [*Some snapshots or postcards would be greatly appreciated, mi carnalita.*]

Sin más,
Su atento amigo y carnal,
raúlrsalinas

•si me escribes directamente favor de usar el número gacho este: #83908. O al New Era.

P.S. Saludos a Mando Y Elda. Dile al Tomás que aquí estoy . . .
[*if you write me directly please use this fucked up number: #83908.
Or, to New Era.

[P.S. Greetings to Mando and Elda. Tell Tomás that I'm here . . .]

■ ■ ■

26 January 1972

Estimado Raúl—

Unas cuantas lineas para saludarte y mandarte el calendario antes de que se pasa más tiempo. Ahorita estamos todos snowbound! Nos cayó una nieve tremenda—se cerró la universidad, todas las escuelas y algunos negocios. Ha sido fantástico, el poder descansar un poco y catch up with myself. Ayer me pasé casí todo el día dormida—fue un día fantástico—la nieve fría y blanca—cubriendo absolutamente todo—todo bajo un silencio lindo y claro—y yo adentro bien calientita! ¡Me encantó! Hoy también estuvo todo cerrado, pero tuve que calificar trabajos de mis estudiantes, preparé algunas cosas para McNeil y leí un libro para una clase titulada literatura y historia. El libro es *Between the Acts* de Virginia Woolf. ¿La conoces? Una escritora de este siglo, de las primeras 3 décadas—muy interesante. Este libro esta escrito en stream of consciousness y trata del periodo imediatamente antes de la segunda guerra mundial y de como cierta clase social de inglatera no sabía como comunicarse unos con los otros—de la inabilidad de enfrentarse con si mismos y su realidad—de la ajenacíon de los seres humanos. Ahora tengo que escribir un trabajo para el lunes acerca del libro, mis reacciones, etc. Bueno—basta de lo que hago yo.

Díme—¿que pasa contigo? ¿Te comunicaste por fin con tu professor que escribió la revista de tu poema? ¿Sigues escribiendo? ¿Escribes prosa también? Tu comment al terminar tu última carta me dejó— absorta—dices que mucha gente te trata, te escribe, etc. pero que no se habla de algún esfuerzo para sacarte de ese lugar—hablemos de ese asunto—¿Cómo se procede—qué se debe hacer? No sé que mas decirte acerca de eso sin que tu nos comuniques tus pensamientos.

Bueno—ojalá te guste el calendario. También quería decirte por si acaso no te dijo Joe, que todos somos tíos y tías—Elda y Mando tienen un niño, le pusieron René Cisneros Mendoza—Es precioso la criatura. ¡Todos estamos muy contentos!

Me despido por hoy. Escribe cuando tengas tiempo. Tomás manda muchos saludos hasta la próxima—con afecto,

[*A few lines to say hello and send you the calendar before more time passes. Right now we are all snowbound. We had a tremendous snow storm—the university closed, as did some schools and some businesses. It has been fantastic being able to rest a bit and catch up with myself. Yesterday I spent most of the day asleep—it was a fantastic day—the snow outside so cold and white—covering absolutely everything—all beneath a beautiful and clear silence—and me inside very warm! I loved it! Today again everything was closed, but I had to grade my students' work. I prepared some things for McNeil and read a book for a class titled literature and history. The book is Between the Acts by Virginia Woolf. Do you know her? She was a writer of this century, from the first 3 decades—very interesting. This book is written in stream of consciousness and deals with the period immediately before the second world war and about how a certain class from England did not know how to communicate with one other—of the inability to confront themselves and their own reality—of the alienation of humanity. Now I need to write some pieces for Monday about the book, my reactions, etc. Well—enough about what I do.*

Tell me—what's up with you? Did you finally communicate with your professor who wrote the review of your poem? Do you continue writing? Do you also write prose? Your comment at the close of your last letter left me—amazed—you say that many people, approach you, write you, etc., but that no one talks about any effort to get you out of that place—let's talk about that issue—How does one proceed—what should be done? I don't know what else to tell about that without first hearing your thoughts.

Well—I hope—you'll like the calendar. I also wanted to tell you in case Joe did not, that we are all uncles and aunts—Elda and Mando have a son, they named him René Cisneros Mendoza—He's such a precious child! We are all very happy!

I must go for now. Write when you have time. Tomás sends his greetings. With affection—]

Antonia

■ ■ ■

February 23, 1972

Qui 'ubo Toña:

Tu tarjetita me llegó el mero día de navidad—día en cual yo tambíen sentía la carga un poco pesada. Gracias por el aliviane. Después, a primeros del año, recibí tu muy agradable y expresiva carta, junta con la postal del Orozco, y tu mini-foto. [*Your card got here exactly on Christmas day—a day in which I also felt overwhelmed. Thanks for the uplift. Later, at the start of the [new] year, I got your very thoughtful and meaningful letter, together with the postcard of Orozco, and your mini-photo*] Again, thanks. You are a kind person.

La razón por la cual no te había escrito mas de volada fue que estaba bien *enmuletado* con el *Aztlán*. Creo que este sera el último (hopefully!) número en el cual yo serviré como redactor. No se, pero aún me fuí lo mas grande que pude. Me gustaría saber que opinas del. [*The reason why I had not written you sooner was because I had been real jammed up with the* Aztlán. *I think that this will be the last (hopefully!) issue in which I will serve as editor. I don't know, but I still went for the best that I could. I would like to know what you think about it.*] Personally, yo pienso que quedó maton de amadre [*I think it came out a killer issue*], aside from the minor technical discrepancies. ¿Sabes, que, 'Toña? No es que me quiero maderiar, pero estos chavos estan pesados por el lado del talento. La otra razón por mi diláto fue que me arrestaron por no cortarme el pelo; y por andar de hocicón. [*Know What 'Toña'? It's not that I want to brag, but these bros. are heavy on the talent side. The other reason for my delay was that they arrested me for not cutting my hair; and for being a big mouth.*] Everything is cool now.

Tengo que agradecer la manera en que defendíste tu posición/profesión. Mucho mas agradezco la explicación del "porqué". [*I want to thank you for the way in which you defended your position/profession. I appreciate even more the explanation of the "why."*] And this is exactly what i was refering to, in part. We know economics, or the lack of, is one of the most negative factors in our situation. Then, why not say this in your introduction; rather than reducing matters down to the level of a racial trip? Tu y yo sabemos lo que ha pasado, no? El yugo de la colonización es tremendo. Esto es lo que esperaba leér en su libro. [*You and I know what has happened, right? The yoke of colonization is brutal. This is what I expected to read in your book.*]

Again, I would like to reiterate this point: if you must look to the society for an explanation, please record your findings for future reference; thereby paving the way for the chroniclers and/or historians of the Chicano experience. You said it beautifully in your letter, and this is what our people need to recognize; the real problem.

O' sí, pesqué tu comentario sobre la explotacíon por "algúnos de nosotros a otros de los nuestros", de aquellas. Esta es parte de la batalla que muchos de nosotros pintos llevamos dentro. Hemos comprendido lo que deberas andabamos haciendo y ahora tratamos de corregír esta debilidad. By the way, acabo de recibír el *Publisher's Weekly* y encontré el primer anuncio del libro de Steiner y Valdez. Suponía salír en hardcover al principio y despúes en paperback. However, el anuncio solo se refiere al paperback. Se portó de aquellas el Steiner. Me mando una carta muy interesante y un chequecíto de $25. Ya sabes como me puse, no? [*O yea, I caught your commentary about the exploitation "of some of our people by some of our own," right on! This is part of the battle that many of us pintos carry out on the inside. We have realized what we really have been doing and we now are trying to correct this failing. By the way, I just received the Publisher's Weekly and found the first announcement of the book by Steiner and Valdez. It was supposed to come out in hardcover at first and then in paperback. However, the announcement just referred to the paperback. Steiner has been real cool. He sent me a very interesting letter and a small check for $25. You know how I reacted, right?*] Trying to decide on whether to use the bread for a pair of much-needed glasses or an order of books. At present, it seems the book thing is winning out.

Tocante al jazz, pues lo he seguído religiosamente desde la época del "Bop" de los late 40's, hasta el "avant-garde" del presente. Fue una de las cosas que me ayudaron a sobrevivir mis "street years." Me considero un estudiante serio de jazz history, con extensa discografía y bibliografía sobre el mismo tema. Un día, quizás, nos sentemos a discutír, at length, las diferentes escuelas del mundo jazz. Incidentally, en estos días pasados, like from november to now, nos han estado tratando de pacificar con toda clase de programs, música, y que-se-yo.

[*Regarding jazz, well I have followed it religiously since the "Bop" era of the late 40's, to the "avant-garde" of the present. It was one of the things that helped me survive my "street years." I consider myself a serious student of jazz history, with extensive discography and bibliography on the subject. One day, perhaps, we will sit down to discuss, at length, the different schools of the jazz world. Incidentally, in those recent times, like from November to now, they have been trying to pacify us with all sorts of* programs, *music, and what have you.*] Fortunately for the jazz lovers, the George Shearing Quintet and the Cannonball Adderley Quintet played a set of concerts for us. Aquí te mando una foto tomada durante una entrevísta que le hicimos [*Here I am sending you a photo taken during an interview that we conducted with him*]. Are you familiar with his "Mercy, Mercy, Mercy"? It's one of his more commercially successful "hits," but he can blow.

Concerning the polemics about what is and what isn't Chicano Art, por derecho que las definiciones se le dejan al crítico [*by right leave that up to the critics*]. We create, they label it. No sé porque un Chicano no podría utilizar las formas o los metodos del Op / Pop / Kinetic, para expresar la experiencia suya, do you? Está como el Dr. Alurista, cual todos por allá en el "West Coast" parece lo estiman bien. Lo respeto como poeta y maestro, y no cabe duda de que sabe las formas distintas de la tradición poética, ígual como conoce la mitología también. Pero, yo preferería que escribíera sus versos o en ingles o en español. Su forma de bilingüe (Chicanismo?) está un poco stilted y afectada. La experiencia del barrio no está suficiente convincing. No la siento. [*I don't know why a Chicano cannot use the forms or methods of Op/Pop/Kinetic, to express his experience, do you? There is, for instance, Dr. Alurista, who everyone out there in the "West Coast" seems to regard highly. I respect him as a poet and teacher, and there is no doubt that he knows the distinct forms of the poetic tradition, just as well as he knows mythology, too. But, I would prefer that he write his verses either in English or Spanish. His way of bilingualism (Chicanismo?) is a bit stilted and forced. The barrio experience is not very convincing. I don't feel it.*] This is what i get from his work. And i say this with all due respect to his education. He does know literature. ¡Que agarrada nos vamos a dar, usted y yo! [*What rap sessions you and I will have!*] It is so difficult to get into raps such as this through the mails. You know, there is so much that goes unre-

solved in transcribing thoughts onto paper. Me gustaría leér algo del
José Montoya o Omar Salinas [*I would like to read something by José*
Montoya or Omar Salinas].

Ya llegó el Eduardo Castro, y éste es el mensaje que me ha pedido
que te envíe: los manuscripts que se llevó la Martha tienen typographical errors y otros mistakes. Para conseguír copias limpias que has de
hablar con el Tony o el Anaya en la "Isla". También quisiera saber si
deseas corresponder con él. La razón por la cual no pudo tomar mas
tiempo en cultivar tu amistad y conversar contigo fue por no faltarle
respeto a los demas carnales allá.

¿No tienes, por casualidad, o sabes quien tenga unas copias rum-
badas en un rincón del "Trotsky on Literature & Art" or "Black
Nationalism & The Revolution in Music?" El uno es por el Trotsky
(naturalmente) y el otro es por el Frank Kofsky. Si te topas con ellos,
ahí vamos, eh?

[*Eduardo Castro just arrived, and this is the message that he has*
asked me to give you: the manuscripts that Martha took have typo-
graphical errors and other mistakes. In order to get clean copies you
will need to talk to Tony or Anaya on the "island." He'd also like to
know if you want to correspond with him. The reason that he was not
able to take more time to develop your friendship and talk with you
was to not disrespect for you or the other brothers over there.

By chance do you have or know someone who has old stashed
away copies of "Trotsky on Literature & Art" or "Black Nationalism
& The Revolution in Music?" The first is by Trotsky (naturally) and
the other by Frank Kofsky. If you stumble on them, send them over,
okay?]

Yo creo ya con esto basta [*I think that's enough*]. i only hope you
don't take as long to reply, as i did. Questions: ¿Qué tan lejos está de
tí la Militant o Pathfinder Bookstore que está situada en University
Place [*How far are you from the Militant or Pathfinder Bookstore that*
is located in University Place]? Is there an alternate (underground)
press in Seattle? ¿No está un vato por nombre de Apodaca en UW [*Is*
there a cat with the last name Apodaca at UW]. A según el Alambre,
he's supposed to be a real rip-off artist.

Te tengo un regalo que espero te guste. Es lo único que puedo hacer
para demostrate mi agradecimineto por el outlet que me das con tus
cartas. [*I have a gift that I hope you'll like. It is the only thing I can do*

to demonstrate my gratitude for the outlet you provide me with your letters.] i'm sure you'll agree with me when you see it, that polemics notwithstanding, "we iz what we iz." It will take from two to three weeks before i can get it to you, but i really think you'll dig it.

Don't hang me up too long. Saludos a todo el sindicato [*Greetings to all the gang*]. Tu recíbe mis más cariñosos deseos [*You receive my heartfelt wishes*]. Hasta la liberacíon, me suscribo, con admiración y respeto,

raúlrsalinas/tapon

(favor de no usar mi nombre por fuera de las cartas [*please do not use my name on the outside of these letters*])

■ ■ ■

2 March 1972

Estimado Raúl:

Unas cuantas líneas para saludarte y mandarte el calendario—creía que lo había puesto en el correo desde enero, pero andaba recogiendo algunas cosas en mi oficina y me encontré el sobre—¡que vergüenza! De todos modos te lo mando y tambíen te mando la carta que te escribí en enero. Armando Mendoza me dijo que le habías escrito y que le habías explicado tu situación. Tambíen dice que te interesa venir a la universidad acá en Washington. A todos nos da gusto y trataremos de hacer lo que sea necesario para ayudar.

Bueno—ahora si me despido para aseguar poner esto en el correo ahorita mismo. Le das muchos saludos a Eduardo Castro de parte de todos acá y tu recibes saludos de Tomás, Joe, Mando, Elda y de mi. El día 12 de Marzo bautizamos Tomás y yo al René—le vamos a hacer una pachanga a todo dar! Antes de que se me olvide, a mediados de Marzo me voy para San Diego, donde estaré por un trimestre—voy a estudiar y a trabajar con Ernesto Galarza, que es un economista Chicano que tiene mucho conocimiento de la historia de los sindicatos—ha estado trabajando en esta area desde los 1930's. Si tienes tiempo de escribir antes del 20 de Marzo porque salgo el 21—no se que será mi dirección en San Diego así es que no te la puedo dar ahorita. Cuídate y no dejes de escribirnos,

[*Just a few lines to say hello and send you the calendar—I thought I had mailed it in January, but I was picking up a few things in my office and ran across the envelope—how embarrassing! Nevertheless I am sending it and the letter I wrote you in January. Armando Mendoza told me that you had written him and that you had explained to him your situation. He also says that you are interested in coming to the university here in Washington. We are all happy about this and will try to do all that is necessary to help.*

Well—now I will say bye so I can be sure to put this in the mail right now. Give my best regards to Eduardo Castro on behalf of everyone here and Tomás, Joe, Mando, Elda and I send you hellos. On March 12 Tomás and I baptize René—we are going to give him the coolest and biggest party. Before I forget it, mid-March, I am going to San Diego, where I will be for a trimester—I will study and work with Ernesto Galarza, who is a Chicano economist who is very knowledgeable about labor history—he has been working in this area since the 1930s. If you have time, write before March 20 because I leave on the 21st—I don't know what my address in San Diego will be so therefore I cannot give it to you right now.

Take care of yourself and don't forget to write us]

> hasta la próxima—
> Fraternalmente,
> tu carnala,
> Antonia

■ ■ ■

March 3, 1972

Querida Toña:

¡Ando mas aguitado! Estos animales me han negado escribir un artículo sobre "Censorship in Prison", para el magazine "Trends". Creo es del Concilio de Iglesias Presbiterianas. Heché pleito y salí corrido. Después pa acabarla de fregar, salieron con una orden permitiendo el uso de bigote, y el pelo un poco mas largo que antes. Como hacía una o dos semanas que me habían cortado el mío, fuí y me razure toda la cabeza. Tambíen el bigote, which is sparse anyway. Ahora andan con la cola parada porque me fuí hasta el otro extremo. [*I am really bumkicked! These animals prohibited me from writing an article about "Censorship in Prison," for the magazine "Trends." I think it is from the Council of Presbyterian Churches. I raised hell and got booted out. Later, just to add insult to injury, they came out with a rule allowing mustaches and hair to be worn a little longer than before. Since it had been one or two weeks since they had cut mine, I went and shaved my whole head. Also the mustache, which is sparse anyway. Now they have a bug up their ass because I went to the other extreme.*] Reprimand!

Sitting here in American History Class, fuming over my row with the porcine elements, and having to listen to the Prof. rant and rave about the American Mind, circa 1750: i had two alternatives for alleviating matters; either cop a sneak at my latest issue of the "Guardian," with news of Angela's release and Genaro Vasquez' death, beckoning me. Or, scribbling a few lines to you, in hopes of eradicating my morbid fit of depression. You win, ni que. . . .

You are probably aware of the fact that Mando has offered me assistance in "raising" from my unexpired bit down yonder, right! He kited me a couple of days ago, and sent the UW Daily. Piensa que puede conseguir mi libertad de los perros aquellos. ¡Quien sabe! [*He thinks he can gain my freedom from those dogs. Who knows?!*] Lo malo es que si continuan arrinconandome mucho mas estos bueyes [*The bad thing is that if these assholes continue boxing me into a corner*], at this stage of my life, i'm going to have some difficulty containing my rage, when i do raise.

Espero que con esto de que el buítre mayor anda tirandole campaña al Chou [*Hopefully with the major vulture courting Chou*] (complete with weather reports from Peking, on the box; chinese cuisine recipes and oriental fashions in the press) nos dejen ordenar escrituras del "Dragoncito aquél" [they may allow us to order writings from "the little Dragon"]. Creo un class action suit sobre esto, sería muy timely y causaría embarrassment a los puercos. [*I think a class action suit regarding this would be very timely and would cause the pigs some embarrassment.*]

Me alegro al leer: que la Angela y el Father Dan han sido liberados, aunque nomas sea temporalmente [*I am pleased to read that la Angela and Father Dan have been liberated, even if it is just temporary*]; the easing of laws on smoke a bit more rational. i'm very excited over Califas abolishing their murder machine. Se salvaran los brothas, conocidos, y las chavalas Mansonias. [*The brothers, acquaintances and Manson girls will be spared.*]

Por el lado de nuestra gente; en la universidad de Tejas (austin) la cosa va mal. Los Drs. Paredes y Sanchez del Centro de Estudios Mexico-Americano han resignado, por motivo de la "mentalidad sur(a)ena (sureña?)" which prevails. [*In regards to our own people; at the University of Texas (Austin) things are going badly. Drs. Paredes and Sanchez from the Center for Mexican-American Studies have resigned, as a result of that "southern mental(sh)ity" [mentalidad sur(a)ena"],* which prevails.] The MAYO youth are enraged. O si, curate, el José Limón, que es asistente del Paredes le hablo al Palmquist informandose si era posible que yo fuera a lecture alla. Pues, le dijieron que estaba loco. Yo no se de que podria hablarle yo a esa gente. En Pharr, al Efrain Fernandez lo hicieron acquit; de aquellas. [*Oh, yea, check it out, José Limón, who is Paredes's assistant talked to Palmquist trying to find out if it was possible for me to lecture there. Well, they told him that he was crazy. I don't know what I would be able to say to those people. In Pharr, Efrain Fernandez was acquitted; right on!*]

Recibí palabra de que el Luis Valdez presentó su teatro en el parque de Chapultepec y que los Mascarones se encuentran bien en Cuernavaca [*I got word that Luis Valdez presented his play in Chapultepec Park and that Los Mascarones are doing well in Cuernavaca*]. Are you hip to Los Mascarones? ¡Jijo! Me dejan bien arreglado. [*Damn! They knock me out!*] Xmas eve, i sat in an empty classroom with two other carnales and heard about ten of their sides, rather than attend the holiday festivities taking place. Que magnífica la manera en que utilízan la musica de las diferentes culturas para presentar su mensaje social. Me gustaría calarme a escribír una canción protesta. El "Sr. Don" de los Boricuas me ha hechado el envite, once or twice. [*It is wonderful the way they use music from different cultures to present their social message. I would like to try my hand at writing a protest song. El "Sr. Don" of the Puerto Ricans has encouraged me to do it, once or twice.*]

Have you read any of the writings on the Tlateloco incident? Ponia-towska or Alba? i get so frustrated at times, Toña, there is so much i want to know about and do.

Por derecho que ya lo que necesito es aire y un buen platon de COMIDA [*For sure what I need now is air and a good plate of FOOD*]. i avoid the messhall as much as i can. A veces me voy vege-terian y en otras ocasiones me la paso a puro snack de la tienda [*Some-times I go vegetarian and on other occasions I get by just on snack food from the store*]. i realize that's not cool for my health, pero ya estoy quemado con todo esto [*but I am burned out with all this*].

But all is not bitterness. There are good moments of peace and con-tentment—though far and few between—you are one of them. Yeah, you bring positive waves into my sometimes macabre existence; sure they trigger off minute "i wonders." And that's valid, as long as it doesn't impose dogmatically on one's trip. "So blow me a jazz horn, let's be real and cry."

By the way, have you heard "Suavecito" by Malo? De aquellitas [*It's tough*]! Their sound is better than "Santana" the elder. More emphasis on the latino than rock. The little dude on trumpet, Luis Gasca, is an old acquaintace from Houston. He's extremely talented. He's made the latin circuit with Orquesta Falcon, Luis Arcaráz on into Mongo Santamaría & Janis. Esta muy loquillo, tambien [*He's really a trip, too*]. The storm must be subsiding. i'm already into a musical rap. See! You are effective. Thank you for being on the receiving end of this outpouring. And then there was you . . .

tapon

■ ■ ■

13 de septiembre de 1972

Estimado raúl:

Por fín me siento a comunicarme contígo—Has de pensar que me habrá tragado la tierra—ya mero—pero not quite! Los últimos meses han sido penosos y difíciles—meses de asesoramiento, de reflección y de redifinición—perdona que no había escrito. [*Finally I sit down to communicate with you—you would think that the earth had swal-lowed me—almost—but not quite! The last months have been painful and difficult—months of evaluation, reflection and redefinition—par-don me for not having written.*]

There is so much to relate that I don't know where to begin. ¿Como estás? Nos dimos cuenta que estabas encarruchado y nos pre-ocupó—además del hecho que estabas allí, nos preocupó que quizá no recibieras el correo. Joe te escribió una nota el primero de septiembre con la cual te mandó fotocópias de la materia y cartas que se habían mandado a Texas. [*How are you? We found out that you had gotten busted and it worried us—aside from the fact that you were there, we worried that perhaps—that you were not receiving mail. Joe wrote you a note on September 1 in which he sent you photocopies of the mate-rials and letters that had been sent to Texas.*] ¿Recibiste esa carta [*Did you receive that letter*]? Let us know. Ahora te mandamos varias otras cosas que tratan de admission y financial aid y nos urge saber que las recibes [*Here we send you various other things that relate to admis-sions and financial aid and we are anxious to know if you got them*]. In a separate envelope we are mailing you all of the information deal-ing with Admission, registration and financial aid. You have been admitted to the UW for fall quarter and you have been awarded finan-cial aid. Since you won't be available until November, the fall quarter admission will be transferred to Winter quarter, Jan 1973, and Zachary's letter indicated that financial aid will start winter quarter. It is imperative that we know you have received the packets, so please answer as soon as possible. We hope to hear from you by September 25. If possible, tu nos puedes llamar [*you can call us*]. El número de Joe es . . . y el mió es . . . . Espero que ya hayas salido de segregation y que te puedes communicar con nosotros. Si tienes preguntas o te hace falta más informacíon—let us know. [*Joe's number is . . . and mine is . . . We hope that you have gotten out of segregation and that you can communicate with us. If you have questions or if you need more information—let us know.*]

Raúl ciertas situaciones han cambiado aquí que quizá influirán tu decisión de venir al UW. Se nos hace justo que debes saber, y quizá — ya te habrá escrito Mando y esto sea innecesario, pero como no sé si has recibido carta de él, yo te lo comunico. Si decides venir al unlim-ited program y entrar al UW en enero, el director del programa no será Chicano. Es que Mando se fue para California el sábado pasado, dimitió aquí y va a trabajar in Oakland, en Mills College, quienes recibieron un federal grant. Creo que va a ser miembro de un team que discute el problema de las drogas y trata de encontrar manera de trabajar con el problema a un nivel más amplio—por ejemplo, creo que tratan cuestiones de drogas y los servicemen, drogas y las communidades Chicanas y Negras, etc.

[*Raúl certain circumstances have changed here that perhaps may influence your decision to come to UW. We think it is only fair that you know, and perhaps Mando already has written you and this may be unnecessary, since I don't know if you have received his letter. I am going to tell you. If you decide to come to the Cons Unlimited Program and enter the UW in January, the director of the program will not be Chicano. It's just that Mando went to California last Saturday, he resigned work here and will work in Oakland, at Mills College, which received a federal grant. I think he will be a member of a team that researches the difficulties of the drug problem in a broader context—for example—I think that they will deal with drugs and servicemen, drugs and Chicano and Black communities, etc.*] Mientras tanto, aquí en Seattle se están entrevistando muchas personas para la posición que dejó Mando, pero el new director no será Chicano [*Meanwhile, here in Seattle they are interviewing many people for the position that Mando left, but the new director will not be Chicano*]—or at least at the moment it doesn't look like it will be a Chicano. There are quite a few applicants most of whom are Anglos or Afro-Americans— la persona que seleccionen sera X-pinto, de eso estamos seguros, pero es todo lo que sabemos [*the person they select will be an ex-con, of this we are sure, but this is all that we know*]. En términos personales, Mando y Elda se separaron. Ella está aquí en Seattle con nosotros, tiene al niño, quién está creciendo, está muy grande y muy lindo. [*On a more personal note, Mando and Elda have separated. She is here in Seattle with us, she has the baby, who is growing. He is very big and very cute.*]

Creo que todos nos encontramos en un período de transición. Pero aun—dentro de las penas y angustias de estar viviendo se necesita tiempo y espacio—hay muchas cosas y muchas razones por tener ánimo y fuerzas.

Bueno—ni—empecé a platicarte lo de San Diego y lo de México— pero lo dejaré para otro día porque quiero mandar esta carta hoy. Hay muchas cosas de interés—la conferencia de la Raza Unida parece que tuvo tremendo éxito. Creo que Ramsey Muñiz tiene chanza de darles en la M en Texas, hay mucho interés aquí en Washington de crear el partido.

A mí se me ha pedido por un grupo de Chicanos que enseñe una clase que trate de la Chicana en los estados unidos. ¿Que opinas tu de tal clase? ¿Como tratarías tu este subject si se te pidiera que enseñaras una clase que trata de la Chicana? Tomás está bien y te manda muchos saludos—

Cuídate y dínos si recibes el material, y que está pasando contigo. [*I think we all find ourselves in a period of transition. But still—within the pain and anguish of being alive and being persons who need time and space—there are many things and many reasons for maintaining hope and strength.*

Well I didn't even begin to tell you about San Diego and Mexico— but I will leave it for another time because I want to send this letter today. There are many things of interest—the Raza Unida Conference appears to have been a tremendous success. I think Ramsey Muñiz has a chance of socking it to 'em in Texas, there is much interest here in Washington for starting the party.

I have been asked by a group of Chicanos to teach a class that deals with the Chicana in the United States. What do you think about such a class? How would you treat this subject if you were asked to teach a class that deals with la Chicana? Tomás is well and he sends his hellos.

Take care and tell us if you receive the materials, and what is going on with you,]

Atentamente,
Antonia

■ ■ ■

8 de Octubre '72

"El Hoyo"

Querida Castañeda:

After putting it off longer than usual, paso a dar contestación a tu muy agradable carta [*I now take the time to respond to your very pleasant letter*]. i had wanted to do so, sooner, but these days i find it difficult to read or write with even a semblance of concentration.

My present situation—conferring with all manner of legal counsel, contacting Prisoner's Rights groups, awaiting the final decision from Texas—is literally too much!

Today, the skies are overcast, like a slate gray canvas, the view dominates my vision. La llovizna cae lenta [*the drizzle falls lightly*] and it has a soothing, almost mesmerizing effect on my senses. Much like you, my moods change with the weather. So, i decided this would be the perfect day to reply to yours. i love (when i'm free) weather such as this. me recuerda mucho de los días de Otoño en Northern Cal: San Francisco, Sausalito y el Monterrey Penninsula. [*I remember well the Autumn days in Northern Cal: San Francisco, Sausalito and el Monterrey Peninsula.*] ¡De Aquellas!

¿Como estás tú, mi apreciable camarada [*How are you, my beloved comrade*]? Many thoughts scampered through my head during your extended silence. Though, i'm sure you too were undergoing extreme personal tribulations. ¿Se ha resolvido todo [*has it all been resolved*]? You must know i really missed you. ¿Verdad [*honest!*]? Dejame saber como te fué por San Diego y Mejícles [*Let me know how it went in San Diego and Mejícles*]. i kept hoping you'd send some flix de por allá. ¡Ja! Wishful thinking. ¿Estás ya para terminar tus estudios, o falta mucho tiempo [*Are you about to finish your studies, or do you still have more time to go*]?

Pues, aquí la cosa marcha so-so. Todavía me encuentro en la silapa. [*Well, things here march on, so-so. I still find myself in the hole.*] The first phase of our lawsuit began last Tuesday in Benton. There was the usual postponement, as we figured. Pero, aún, los sofocamos con cuatro plaintiffs y catorce witnesses. Puro animal de uña que les enseñamos. [*There was the usual postponement, as we figured. But, still, we blew them away with four plaintiffs and fourteen witnesses. We showed them our claws.*] Ha-Ha! We are due back in court next week, date unknown as of yet. Slowly se están mobilizando las tropas con la publicidad [*Slowly the troops are mobilizing the publicity*]. Hopefully, things should work out for the better. If only to secure the release from lock-up of 140 brothers. You must have spoken to Mando prior to his departure, if you knew i was boxed in que no? Oh! Yeah, I made a request for a phone call, unfortunately, los perros me tiraron a león [*the pigs just ignored me*]. Only under extreme circumstances will they consider an emergency call. As if preparations relevant to my freedom were not an emergency. ¡Se salen, los pendejos! ¿No crees? [*They got some nerve, those assholes! Don't you think?*]

¿Disque el Señor Mendoza se descontó pa Bay Area, eh [*They say that Mr. Mendoza split to the Bay Area, huh*]? The field he's gone off into is a delicate subject with me. A según me siento [*As far as I am concerned*], i wouldn't care to be a drug crusader. i am done with hard drugs y total. On my end, this undoubtedly means Resident Release (cons unlimited) Project is out. Such being the situation in Seattle, i better start thinking of obtaining suitable (lava platos [*dishwasher*]) employment. Correction: i better start hoping i get cut loose. ¿Que clase de trabajo hay por allí [*What kind of work is there out there*]?

Lo de la separacíon me cayó mal de amadre [*Regarding the separation, it hit me real fuckin' hard*]. What can i say? i am ill-equipped to attempt expressing through words what can help alleviate the pain felt by María Elda, and by you, as a result of your proximity to them. What's to become of María Elda, will she continue in school? Is there any chance for reconciliation? Will this have any bearing on my coming up? No me quiero sentir guiltón al llegar [*I don't want to feel uneasy when I get there*]. You know what i mean? The only people i will know there seran ustedes [*will be you*]. Para caer en un scene que esta triste al momento está poco cabron [*To fall into a sad scene at this time is kinda fucked up*]. No, i shall go (sí acaso [*if possible*]) and try not to impose unduly upon the generosity of you good folks. Okay? i almost forgot to tell you, my official release date is November 27, which means i should be there the first days of December. Isn't that grand? Solo que, save me a slice of bird, will ya? You will be there, right? That is, someone will, huh? Como que me estoy chiviando [*Looks like I'm getting cold feet already.*]. ¡Ja!

For sure, i thought someone in your group would've attended the Raza Unida Conference. Aside from some bland reports in the Austin Statesman & Denver Post, the only good, accurate (we think) accounts came from the Militant newspaper y un analysis socialísta por correspondencia [*and a socialist analysis by mail*]. These were, at least, favorable, and when critical of the Partido's structure, explanations were given. The prensa reaccionaria [*reactionary press*], on the other hand, tried to make an issue of the expressed differences in filosofía between José Angel & Corky. There, were as you undoubtedly heard, the tragedies, Ricardo Falcon in NM and another in Jauritos—which the establishment press also tried to exploit. No CPA publications here, so our sources are limited. By the way, do you know Rudy García from Denver? He wrote 3 excellent editorials in the post. Especially the second one, it was very perceptive observations that he made. Do you think you could write the paper and ask for these? (9-26, 10-23, 10-30)? If you should happen to score, hay vamos con unas copias [*send us a few copies*], okay? We also wrote the RU office in San Anto, and to José Angel for some info on resolutions, position papers, lectures, etc., but so far no reply. Se me hace que los derechos del Pinto no fueron discutidos [*I think that prisoners rights were not discussed*].

Me gustó mucho la respuesta de Muñiz, a sus opponents [*I liked Muñiz' response to his* opponents], Briscoe & Grover at a rally in Austin. Their response to his challenge for a public discussion of issues, was to send hired public relations firms, instead. Les dijo "I don't have to go to New York or Tennessee to hire a public relations firm. All i have to do is go to Crystal City and we have our public relations (Raza Unida) firm there." He was at that time adhering to José Angel's "Balance of Power" theory, which has since the conference—been disregarded for the more independentista party line, proposed by the Colorado delegation. Another (put down) article i read was on the deplorable conditions and decline of Cristál. How people were moving away y todo ése pedo [*and all that shit*]. Me puso en mente lo que he leído y las noticias que nos llegan "abajo de ala" de Cuba [*It made me think about about what I had read and the news that gets to us "underground" from Cuba*]. You know, the same struggle por el desarollos [*for development*]. One of the things i plan to do upon release is challenge the unconstitutionality of the Pintos' loss of voting rights. Naturalmente, que quiero la oportunidad de votar Raza Unida [*Naturally, I want the right to vote for Raza Unida*]. However, si se me hace un sapo [*if I can pull it off*], it would set a precedent for other ex-pintos to follow. Tambíen está el case de [*There is also the case of*] Morton Sobell regarding his right to travel, on parole, to attend political events. i want to check that out, also. ¿Creés sería buena idea [*Do you think it would be a good idea*]?

Now then, i'll attempt to answer your pregun-to-to-ta [*Q-Q-Question*]! Primeramente, tendríamos que establecer [*First, we would need to establish*] what is meant by Chicanas. Whether all Raza women since the rip-off of Aztlán, or 1st & 2nd generation estadounidenses [*U.S. born*]. Vez, yo hago relate lo [*You see I refer to the*] Chicano experience from 1910 to now, in a particular sense. En terminos mas general, pues todo Mejicano y Latinos [*In more general terms, well all Mexicans and Latinos*]. Wow! You pose a helluva question! ¡Me pones, en la cruz de amadre, mujer [*You've backed me up against a wall, woman*]! Okay. Quizás sería necesario un breve resúmen sobre la mujer latina [*Perhaps it would be necessary to give a brief overview of Latinas*]: heróinas como [*heroines like*] Gertrudis Bocanegra, Maríanna Bracetti, Juana Gallo, La Coronela y otras soldaderas [*and other women warriors*], poetíza [*poet*] Lola Rodriguez, Tió, etc. Then you could define their role in this society. A depiction of the Chicana as a migrant worker, as a wartime wife, student, and La Nueva Chicana en el Movimiento. Oh! And don't forget las pachuquitas [*those pachucas*] of the mid '40s and early '50s. Recuerdo que en Houstón se llamaban [*I remember that in Houston they were called the*] "Black Skirt Gang." Portaban sus pompadours donde (a segun el mito) cargaban sus fileros [*They wore their pompadours where (according to the myth) they carried their switchblade knives*], tailored mini-skirts negras, camisas (o sweaters) negras, y calf-length socks blancos [*black shirts (or black sweaters), and calf-length white socks*]. En Austin eran "Las Jitterbugs" y se trajeaban con suits tailored igual [*In Austin they were the "Jitterbugs" and they dressed up with suits tailored exactly*] (same cut & material) que los de los chucos [*as the ones the chucos wore*]; mini-skirts con finger-tip coats. Sort of an early-day uni-sex trip. Ha! En San Jo había las "Alley Kats". Estás ya venian siendo de otra época. Con sus Levi-ses arreglados [de] diferentes maneras, bien cáidos abajo de la cintura. [*In San Jo there were the "Alley Kats." These were already from a different era. With their Levi's worn in different ways, real low below the belt.*] Con men's hawaiian print or solid color gabardine shirts, buttoned up to the collar; sus calquitos blancos con calcetínes [*with white socks*] rolled down below the ankles, where they sport stars, crosses or initials tatuteadas [*tattooed*]. Wacha por donde ando. Me salí afuera del traque. ¿Verdad? [*Check out where I'm headed. I sure got off track. Right?*] Perdoname pero estó es todo lo que yo conozco [*Forgive me but this is all that I know*] and, it probably wouldn't have any place in a class such as you mentioned. ¡Chingao [*Goddamn*]! Me siento mal porque no puedo expresarme a tu nivel, a veces [*I feel bad because I can't express myself at your level sometimes*]. This wasn't what you asked and, certainly you deserve a better reply. Cuando nos veámos, hablaremos más sobre este tema [*When we see each other we will talk more about this topic*], because i don't consider it a satisfactory (in depth) respuesta [*response*]. Okay? Te digo, siempre tengo que salír por debajo de la mesa. Están cabrones estos mental blocks. [*I tell you, sometimes I always have to blow it. These* mental blocks *are hard ass.*]

Cúrate, aquí en bartolina nos dan un rato de radio por día y acaba de empezar un jazz program del colegio. Ya sabes como me pongo, no? [*Dig, here in isolation they give us daily radio time and a jazz program from the college just started. You know how I get, right?*] They kicked it off with a very tight composition by pianist Herbie Hancock, entitled "Maiden Voyage." His quintet consists of a 2 horn frontline with rhythm section, headed by the crisp and fiery trumpet stylings of Little Freddie Hubbard and the forceful surging tenor sax of George Coleman. ¡Jijo! It's really nice. O'si, [Oh, yea] i heard "Vickie en Español" the other day. And though i've never dug on her "pop" style, nor did i care for her bourgeoisie mentally (which she is seemingly trying to shuck, in recent times) i have to, at least credit her for this recording. Her choice of selections which have not been overworked, lends a fresh quality to the overall production of this latest effort. It is much in the manner of Eydie's "Amor" & "Mas Amor" with the Panchos of several years back. Would you believe, i also heard "La Tariacuri" once? Now that's a real treat! i'm going off into another brain lock for lack of something more relevant and interesting to tell you. so rather than prolong the boredom i may be carrying you through, i'll start tapering off.

One thing for sure Toña, i am most anxious to hit the ground. How are the parks and libraries up there? You know when i got here, i'd gone for about 3 years without exercise or sunlight. Pues, i started running a mile daily and doing calisthenics, ya estaba bien prieto otra vez [*i was real dark again*]. Now, i'm out of shape again and my "prison-pallor" has returned.

Confined as we are in seg., the senses become very distorted. Like, one's sense of equilibrium goes all out of kilter. A veces me levanto del bunk y me mareo. [*Sometimes I get up from my bunk and feel disoriented.*] Or like there may be a dark spot on the floor, and while i'm writing i'll catch it with the corner of my eye and it seems to move. No creas que se me "estan" volando, [*Don't think that I am losing it,*] it's just a perception thing. To write I lay a blanket on the floor. Every time i start getting restless, i run the few steps in my cell from front to back. Ahora comprendo porque los animales de la selva [*Now I know why wild animals*] pace back and forth in their cages in the zoos.

Bueno, te daré barra por esta vez. [*Well, I'll give you a break for now.*] Don't let me scare you away. Please write when you find time and the spirit moves you. Okay? Incidentally, i may be repeating myself but did i ask you about your lunar? Or your relationship to the author of "Crónica Personal de Cristal" [*"Personal Chronicles of Crystal City."*] I'd say she's your jefita [mother]. Do you know a Phillip Ortego or Dorothy Harth? ¿Qué pues con el libro [*And what's up with the book*] "Los Chicanos" by Feliciano Rivera?

Please extend my best regards to María Elda & Rene, Prof. Sommers. Tu recibe mis más sinceros deseos. [*You receive my most sincere wishes.*]

Affectionately,
raúl r.salinas

■ ■ ■

[circa mid-October 1972]

Estimado raúl:

domingo por la noche—noche de brisa suave de otoño en Seattle—entre los gritos lastimeros del René que no se quiere dormir y el bulto silencioso de mis libros abandonados—unas cuantas líneas para saludarte.

Joe y yo pensábamos en tí el día 2 de octubre—tanto por ser el día del trial como por ser el 4 aniversario del Tlatelolco ¿Cómo salió el trial? La semana pasada recibí copia de la carta del abogado de Southern Illinois. Me interesó mucho—especialmente porque yo no conocía los detalles de la manifestación.

Creo que Joe ya te habrá escrito acerca de su conversación con Tippy. ¿Que han sido las reacciones por allá? ¿Si te ha dicho algo? ¿Mandaste tu una petición a Texas? Nosotros no sabíamos sí habías enviado petición alguna a Texas o si Tippy lo estaba haciendo, o como se estaba arreglando ese aspecto del release. Nos dices si hay más trámites con que cumplir.

Nos da mucho gusto que opines bien del libro—todavía esperamos una crítica de parte tuya y de los compañeros de Marion. En diciembre sale un 2nd printing y esperamos poder incluir tres trabajos (poemas) de Tino Villanueva—se avienta! No es 2nd edición sino hubieramos hecha mas sustituciones, pero ya veremos—si nos toca otra edition—hacemos algunos cambios—desgraciadmente se nos pasaron algunas obras muy buenas, algunos autores importantes—pero de todos modos—las obras que no incluímos nosotros se están publicando, se están conociendo, que es lo más importante—y aún más todavía—cada día hay más y más literatura chicana.

Espero que ya salíste de segregación, que palabra tan horrible—y que hayas encontrado todo tu "yonke" en su lugar.

Las cosas aquí van bien—ya se ven más y más caras morenas en este campus donde hace poco eramos solo unos cuatro gatos—it's a gorgeous trip to see all those students on campus—tho' never enough—from 5 or 6 to 200 + in 3 years is a start.

Bueno raúl—me despido—tengo que escribir un trabajo para una clase de historia—aunque apenas empezó el trimestre ya estoy bien atrasada. Cuídate—escribe—y nos dices si se necesita más papelerio.

[*Sunday evening—a night of cool Autumn breeze in Seattle—amid the sad cries from René, who doesn't want to sleep, and the silent pile of my abandoned books—a few lines to say hello.*

Joe and I were thinking about you on October 2—at once because it was the day of the trial as well as the fourth anniversary of Tlatelolco. How did the trial turn out? Last week I received a copy of the letter from the lawyer from Southern Illinois. It really interested me—especially since I did not know the details of the demonstration.

I think Joe must have written you about his conversation with Tippy. What have the reactions been like over there? Has he told you anything? Did you send a petition to Texas? We did not know if you had sent any petitions to Texas or if Tippy was doing it, or how that part of the release was being arranged. Tell us if there are more details to complete.

We are very pleased that you think well of the book—we are still awaiting a critique from you and the brothers from Marion. The second printing comes out in December and we expect to include three works (poems) from Tino Villanueva—he's right on! It is not a second edition or we would have made more substitutions, but we'll see—if we get another edition—we'll make some changes—unfortunately we overlooked some really good works, some important authors—but nonetheless—the works we did not include are being published, they are becoming known, which is the most important thing—and even moreso—everyday there is more and more Chicano literature.

I hope you are now out of segregation, what a horrible word—and that you have found all your "junk" in its place.

Things here are going well—one now sees more and more brown faces on this campus where not too long ago we were just four stray cats—it's a gorgeous trip to see all those students on campus—tho' never enough—from 5 or 6 to 200 + in 3 years is a start.

Well raúl—it's time to say goodbye—I must write a piece for a history class—even though the trimester just began I am very behind. Take care—write—and tell us if you need more publications.]

Atentamente,
Antonia

■ ■ ■

Octubre 23, 1972

Querida Toña:

The long drawn-out, no-nothing scribblin's of the 8th were the result of an extremely frustrated state of mind. You shouldn't be subjected to such insane outbursts, but who else? If nothing more it provided you with a peep into another facet of my erratic personality; a glimpse of a man in his weak moments. Essential moments, if one is to remain undaunted in the face of adversity. i find the need to utilize these escape valves in my refusal to be broken by the enemy. / the spirit of Bro. George J. seems to hover close by.

It is quite evident that our rhythmic waves were sure enough hooked up to the seasons, somewhere out in the universe. The gentle wooing of Autumn seeemd to affect us jointly. No? However, you lay it down much more poetically—more beautifully. ¡Estás pesadísima! [*You're real heavy!*] Your letter proved to be—as usual—the ever-welcome panacea.

There was reference in my last one, to our trip downtown, so you know how matters stand in regards to our lawsuit. Everything is at a standstill up to this point. Nos golpearon a uno de nuestros plaintiffs, detalles later. [*They beat one of our plaintiffs, details later.*] Yes, the trial date coincided with the Tlatelolco Massacre, we ran it to our non-Latino brothers. Incidentally, did i ever ask you about some writings concerning Tlatelolco? Anyway, have you read anything on it? Ni recuerdo donde leí de ello, [*I don't even remember where I read about it,*] but there were supposed to be four books covering the incident y me parece que [*and it seems to me that*] Poniatowska & Alba somebody were a couple of the authors.

Listen Toña, when you received the letter to Mike Deutsch, were there any complementary materials enclosed? Se ha preparado un paquetón de escrituras, ensayos, y exposés contra ésta pinta, por varios brodas. [*A big packet of writings, essays and exposés against this joint were prepared by various bruthas.*] i understand that El Grito del Norte, & Mario Cantú de San Anto are supposed to be coming through with active support, whenever/if ever. Nos están jugando un cuatro con sus tacticas dilatorias. [*They are playing a number on us with their delaying tactics.*]

In regards to the Texas situation, a very informal petition was submitted. Rather than a petition, it was a letter expressing my feelings toward reinstatement. This was sprinkled with comments by leading authorities in the field of correction and penology, supportive of my statements. Along with the letter was included an information sheet, listing amount of college credits, magazines in which poems were published, writing awards, 7 names of persons who could verify the information. Prof. Ruiz and a dude from Notre Dame, Ind. wrote some very impressive reference letters. Tu sabes, me subieron al caballo, de amadre! [*You know, they had some cool things to say!*] The final decision now is for Texas to decide. O' si, Tippy came by and informed me that the latest he had was a communique *from* Texas *to* the State Parole board in Seattle, asking if they'd accept me. That was last week, solo que [*yet*], who knows? i'm just waiting now.

Prof. Sommers had mentioned Villanueva before. In fact, he promised to send me a sample of the brother's work, if he copped. Do you have the 3 pieces you referred to? Could you run me unas copias? Estoy interesado en leer al chavo. Aquí te van unas cuantas líneas del carnal Boricua. [*I'm interested in reading the guy. Here's a few lines from the Boricua brother.*]

Bueno, hermana, pues mi compa Raúl me pregunta que porqué no le escribo unas letras a usted y yo me digo: bueno ¿y por que? Soy Rafael, hijo de la Patria borincana de La Raza. Leí y comprendí "Literatura Chicana: Texto y Contexto." Y le digo que quisiera que mi pueblo la leyera, pues leyéndola no solo se realiza la situación del Chicano y los porqués de esa situación, y sí que también la situación del Puertorriqueño y los porqués de su situación. Nuestras vidas corren casi paralelas y quizás por éso, mientras mejor nos conocemos, más cercas nos sentimos unos de los otros. El mismo enemigo ha querido mutilar, y si posible, hacer desaparecer nuestras culturas, tan parecidas una a la otra, y sin embargo, tanto el Chicano como el Boricua hemos podido salvar nuestra idenitidad cultural, nuestra personalidad, y "Literatura Chicana: Texto y Contexto," es una prueba de ello! Atraves de tan rica antología, no solo conocí mejor el alma del Chicano, y sí que también me alma borinqueña. Y le doy un ramo de gracias a usted u sus asociades por la parte dedicada a la literatura de mis compatriotas. Nuestros poemas se parecen tanto en alma y contenido, que si no lo especificáramos sería algo dificultuoso saber que poema escribió un Chicano y cual escribió un Portorro. Especialmente entre uno escrito por un Puertorriqueño de los nuevayores y un Chicano. En ese caso hasta la forma sería casi, si no del todo, similar. ¿Ha leído poemas de Lola Rodriguez Tío, Pachín Marín, Luis Llorens Torres? Sus poemas son profundamente Puertoriqueños y cubren varias épocas. Y hoy tenemos una legión de magníficos jóvenes poetas y veo con tremendísima alegría, que mi Raza de por acá, de Aztlán, también está en pleno apogeo en su literatura. Es un sublime orgullo para mi haber cultivado la fraternal hermandad de un poeta de Aztlán: raúl! Todo su pensamiento es un poema para La Raza, lo afirmo con la sinceridad de quien solo elegia a quien lo merece. Pa'lante siempre, mi hermano, que aunque muchas espinas lastimarán nuestros corazones, muchas rosas también encontraremos, y cada una de esas rosas, las rosas de la Raza, bien valan cruzar cualquier sendero espinoso para alcanzarlas! Espero que a la rica antología "Literatura Chicana: Texto y Contexto," sigan otras obras que tanto elevan nuestras almas al leerlas. Le admira—Rafael.

[*Well, sister, my comrade Raúl asks me why don't I write you a few*

lines and I tell myself: well, why not? I am Rafael, son of the Borin-
quen land de La Raza. I read and understood "Chicano Literature:
Text and Context." And I tell you that I wish my people would read it,
since by reading it one not only understands the Chicano situation and
the whys of that situation, but also the Puerto Rican situation and the
whys of our situation. Our lives run almost parallel and perhaps
because of this, as we get to know each other better, the closer we will
feel to one another. The same enemy has sought to mutilate, and if
possible, annihilate our cultures, so similar to each other, and nonethe-
less, both the Chicano and the Boricua have been able to preserve our
cultural identity, our personality, and "Chicano Literature: Text and
Context," is proof of this! Through such a rich anthology, I not only
got to know the Chicano spirit much better, but also my borinquen
soul. And I give a lot of thanks to you and your group for the part ded-
icated to the literature of my compatriots. Our poems are so similar in
soul and content, that if we did not specify, it would be a difficult thing
to know which poem was written by a Chicano and which was written
by a Puerto Rican. Especially between one written by a Puerto Rican
from New York and a Chicano. In that case even the form would be,
for the most part, if not totally, similar. Have you read poems from
Lola Rodriguez Tío, Pachín Marín, Luis Llorens Torres? Their poems
are profoundly Puerto Rican and span various eras. And now we have
a legion of magnificent young poets and I witness with great joy, that
my Raza from here, from Aztlán, also is at the full peak of its litera-
ture. It has been a profound honor to have been able to cultivate a
solid brotherhood with a poet of Aztlán: Raul! All his thoughts are a
poem for La Raza, I assure you with the conviction that I only cele-
brate those who deserve it. Always forward my brother, even though
many thorns will wound our hearts, we will also find many roses, and
each one of those roses, the roses of La Raza, are well worth crossing
any thorny path to reach them! I hope that the rich anthology "Chi-
cano Literature: Text and Context," is followed by other works that
also elevate our souls when read. I admire you—Rafael.[7]]

And just about the time brother lays down his heavy rap, i gots to
cop that, at present, my total pensamientos [thoughts] don't add up to
even half a poem. ¡Ja! Myself, i haven't written a thing lately. Espero a
la *musa azteca* por aquello de la media noche [*I am waiting for the*
Aztec muse right around midnight] and she just won't show. i guess

she ain't doing no vamping these days. A few more "chácharas" [personal items] were allowed me this week, which included the poems. En ratos los leyo y me caen, porque (naturalamente) son míos, pero a veces se me hace que están muy chafas. [*At times I read them and I like them because (naturally) they're mine, but at times they seem to me to be real lame.*] Remember we almost got into a Chicano / Non-Chicano art thing and (mostly) about folks i have known. No son muchos los que tengo con tema—strictly Chicano. [*There are not many I have with a—strictly Chicano—theme.*]

They are, moreso, people poems. These are in the form of elegies and tributes to poets, musicians, tecatos, and revolutionaries, y algun erotic escapade u otro [*and an erotic escapade or two*]. No love, pastoral, or mistico-philosophical numbers here. i found one about García Lorca written in '58 or '59, it really gassed me. Literary wise, it's not a good poem, but i can still recall how good it felt when it was written. My work runs the gamut from the traditional to the absurd— o fractured modern. Tenía pensado mandarte todos [*I had thought of sending you all of them*], a couple at a time within the next 30 days— by the way, hay chansa [*there's a chance*] that i may leave on the 24th, rather than the 27th—but they (most of them) are rough and need much revision. So i decided to hold off, at least until i received positive confirmation from texas, or found out how you felt about it. Perhaps you can help me get them together, when i raise. Okay? Tengo como tres [*I have about three*] short, short stories which i think could be correlated into one, if i ever find the appropriate connecting thread. Una es de un velorio de un tecato en el barrio ('64), otra es de "La calle", los characters son los pimpos y talonas callejeros ('70), y la ultima es de "la embarcación," getting el troque ready pa' los trabajos ('69). [*One is about a wake for a dope fiend in the barrio ('64), another is about "the street," the characters are pimps and streetwalkers ('70), and the last is about "the caravans," getting the truck ready for the fields ('69).*] i read one of Tomás Rivera's stories in the Steiner-Valdez anthologies, and mine are similar in style, though cruder. También tengo un jazz story escrita en 1964 que no está related. [*I also have a jazz story written en 1964 that is not related.*]

Míra, what upset me last time in running the pachuquita thing by you was that so much was pressing on me from all sides and i could not give a better account. For instance, i dwelt mostly on their manner of dress, rather than attempt to point out the social conditions which produced them. Their refusal of mainstream american conformity has some importance, as well as showing that the rebellion was against an oppressive & culturally stifling society. There was also the contradictory, defiant assertion of self, in conflict with an almost nihilistic attitude—at a time when it can be said, our roots were being viciously lacerated. To show why their particular milieu was so affected and whether their behavior wasn't a defense mechanism directed against an indifferent social system. And try to deduce if these mechanisms (behavior) were valid. As i run this trip through my skull, i wonder if by some strange osmosis, these "auxiliares" weren't an extension of our soldaderas of the past?[8] But let's not get into that again. ¿Ahí que muera, eh? [*Let it ride, eh?*] Ha-ha! No, i'm not as sick as i was last time.

Bueno, my tolerant camarada, te digo bye por ahora [*I'll say bye for now*], because i want to get a couple of hours sleep (son las 3:00 a.m.) before i pick up the pen once more. By the way, i received a letter from Mando, running down his whole program. Saludos al Profe, María Elda, y al compita René. Tú, recibe mis mas calurosos y sinceros deseos, de que todo esté de aquellas contigo. [*You receive my warmest and most sincere wishes that all is cool with you.*]

Cariñosamente,
raúlrsalinas

■ ■ ■

Nov 2, 1972

Estimado raúl:

Unos cuantos garabatos escritos rápidamente pa saludarte—deseando que te encuentres bien—estamos en medio de los mid terms y tengo una clase de economía que no entiendo ni jota—me esta llevando el pingo!

Lo más inmediato es acerca de housing para cuando llegues—no se sí te ha escrito Maríana Griego—dijo que te escribería. Como no sabiamos que te interesaría en términos de aparamento, etc, una pareja, Pablo y Maríana, dijieron que les daría mucho gusto si te quisieras quedar con ellos por un tiempo hasta que encuentres tu propio lugar y te establezcas. Son personas muy buenas, muy interesantes. Y creo te cairán bien. Ella ahorita trabaja con E.O.P. y el es estudiante y trabaja en la oficina del public defender downtown. Pablo vino el año pasado como uno de los primeros en resident release antes de que hubiera programa de resident release. They are buenos carnales. Pablo also put us onto some possible employment pa tí pero quisieramos saber que te interesa en términos de empleo. ¿Quieres algo temporary nomás pa tener jale cuando llegues? ¿O quieres algo más permanente desde un principio? Also, let us know what kind of jobs you'd be interested in— What would best suit your needs, interests, etc?

I started a letter to you last week at home pero no la he podido terminar y ahorita estoy en la oficina y decidí escribirte de una vez porque things here aren't getting any better in terms of time—besides the mid term in econ I've a paper in another class, a presentation to conceptualize and deliver in Sacramento in Mid-November, the Chicana class to work up, etc, etc. and thought you might be wondering about arrangements for your arrival. Joe me dijo que té había escrito about his conversation with the woman in charge of your case here—nosotros estamos operando bajo la creéncia que vienes en diciembre—¿Como estás?

Dispensa lo messy y hastiness of this letter, pero hay más allá platicamos con some semblance of calmness! Cuídate y let us know about job interest and housing, should you not want to stay with Pablo y Maríana. Se me olvidó decirte que she's pregnant, that they both work and you'd have some privacy during the day, at least, while you're there. Again—dispensa esta cartita—it's disoriented, disorganized, and rather off kilter—pero hay se va—Antonia

[A few quick lines to say hello—hoping that all is well with you— we're in the middle of midterms and I have an economics class in which I don't understand a thing—it is driving me crazy!

The most urgent thing concerns housing for when you arrive—I don't know if Mariana Griego has written you—she said she would write you, since we did not know what you were interested in regarding apartments, etc. A couple, Pablo and Mariana, said that they would love it if you stayed with them for a time until you find your own place and get settled. They are very good people, very interesting. I think you'll like them. She currently works with the E.O.P. as a counselor and he is a student and works in the office of the public defender downtown. Pablo came last year as one of the first of the resident releases before there was a program of resident release. They are good people. Pablo also put us onto some possible employment for you but we would like to know what interests you in terms of work. Do you want something temporary just to have work when you arrive? Or do you want something more permanent from the start? Also, let us know what kind of jobs you'd be interested in—What would best suit your needs, interests, etc?

I started a letter to you last week at home but I have not been able to finish it and right now I am in the office and decided to finally write you because things here aren't getting any better in terms of time—besides the mid term in econ I've a paper in another class, a presentation to conceptualize and deliver in Sacramento in Mid-November, the Chicana class to work up, etc, etc. and thought you might be wondering about arrangements for your arrival. Joe told me that he had written you about his talk with the woman in charge of your case here—we are operating under the assumption that you come in December—How are you?

Pardon the messy and hastiness of this letter, but we'll talk later with some semblance of calmness! Take care and let us know about job interest and housing, should you not want to stay with Pablo y Mariana. I forgot to tell you that she's pregnant that they both work and you'd have some privacy during the day, at least, while you're there. Again—pardon this letter—it's disoriented, disorganized, and rather off kilter—but there you have it—Antonia]

■ ■ ■

November 14, 1972

Querida India,

Your "garabatos" arrived and in spite of the hastiness, i still felt you! especially the little trip you carried me into by writing all around the page. It wasn't pay back for the number i pulled off with my "weirdie" letter of long ago, huh? Ha-ha!

A few days ago after yours arrived, i did receive word from Maríana. A very nice letter it was, too. i have since replied, informing her & Pablo that i would be delighted to stay with them. On the other hand, the lady parole-officer also wrote, and she referred me to some Antonio Cardinas (Cardenas?) connected with the Minority Affairs office, for possible lodging. However, he & his wife already have 2 students living with them. And, i much prefer your choice.

Term papers, economic classes, chicana class, speeches to deliver, WOW! ¿Cuando descansas, mujer? i mean, you do rest now and then, huh? Y que es eso de *conceptualize*? Ooh! That was sneaky! Break that down to street corner level, okay? ¡Ja!

Regarding your creencia of my release date: it is November 27, which means that i have exactly 12 days and a cup of coffee. i am literally at wits end. Yes, the Prof wrote and i have yet to answer. i have sort of fallen into a catatonic state, just laying up on my bunk, staring at the ceiling. i want out so bad, my senses all dictate "*FREEDOM.*" Listen, i am curious to know whether you received my last two letters dated Oct 8 & Oct 22. Dejame saber, okay?

Oh! Let me tell you, we had our initial hearing (al fin!) on Nov. 2nd & 3rd. Fuimos p'al town todos wrapped up muy neat with chains, cuffs, leg irons and many locks. We stayed gone both days. It was one experience with much mud slung back and forth, mas detalles later. Cuando volví the thin volume of Tino's poems was laying on my bed. Lo comprendo bien. He is a damn good poet, found his early influences like mine—were into Dylan Thomas & Co. Lorca was the closest hook-up to our roots. He's got such a beautiful command of the Spanish language. ¡Jijo! i really think he's been re-born.

By the way, José Angel asked for a tape of some of my work. Ortego asked for permission to use both poems in Literatura Chicano. Even though i consented at first, lo tiré a león for several reasons, i'll run it down to you later. There is a sister in Rhode Island and one in New York who also want to use some of my poems. There is Profe Ruiz in K.C. who still wants to do a 50 minute documentary film of "A Trip . . ." What i am getting at is that, should Texas not come through with their reinstatement (which is par for the course) voy a formar gran lío. To deny me access to these responsible & constructive offers will be highly unethical and quite contrary to the myth of rehabilitation which they so religiously claim to uphold. Pero, a ver que pasa.

Until our next exchange, or eventual meeting, regards from my compañeros. Hello to Elda & Rene, El Profe and others. You receive my very best. Take care and rest once in a while.

Cariñosamente,
raúlrsalinas

Letters upon Leaving Prison

[circa late November 1972]

Friend Raúl!

You are a very gifted person my friend! And only thru your super strength has this gift and your entire character bloomed so thorough.

I followed your moods thru those 15 odd years & your position (en La Causa) is evidenced early in your life. That you will not digress upon release is written so well. I am so glad to have met a man who does not use the cause of his people for his crutch as so many in prison do. I am not a man of the arts but I do know why I read a man. Siempre fidelity,

Jay Lewis

P.S. Thank you for the opportunity of letting me do so!

■ ■ ■

November 26, 1972

My Brother Alberto:

Today, when they are most needed, words—which are my daily tools—fail me in attempting to express my feelings toward you, with some semblance of relevancy.

Perhaps there is more significance in these silent moments than we can ever hope to realize.

For 3 years we have studied & learned together. We argued and conversed. We disagreed and thought alike. All for the mutual benefit of our cause. At times we were lax in our duties, other times we contributed our share, whole heartedly. We made mistakes and overcame them. We were—above all—sincere & dedicated in our struggle.

In leaving prison, i do so with my manhood intact. Though i am free, so long as there are loyal brothers in prison, i am not free. i leave my spirit here with you—and the rest of the brothers. May it linger forever with the men who refuse to be broken.

Thank you for your understanding, i shall never forget it. Your faith in me, i shall not betray.

Stay strong my Beautiful Brown Brother. i remain in service to the prisoners, in the struggle of the oppressed.

Con Amor Revolucionario,
Tu Hermano
raúlrsalinas—"Tapon"

"A Revolutionary must
always be patient, calm,
and vigilant."

Nguyen Ali Quoc
(Ho Chi Minh)

■ ■ ■

T. J. Craven

#86419
Jan. 25 (1973)

Hey!

In these difficult times of our striving for a brotherhood and togetherness of the spirit, many of us wonder what happened to that messican fella from Austin. We feel much like "out of sight out of mind?" Just a brief note to one of us will alleviate our sincere concern.

Everybody continues to do well and avoid the wrath and oppression that present circumstances sometimes afford us. It's really encouraging to see so many of "our people" getting their head's in such nice places. It makes me predict an exceptionally high rate of success for our brethren, once the opportunity of freedom presents itself again. I'm really optimistic, Tap. So many of the dudes are going to go out of here without ever having to face the risk or possibility of returning. They are going to be able to do this because they are finally going out there into things that they *want* to do. Hasn't this been one of the prevailing problems of the past for many of us? Hitting the front door with an attitude of "getting even" or needing to "catch up?" I like to think that via the loose amalgamation of our association, we have given each other something. We have all contributed our small part to helping each other find a new direction. I see it happening all over the county, so I don't think I'm making an overly idealistic or invalid assumption.

Until I hear from you, my friend, I shall not take up any more of your time. Take care in all things. In strength and unity,

Tony

■ ■ ■

Febrero Uno, año '73

Seattle

Querido Hermano [Rubén Estrella]:

i think you've been ignoring me . . . ? y sabes que Indio-Feo-Prieto-Cabron? You too, were sent a postcard from the Dallas airport. Blame the faulty postal facilities on your end for that loss. Okay?

No, en serio . . . i am running ragged. La comunidad total needs help. There is so much to do and not enough people to appeal to for support. Our MECHA group here on campus is going through painful stages, however i'm confident that these stages will soon pass and we can become a more effective Chicano student body. For the good of the campus people and for Raza community as a whole. The Indian brothers need our support in their protests against loss of fishing rights. The Community College in the Yakima Valley has suspended & jailed 8 Blacks and one Chicano and so the Black Student Union and MECHA took us on a trip last friday over the mountains to picket the school and attend their plea proceedings. i covered it for the Daily at the same time. Articles, clippings, etc. to follow. O yea, i dug a Posada (you know the dude that does the calaveras?) book that contains a magnificent selection of his works. Let me know what i have to do to send it. i stumbled on it at a little import shop.

Po si, Carnalito . . . ya'stuvo. i am OUT!! Ahora solamente faltas tu . . . y así también después los demás. Tenemos que hacerle huelga a esos pinches cantones. [*Well yea, little Brother . . . It's done. I am out!! Now all we need is you . . . and also all the others later. We have to start boycotting those fucking joints.*]

There's a couple of young Chicano artists here, who—because of fucked-up societal conditions—are still caught up, grappling with themselves. Hoping to hook you up with the Con Safos artistas, Prof. Ybarra copped some addresses on his yuletide trip to San Anto. We'll kite them for you as soon as we catch a free moment. ¿Esta de aquellas? [*Is that cool?*]

Dig Bro. your arte is not known in these Northwest sectors of the so-called united states, so we got to get our stuff in order, for that very purpose. Okay? The kicker could be a mural—if you can swing a mural without any hassle—for Beacon Hill (El Centro de La Raza) School. This would be a good exposure for your talents, as well as a contribution to the people—which is where *i know* your HEART is at.

El Centro was an abandoned school, located in an Asian community, which the Chicanos took over last fall; to symbolize minority community's needs. It has been an issue of much controversy between the City Council, School Board and Chicano/Blacks since the occupation. Pero al fin, se hizo el güiso. [*But finally, we got the bird in the skillet.*] Now, it has taken on a very tasty 3rd World flavor. The caravan of Native American brothers who figured in the "Trail of Broken Treaties" thing in D.C., had a session there complete with indíto band. Despues se arranó el guitarron del Centro con una compañera de Houstón en indian-style ceremony. Estuvo suave, muy simple, muy poetic. [*Later the leader of El Centro hooked up with a sister from Houston in an Indian-style ceremony. It was cool, very simple, very poetic.*]

About your marvelous rendition of the lady-professor's portrait. It really laid her out. ¿Quedó encantada? No encontró palabras, la sofocáste, carnal. [*Did she love it? She was speechless, you shocked her, brother.*] She is a very sensitive woman, who understands el friendship tuyo y mío [*this friendship of ours*]. For this, and for all the other reasons that a sensitive carnala is able to, she digs you. Even if yo' ancestors the Moors wuz niggggaaahhs! Ha-ha! It still hasn't been framed for lack of leisure (only rest periods) time in which to do. Hopefully, i can somehow cop one from El Estado, no?

Hay mucho que contarte, pero lo principal es que te envíe esta papira. [*There is much to tell you, but the important thing is that I send you this kite.*] At the time i started sketching out this letter to you, i was down in the basement of my crib doing the old laundromat bit . . . contraptions for which i have no eyes. As careful as i was, i still came out with some red socks & green jeans. Ha! O sí, i dug your cartita in La Raza magazine. Es todo, Compa, pongale por la puerta. Y que me cuentas del grupo CORA? ¿Lo quebraron los melaseros or does it still exist? [*Right on, Bro, let 'em have it. And is there anything to report about the CORA group? Did the pigs break it up or does it still exist?*] Are *Aztlán* & *New Era* coming out regularly? Ahí vamos. [Send us some.]

Por el lado de social life, nomas a un borlo he ído [*I've only been to one dance*]. i was scared to death, jack. Al fin, i mustered up enough courage to dance a valse, it got good, and i decided that i would be ready for the last good, getting-into-it bolero at the end of every dance. Well, since you know how salado [jinxed] i bees, that valse was the last number of set. Me quedé malías! [*I was bummed!*] Dug "Lady Sings The Blues" on xmas eve. i just snapped, otra casa que podemos hacer es exhibit a collection of your works during the UW's Semana Chicana in May. You could sell some & show some. ¿Como la ves? [Are you game?] By the way, remember Jaimy? The teacher from Brown University is ready to put out her intended booklet of my poems. She said i could have some pen & ink (charcoal?) line drawings in it. There's no bread, merely exposure. ¿Te anímas? [*Excited?*] She is definitely using "Trip" & "Journey II." So if you care to whip up some of your goodies, dale dado [*go ahead on*]. Still trying to find the right Orozco. Let me know what you need in the way of books or whatever, and i'll manage to send it to you somehow. Just let me know what and how to send. El Profe will have some brochures & pamphlets. Puro yonke, pero se los quería mandar anyway. [*Just junk, but I wanted to send them to him anyway.*] Oye mugrosote [*Listen up you dirty bum*], i dug the painting of that dude in chains at the Profe's pad. Está ferozo. Yo te miro. [*It's tuff. See you later.*] Take care, regards to all the carnales que tanto me ayudaron a sobrevivir esa muleta [*brothers who helped me so much to survive that cage*]; al viejo Bossman, al

Indio wino, a Maíque & all the miembros of C.O.R.A. / *Aztlán* / Leavenworth. Me despido con admiración y respeto.

Hasta la liberación total,
your brother
tapon-poeta

■ ■ ■

[circa Fall 1973]

Greetings Dan, Ana, and other friends/acquaintances sitting at the bar⁹ : hacking away at the keyboard this gloomy "early autumn" seattle afternoon, in the solitude of my room . . . happy-sad memories of you and the rest of the people who helped shape & form the entire course of my life, stroll through the thoroughfares in my head.

It did my heartsoulmind good to return and be with folks from whence i came. So much so, that there is a poem in the making which expresses my feelings during the recent trip home. The title of same is entitled simply: "Austin, Tejas: Revisited." Eventually it will (as everything else) find its way to you. There were, however, many things left unsaid, unexplained. Good valid questions were posed by all. Questions which merit attention and response. Because the mood was such, and because they are questions which must be answered honestly and in great detail, it was not possible for me to comply while there. I will attempt to do so now.

How easy it would be to assume a position such as some writers of the dominant society who say "read my poems, it's all there." Fortunately, i am not of that class, not would i care to be; therefore i stand accountable to the people. One of the most asked questions was "what are you, what do you do?" Had i replied that i am a servant of the people, it would not have sufficed. Allow me to explain that position first. In serving the people, one cannot devote 8 hours y se aca. It requires a total commitment. That's why there's so few of us around. The nature of such service takes on the form of counseling Chicano students in personal & educational matters; interpreting for immigrants (what an absurd term in regards to our people) and other non-literate grass-roots gente; supporting all raza causes by actual participation (as well as other third world causes) and community organizing, setting up political workshops; and much hard, 'round-the-clock, WORK!!!

As to what i do (aside from all this), i write poetry every chance i get; write political papers for progressive publications, whether they be Raza, Marxist-Leninist, Socialist, Black—Native American, or Prisoners Rights periodicals; i do lectures before students & educators on Chicano Literature, Third World Literature & Prison Literature; i give poetry readings throughout the country (be on point for the FIRST Chicano Poetry Festival, to be held—supposedly—in Sept. or Oct. in S.A.T.). My poems have been included in three major anthologies of Chicano Literature ("Literatura Chicana: Texto y Contexto"—Antonia Castaneda, Joe Sommers, Tomas Ybarra Frausto—Prentice Hall 1972 "*Aztlán*: An Anthology of Mexican American Voices"—Stan Steiner—Luis Valdez—Viking 1972/"We Are Chicanos"—Philip Ortego—Washington Square Press 1973). i have had small volume of poems published ("Viaje/Trip"—Hellcoal Press—Brown University 1973), another is already at press ("Seattle Blues" Centro de Estudios Chicanos—University of Washington). and plans for poster poems are being discussed. i do these things partly for benefits or because i have to and partly for hotdog coin. My summer job was paid for by a Quaker organization American Friends Service Committee (for $300 clams per) as (according to them) Director of Chicano/Farm Labor Affairs. What a title, when WORKER is more appropriate . . . and simple! Am taking classes in sophomore year centering around Communications and Chicano Studies with a side-order of English. The university is another trip. Politically i can't accept it because it grooms people into becoming slaves to the monster by the competitive concept, and because the process is so dehumanizing that it robs our communities of much needed man/ woman power. Yet, on the other hand, i receive $700 bucks each quarter to survive on. My only justification is in that i challenge rather than attend classes, i'm not sacrificing my ass for a degree, therefore i don't bow down in obeisance to the rigid gospel of academia and i don't think of paying back the loans, which are—for all intents and purposes—federal funds. Chale! That's me, jack.

But what does all this imply? Better yet, what does it say? Basically, my brothers and sisters, i am still the same dude. i still possess the same bad & good qualities, hang-ups & contradictions. However, i also think/feel that i have become a new man . . . more humanistic, more genuinely concerned for man/womankind. i learned much from my past experiences and now i share that with the world. i have dealt with my weaknesses and strengths. i have grappled with suffering inflicted by and upon me. Out of the depths of degradation & despair i have emerged a new person . . . triumphant! Oh, i still feel the same way . . . brought on us by madness of Capitalism, i still have the same . . . frustrations and desires. Even hatred, but i deal with these emotional states in a political sense (to better analyze my situation) . . . out of our daily struggle. Liberation's GOT to come.

Underneath it all, as i said before, i'm still just me. Erratic & cool, complex & simple, arrogant & humble. i respect this guy who can respect you and our kind. i sincerely hope you get to know him and are able to render the same respect accorded you.

As to my politcs—my politcal stance . . . which may have offended or turned off someone . . . as may have my appearance. Neither of which have to do with my feelings for humanity at large. i can state my views honestly and sincerely because of a political orientation and a rude awakening to the need for social changes in this country. De todos modos . . . i have very strong socialistic tendencies, rather than being a socialist; i live in a communistic environment, but am not a Communist. i relate to the Cuban and Chinese forms of Socialism and less to the Moscow line. i support all progressive people's struggles and champion all aspects (with much constructive criticism in-between) of the Chicano Movement. By the same token, i will oppose by any means necessary, the reactionary forces (which middle-class Mexican American bourgeoisie is a part) who would obstruct and exploit instead of providing service to the working class peoples. Raza, i have met many brothers and sisters who are dedicated in the various national and international struggles for liberation.

My reasons for returning to the homelands was multifold. i had to evaluate a migrant program in the Rio Grande valley for the above mentioned firm i work for; to see if i had changed—if things had changed (for i believe i have changed . . . we've all changed); to see what could be salvaged of a beautiful family which i helped devastate. That was for me the most painful, but since i'm dealing in honesty, i had to deal with it. At any rate, i saw that some of the elements in the relationship, whereas others were not . . . were very much there.

That's why i had to come to Austin. And in doing so, i was determined not to relinquish my position in life—such as it is now—for anyone or anything. Not even my own mother. Sometimes i wonder if i will ever waver from this position back to what once was.

   i don't know that i will ever be able to provide these services, these talents at home. i don't know if i will ever return home to stay. Nor do i know if that is still home. So much has transpired. The years have left their scars upon our lives, but i carry you in mi corazón wherever i go. Adios people who gave me yourselves. Farewell gente who gave me myself.

respetamente,
para un mundo mejor
raúlrsalinas

■ ■ ■

3 de enero de 1974

Querida India:

   Al fin paso a terminar tu pápira. Han pasado tantas cosas que quiero compartír contígo [*Finally I get to finish your letter. So many things have happened that I want to share with you*] that who knows how this kite will turn out. At any rate, aquí te voy con las carta primera del 27 de noviembre, despúes la de crís-mas y noo year, and then hasta ayer con mando y tomás [*Here goes the first letter from 27 November, then the one from X-mas and noo year, and then the one from yesterday with mando and tomas*]. Okay?

   11/27/73—What to say about anoche's plática tan sarbrosona [*last night's wonderful conversation*]??? . . . it feels good to correspond with you again as we once did en aquel ayer . . . pero basta, todavía te quiero un chingo [*in the past . . . but enough, I still really love you a hell of a lot*]!

   Today . . . the DAY of days, i am taking "time out for *TIME OUT!*". Fíjate [*Check it out*], a year ago the prison doors were opened; i like to think that, at least, a baby dragon flew out. Todo un calendario [*A whole calendar*] just shot past me and in my hi-speed strut, i almost forgot to rip it off my wall.

"Hace un año que yo tuve una ilusíon,
hace un año que se cumple en este día . . . "

Por derecho que no me dí ní quebrada [*To be honest I didn't even
take a break*] to count the months-weeks-days-hours-minutes-seconds.
There was no time to count the bricks on my wall nor the bars on my
cell. Instead, i ran like mad/ness trying to get in tune with my lost self;
attempting to retrieve my youth forgotten and waylaid on some dark-
ened streetcorner of the world. Doing it! Desperately wanting to do it
all! Wanting to devour humanity with a hungering, passionate love.
Giving (hopefully not taking) and receiving.

Still, at times, i shiver in the frightening chill of my Seattle nights.
Me estremezco [*I shudder*] at the thought that this might all be but a
dream from which i'll soon be waking up. ¡Ójala que no! [*Hopefully
not!*]

Entire panoramas of post-Crash Landing actividades & involve-
ments flash through my drunken, smoked-out head. Chingao! i only
hope i've contributed something worthwhile to someone, somewhere,
during this serene/turbulent/joyful/triste year. No se que haré durante
la navidad. Creo lo pasaré aquí como el pasado. My bread is low and
no bucks are forthcoming in the immediate mañanas. Mi chavala se
aníma más cada día. Dice que quiere venir a "scope out the dudes and
the dances". Está muy loquílla. El niño menor aparece muy sano . . .
muy gentíl; unlike como de nosotros (his insane familia). El vato mas
calote, pos todavía traí las pistolas puestas. Pero ahí se va. [*I don't
know what I'll do during Christmas. I think I'll spend it here as in the
past. My bread is low and no bucks are forthcoming in the immediate
tomorrows. My little girl gets more excited each day. She says she
wants to come to "scope out the dudes and the dances." She's a real
trip. My youngest son, on the other hand, seems to be the most sane,
real considerate; unlike the rest of us (his insane family). My oldest has
issues. That's the way it goes.*]

En terminos de mis intenciones y desarrollo personal, pues quiero
apañar as much teaching experience (intercambio de informacíon) [*In
terms of my goals and personal development, well I want to soak up as
much teaching experience (information exchange)*] as i can possibly

obtain without a teaching certificate or degree. i will be doing a Contemporary Chicano Poetry at the downtown YWCA in January. The class in Chicano Studies, which i felt could be dynamite, will not come off as anticipated. There were too many areas of involvement which prevented me from processing my course outline on time. Pero está scheduled pa'l spring. ¡Y alálba! [*But it's scheduled for the spring. And watch out!*]

i am somewhat into Ricardo Flores-Magón. During the course of my hectic days, i manage to catch bits n' pieces from his antología . . . which i think belongs to you. During our stay in Vegas, La Betita and i rapped some on his short stories; two of which she laid on me then. Solo cuando llegó al canton, voy pa' la oficina del mickey mouse y lo wacho en la shelf [*But when I got to the pad, I went to mickey mouse's office and see it on the shelf*] (el libro no el mickey) and i say bring it!

Aztlán Journal, también is preparing some of Magón obras for a future publication. O' si, Madrid's Pachuco piece is also scheduled for publication in the next *Aztlán* Journal. Have you read it? Hablando del Chuco, 'hora que fuí pa' Los, les heché ka-ka a los señoritos eruditos quienes 'tan diliando con ese tema. [*Speaking about the Chuco, last time I went to Los, I gave shit to the erudite old men who are dealing with the topic.*] Perhaps i'm being overly / unfairly critical, pero la verdad es que me apañan el chivo de amadre [*but the truth is that they bug the shit out of me*]. Los envité a leér en [*I invited them to read in*] Chino & i guess all the front-rowers (to whom i was mainly addressing myself to) Rodolfo Sanchez (Los 3 del Barrio) read his "Proletarian Poems" and spoke of the repression in the joint. i sure hope you can eventually check out the film presentation of my reading at Festival Flor y Canto. i would like to share your comments. At the time i was in L.A., I met Chuy Treviño, a film-maker at KCET-TV "Chicanos en Acción" and discussed the possible filming of "Trip." It came about as a result of Joe's sending him a copy of "Viaje/Trip and Dorinda's constant rapping. Pero, no se: me chivéo. ¿Como la miras tú, India? [*But, don't know: i get freaked out or spooked. What do you think, India?*]

Aside from all this, i like to think that all is cool with my vida personal; pero quien sabe. A veces tristes/blue moods overcome me y me desgracian todo mi balance. También cuando me voy en tripe de ti and how i loved you a la bravota, sin control . . . unleashed & good . . .

risking whatever, me pregunto que si híce mal, and if so, ¿como y porqúe? i ask myself que si pensarías que era puro pedo lo que yo the expresaba. i also know that you feel incomoda when i tell you these things, solo que, end of rollo, okay? [*Sometimes sad/blue moods overcome me and screw up my balance. Also when I go on a trip about you and how i loved you all the way, without control . . . unleashed & good . . . risking whatever, I ask myself if I did wrong, and if so, how and why? i ask myself if you think what I expressed to you was all bullshit. i also know that you feel uncomfortable when i tell you these things, therefore, end of rap, okay?*]

Diciembre—Qui'ubo Chava: La cena on the 27th estuvo matona. El Moses García y su ruca Sylvia se aventaron un platón de aquellas. Fuímos el Barbas, Nina, Jean, Tomás y yo. Todos nos pusímos hasta el quéque. On the 30th, La Nina me tiró un anniversary porazo bruto [*December—what's up Girl: the dinner on the 27th was killer. Moses García and his wife Sylvia put out a real good spread of food. We were Barbas, Nina, Jean, Tomás and me. We all got wasted. On the 30th, Nina threw me a hell of an anniversary party*] where all the Centro & UW Raza, along with some Black sisters and brothers rapped, danced, smoked and DRANK! Comunicaciones de La Raza ever at work resulta en muchas fotos. [*La Raza Communications ever at work result in many photos.*] El veintiuno de diciembre we held a benefit dance to complete remodeling of the Centro. Estuvo ferozo y de allí salio otro [*It was tuff and from there came another*] radio program on KRAB, making it a total of three. Se llama "Nuestra Obvía realidad" [*It's called "Our Obvious Reality"*]. It deals with political (only) happenings of Raza on a local, national, and international level. Los otros dos son "Sonidos Latinos" [*The other two are "Latino Sounds"*] and "City Forum." We have finally managed to wrest Jim Cantú from "Sonidos" because we need him elsewhere. Either Epi, Ramiro, or Moises will deal with it. We did a show prior to Joe's departure. We bade him farewell on the program on behalf of MECHA, UFWA, EL Centro & 3rd World Coalition. Después nos fuímos a su canton [*Later we went to his pad*] and did some very serious drinking with him & Jean. El show se trató de un recap del año [*The show dealt with a recap of the year*]. Cruzita, Jim, David Silva, Adrian, Barbas & me did the thing. Mas fotos; i will definitely have to get you some prints made of all our happenings. Traigo una camara Minolta que esta perra [*I have a tuff Minolta camera*]! Dennis (Barbas' cuñado) is teaching a phtog. class, Daniel Desiga is starting on the mural, and Pablo Griego is doing silk-screen classes. Hopefully, un día de estos se nos hace sapo [*one of these days I'll make it*].

Año '74—Wow! i've been on this kite for a year now. ¡Me salgo de amadre [*Shame on me*]! This will the wrap-up. Estuvo el Mando aquí y andaba bien caido. Cometió a la ruca al hóspi en Tacoma pero to no avail. Pobre cabron, pero no capéa de que tiene (como todos nosotros) ciertas debilidades. No quiere pity, solo que sospecha todo. Me recuerda de otro cabroncito que conozco bien. [*Mando was here and he was real down. He committed his old lady to the hospital in Tacoma but to no avail. Poor fucker, he won't admit that he has (like all of us) certain weaknesses. He doesn't want pity, it's just that he is suspicious of everything. He reminds me of another little bastard I know well.*] Aún, we did what we could to ease his mental pain. He couldn't get over the fact Tomás received him well y que el Barbon & Boca went all over town with me looking for him, because they just wanted to rap. When he expressed an interest in an MA in the school of social work, Boca & Juan Sanchez agreed to assist him. Quien sabe. Le díje que estabas pensando llamarle, dijo que [*We told him that you were thinking of calling him, he said that*] it wasn't fair of you to condemn him. i assured him that you weren't and had been dealing with that and would contact him. Se alegró [*He got happy*]. Se reveló conmígo [*He opened up to me*] like never before.

¡Jíjo! Ando bien crudo [*¡Damn! I'm really hung over*] . . . had a serious tavern meeting (y ya me esta pegando el malecito otra vez [*and the sickness is hitting me again*]) which carried over into 4:45 am. Se trato de que [*It was about*] Chávez sometime in Nov. tomo una posición política pro-Israelita [*took a pro-Israeli position*]. Since we had publicly taken a pro-Arab stance (which brought a bit of pressure down on the Centro & UW Chicano comunidad) a couple of months ago, we maintained that same position in criticizing Chávez' move. We felt that it was an incorrect position and that we as supporters (constituents) have a right to criticize our leadership whenever we feel that a mistake has been made. At any rate, we decided NOT to discontinue our picketlines simply because the campesino situation still remains sad. And since they, and not César, are whom we are struggling for, we will provide our usual support. We have asked him to retract his statement in the interest of the struggle.

Pues, 'hora si, Indita de mi vida . . . se áca. No te dijo Tomás del Mickey Mouse que le compre en Los? [*Well, for now, dearest India of my life . . . it's done. Didn't Tomás tell you about the mickey mouse I bought him in Los?*] Estaré en Olympia en un Symposium on Chile on the same bill as Malvinia Reynolds who is doing the late Victor Jara's protest songs, on the 25th & 26th of this month. Estaré con [I'll be with] Ernie Vigil de Denver en Eugene, Oregon for a 3rd World Seminar on the 16th. Estoy jalando de consejero, como la ves? El Robe dice que . . . [*I'm working as a counselor, can you believe it? Ol' Rob says that . . .*] oh, fuck him, and his bearded ass. No dice nada. [*He ain't saying nothing.*] Drifters while in the process of this letter say: Hi, the baby feels active, due in Feb. (Rita), te quiero un chingo [I love you a lot] (Freddie Mata), cuidado con los parejes [careful with the twins] (Esteban), halo de yo y Epifanío [*hello from me and Epifanio*] (mi comadre Norma). Oh, yea, i found the book "Women, Resistance & Revolution" while in NY. Tambien "Mujeres de la Revolución" & "Part of the Solution" por Margaret Randall. Te miro, cuídate y déjame saber de tí. Saludes a loca Isabel.

Con muchisimo carino [*I'll see you, take care and let me know what's up with you. Say hi to crazy Isabel. With very much love*],

> tapon/poeta/cucaracho del
> norte de Aztlán,
> raúlrsalinas

Notes

1. These five notes to Salinas were handwritten on a single sheet of paper on the occasion described. They are especially important because they mark the beginning of lifelong relationships with people who were to be instrumental in Salinas' release and continuing development as a writer and activist.

2. The reference is to McNeil Island Federal Penitentiary in Steilacoom, Washington.

3. This note about the proper way to address correspondence was standard for all of Salinas' outgoing mail. To avoid redundancy, the repetition has been eliminated. Likewise, identifying markers like addresses and phone numbers have been eliminated from all correspondence so as to save space.

4. Prisoner moniker for Leavenworth. Chicanos often referred to Leavenworth as "once," or "eleven" in English.

5. Message from Rafael Cancel Miranda to Armando Mendoza. These interjections in letters are not uncommon, especially as a means to circumvent punitive letter writing restrictions imposed on certain prisoners.

6. Peter Camejo and brother, writers for *The Militant* and members of the Socialist Party.

7. Message from Rafael Cancel Miranda to Antonia Castañeda.

8. Salinas' poem "Homenaje a la Pachuca (Blues for Blood)," dedicated to Antonia Castañeda, explores this theme more fully. The poem is part of the collection *East of the Freeway: Reflections de mi Pueblo."*

9. See Introduction, note 9.

UNITED STATES DEPARTMENT OF JUSTICE
Penal and Correctional Institutions

UNITED STATES PENITENTIARY
(Institution)

MARION, ILLINOIS
(Location)

Certificate of Mandatory Release

UNITED STATES BOARD OF PAROLE:

It is certified that ____ ROY SALINAS _____, ___83908-132_
(name)   (register no.)

now confined in the_____ U. S. Penitentiary, Marion, Illinois _____
(76 EGT & 103 EGT)

is entitled to__871___days statutory and extra good time deductions from the maximum term of

sentence imposed as provided by law, and is hereby released from this institution under said sen-

tence on____November 27_____, 19_72_. Said person is released by the undersigned according

to Section 4163 Title 18, U.S.C.

    Upon release the above-named person is to remain under the jurisdiction of the United States Board of Parole, as if on parole, as provided in Section 4164, Title 18, U.S.C., as amended, under the conditions set forth on the reverse side of this certificate, and is subject to such conditions until expiration of the maximum term or terms of sentence, less 180 days on__October 19_____, 19__74. He is to remain within the limits of ____Western District Washington_____.

    This certificate in no way lessens the obligation of the person being released to satisfy payment of any fine included in the sentence; nor will it prevent delivery of said person to authorities of any state otherwise entitled to custody.

G. W. PICKETT, Warden _____

E. J. FISCHER, Administrative Assistant
xxxxxxxxxxxxxxxxxxxxx

    This CERTIFICATE will become effective on the date of release shown on the reverse side. If the releasee's continuance under supervision becomes incompatible with the welfare of society, or if he fails to comply with any of the conditions listed on the reverse side, he may be retaken on a warrant issued by a Member of the Board of Parole, and reimprisoned pending a hearing to determine if the mandatory release should be revoked.

Adviser _____ Proff. Joseph Sommers, Washington University, Seattle, Wash.

Probation officer J. Eldon Mincks_____
Post Office Box 1870
Seattle, Washington 98111

Facsimile of Salinas' "Certificate of Mandatory Release" from Marion Federal Penitentiary (1972)

Salinas at the Peoples' World Rally in Seattle (circa 1973)

Salinas reading at First Annual Festival Flor y Canto at the University of Southern California (1973)

Salinas with students at the University of Texas at Austin (circa 1973)

THE WRITING ON THE WALL
A Reading of Texas Inmate Writing

Salinas editing "Un Trip through the Mind Jail" in 1979. Photo used for special issue of Tonantzin, San Antonio Guadalupe Cultural Arts Magazine, *on Prison Writing (1985)*

Salinas at Resistencia Bookstore (circa 2002)

Resistencia Bookstore in South Austin (2004).
Photos courtesy of Valentino Mauricio.

Salinas's Resistencia.

Photo by Mary K. Bruton, MKB Photography

The Marion Strike

JOURNALS FROM "EL POZO"

The documents in this section all pertain to the prisoner-guard conflict and subsequent work stoppage and strike between prisoners and officials at Marion Federal Penitentiary in the summer and fall of 1972. Raúl Salinas was one of four plaintiffs in this first lawsuit against Marion, which was to become one of many over the next few decades that would attempt to expose and eliminate Marion's notorious behavior modification program and control units that were instituted in the early 1960s. After undergoing a period of intense involvement at Leavenworth in prisoners' rights activism and political journalism, which included direct and indirect involvement in three work stoppages, Salinas and several of his comrades at Leavenworth experienced a punitive transfer to Marion on April 8, 1972. This followed a March 31 prisoner strike at Leavenworth. As Salinas indicates in letters in section 2, this transfer occurred at a time when Marion had been designated as the supreme maximum security prison designed to handle the "most dangerous" prisoners, particularly those identified as agitators. That spring, prisoners were bused in from McNeil Island, Atlanta, Georgia, and Leavenworth, Kansas. The result was an intense concentration of politically conscious prisoners who were experienced in prison reform, knowledgeable of their legal rights, and articulate in giving voice to their protests. As Salinas says to one recipient of his letters, these are "men who are dedicated to the proper implementation of prisoners/human rights, in the area of penal reform."

Cognizant of the psychic manipulation occurring in Marion's behavior modification program, the prisoners coordinated a national campaign against the inhumane treatment of federal prisoners via the Federal Coalition of Prisoners. The result was the July 5, 1972, submission of a Human Rights Abuse Report to the United Nations Economic and Social Council.[1] It was submitted by attorneys from the Center for Constitutional Rights, the New York American Civil Liberties Union, and the NAACP Legal Defense. In a 1974 post-prison interview published in the *Sunfighter*, "Resisting Mindfuck," Salinas describes in vivid detail many aspects of the psychic manipulation and physical abuse they endured at Marion. This interview is reprinted in its entirety in section 4.

The prison journal that follows is a day-to-day account of the events of the Marion Strike of 1972. This journal of events, beginning on July 15, 1972, was maintained in handwritten form by Raúl Salinas and Rafael Cancel Miranda while they were in "el pozo,"[2] or administrative segregation. Written under duress and often in brief note form that includes third-person references to themselves, the writings provide a sketchy but simultaneously vivid glimpse into the intense physical and psychological war between guards and prisoners. The original journal exists in the Salinas files in two forms: (a) handwritten pencil and pen writings on loose-leaf paper and (b) typewritten summations that were created for attorneys and smuggled out to be used by lawyers and other outside supporters. There are two entries and accounts for some dates, in which case they are both included here. The journals document the actions leading to the Marion Strike, subsequent retaliatory actions by prison authorities, and legal actions taken by the prisoners and their attorneys, Michael Deutsch and Arnold Jochums of the People's Law Office (in Chicago and Carbondale respectively), with assistance from Allen Ressler of the Legal Aid and Defender Society of Kansas City, Missouri.

The statement "Aftermath of Federal Prisoners' Work Stoppage, July 1972," which contains a "Brief History" of events from July 15 to August 4, 1972, is taken from a document released by prisoners on August 5, 1972, as a means of generating public support. The daily entries included in the original document (July 25–August 4) are not repeated here, but are included in the complete journal entries that follow, which extend from July 15, 1972, to November 3, 1972, the concluding day of the trial held as a result of a lawsuit filed by four prisoners in a class action lawsuit against Marion Prison.

The approximately 150 prisoners held in "I" and "H" units were retained in segregation from July 24, 1972, until the final disposition of the case in September of 1973, at which time Judge Foreman of the U.S. District Court for the Eastern District of the United States ordered Marion officials to hold hearings for each prisoner in a manner consistent with established guidelines. A complete transcript of Judge Foreman's decision is available in Stanford University's Salinas collection. This decision constituted a victory for the prisoners who were seeking to put an end to unlawful, inhumane, and punitive practices against those who sought to exercise their legal rights while incarcerated.

Also included here are two other important documents related to the strike: (a) a July 17, 1972, call for action designed to solicit support from fellow inmates for the impending strike; and (b) a manifesto issued by the Political Prisoners Liberation Front in August 1972.

August 5, 1972

Seeking Justice and Liberation: Aftermath of Federal Prisoners' Work Stoppage, July 1972

Freedom of Expression Committee
Federal Prisoners' Coalition Intra-national
Marion, Illinois Chapter

Brief History

ON JULY 15, 1972, an altercation took place between prison guard Donald Hillard and prisoner Jesse Lopez. The incident occurred after Hillard provoked Lopez into striking at him, at which point the guard reached for a blackjack—considered an illegal weapon in possession of an official on regular duty, in any government institution—and struck Lopez twice on the head, before summoning two other guards to help subdue the prisoner and march him into a segregation unit.

As a result of this incident, a work stoppage was affectuated on Monday, July 17, 1972. This peaceful demonstration was to protest the jailing of Jesse Lopez and to demand the firing and/or prosecution of guard Hillard. This expression of dissent was met with a general lock-up, which went into effect at 12:30 p.m. of the same day, lasting until July 25, 1972. During the general lock-up, the prisoners were fed sack lunches three times daily.

On the evening of Monday July 24, 1972, prisoners were allowed outside their cells for an exercise period. The following morning, breakfast call was sounded, as per "normal operation status." At 7:30 A.M work call was sounded, resulting in mass confusion. A few men went to work while the rest mingled in scattered groups throughout the yard. At noon, some administration appointed (our regular ones were fired) inmate councilman informed everyone that the yard would be open like on any normal day and that the commissary would also be open at 1:00 P.M. On the basis of this information, the corridor was teeming with prisoners; some by the yard door and others by the commissary. This caused the guards to become uptight.

When the afternoon work call sounded, very few men responded to it. By 2:00 P.M., a recount was called and the general lock-up order was again re-instated. At 6:00 P.M. word got around that a mass raid was underway. Prisoners were being picked up indiscriminately from all cell-houses and lodged in I-Unit—a semi-honor block, while the occupants of same were being housed in the cells vacated as a result of the arrests. This dragnet was carried on into about 1:00 in the morning. Following is a chronological account of what has since transpired, in the I-Block "Special Control Unit."

[*Following 8-4-72 entry in original 8-5-72 document*]

Respectfully submitted to all concerned individuals. For the convicted masses of the world, we remain in unyielding solidarity:

The Marion Story

July 15, 1972—Saturday. Donald Hilliard, Correctional Officer, provoked inmate Jesse Lopez into striking him, at which point Hilliard, armed with a *Black Jack* (which is considered an illegal weapon for an on duty officer at any governmental correctional institution) hit Lopez over the head twice. Two other guards were than called in to help, taking Lopez to the segregation unit.

July 17, 1972—Monday. A peaceful work stoppage went into affect. It was called to protest the jailing of Jesse Lopez and to demand the firing and/or the prosecution of Guard Hilliard. at 12:30 PM the same day, began a general lock up which lasted till Tuesday July 25 1972.

During this general lock up the prisoners were fed sack lunches three times a day.

July 19, 1972—Wednesday. One inmate reports that on this day an officer passed by his cell and placed a small piece of paper on his cell door. No explanation was given by the officer to the inmate. The paper consisted of a ballot of some sort asking whether or not the inmates wanted to return to work, but it stated no facts.

July 21, 1972—Friday. At about 4:00 PM a typewritten letter of several pages which consisted of a list of grievances was handed to the inmate. The list had ten grievances. The list was thought to be compiled by the inmate council. (Who, many inmates claim, is recognized by few other inmates).

July 20 or 21, 1972—Thursday or Friday. An inmate reports being taken from his cell to be interviewed by someone in civilian clothes. Actually he was going in front of some board. The men present had no name tags, so they were not identified. A man seated in the center said that if the inmate signed the paper he had "at the bottom, you might forfeit your good time." Frightened and ignorant of what was happening, the inmate rapidly returned to his cell.

July 23, 1972—Sunday. On this date the first inmate was taken to segregation resulting from the work stoppage, Vern Thogmartin. On this day Eddie Adams was also taken to segregation. On or about this same date Dillard Morrison was taken to segregation.

July 24, 1972—Monday. at 7:30 AM work call was sounded resulting in mass confusion. A few men went to work while the rest mingled in scattered groups thruout the yard. At noon some administrators appointed inmate councilmen (the rest were fired) informed everyone that the yard would be open like on any normal day and the commissary would be open at 11:00 AM. When the afternoon work call was called very few men responded to it. By 2:00 PM a recount was called and the general lock-up was reinstated.

July 25, 1972—Tuesday. 11:00 P.M. Arrived at cell #9, on C-Range. Cell has been stripped of all vestiges of habitation, i.e. half-mirror writing table, and medicine cabinet. All that remains is a commode/sink combo, bunk mattress. By 1:00 A.M., all 18 cells have been filled. There are (coincidentally) 6 Blacks, 6 Anglos, and 6 Chicanos. All were held incommunicado, not allowed to write. Denied writing materials, tobacco and personal hygiene/cleaning supplies. These items are re-issued, always, upon being placed in the H-Block segregation unit.

July 26, 1972—Wednesday. There are 72 men confined here in I-Block (where we conclude, we are on isolation rather than segregation status), and 78 in H-Block segregation unit. We were allowed to receive mail and newspaper. Otherwise still incommunicado. We can look out the window to the main corridor and see the "inmates" going to work. Much razzing takes place.

July 27, 1972—Thursday. This is the first day of showers since we were placed in segregation. Regular meals were served on paper plates. This is the day the Special Disciplinary committee started meeting, calling each inmate individually, most without notice and reading their charges. The charges range from instigating and agitating to inflammatory remarks and congregating in groups. A blanket charge was filed accusing all prisoners of rattling bars and hanging bunks when inmates went to and from work.

July 28, 1972—Friday. Committee continues bogus session. Medical Assistants make their rounds, providing BAD treatment.

Saturday, 7-29-72—Mop and broom passed around for cell clean up. Writing materials issued (2 legal sized envelopes, 4 sheets of brownish poor-quality writing paper, and cut-in-half #3 pencils. Windows in corridor across the way are frosted with spray paint. The workers can be seen no more. A prisoner receives letter informing him that his mother suffered a mild stroke after hearing news of Marion situation. He asked to be allowed the customary phone-call and is denied. At shower-time he walks out on the range, sits down, refusing to budge. A 5-man goon squad comes in and begins to manhandle him. All the prisoners start shouting that they not beat the brother up. At this point, the goon squad makes every effort to let us know—verbally and visually—that they will not harm the prisoner. The brother is shoved into his cell.

July 30, 1972—Sunday. An inmate in I unit had an epileptic fit/seizure. After much noise and protest by other inmates, medical attention was given.

Monday 7/31/72—Dentist calls for visit with men. Excellent treatment. He expresses genuine concern, is upset because imposed security measures prevent him from calling more men out to the hospital. Medical assistant still coming through with shitty attitudes. Tranquilizing drugs (librium and valium) dispensed quite freely. Most brothers not going for it. Others do, failing to see the implications of restraint and domination on them.

August

Tuesday August 1, 1972—caseworkers show up en masse, promising everything and granting nothing. They do serve to allay the anxiety & desperation of a couple of brothers. The chaplains make their rounds promising greeting cards and prayers.

Wednesday, 8/2/72—Tobacco passed around. Limited property (toothpaste, soap, toothbrush, & photos) also issued out.

Thursday 8/3/72—Dinner was lousy. 1 frankfurter, 1 ice-cold hot dog bun and heated kool-aid/Complaint voiced. Altered commissary list (shaving lotion, lotion, but no razor—cigarettes but matches have been restricted. MTA prescribes medication to two brothers for back ailments. When he is asked to make the necessary application, he refuses. When other prisoners request they be allowed to apply medication, request is also denied. People's Lawyer comes to visit this writer from Carbondale. Envelope supply restocked. All backlogged newspapers released. More *hot* kool-aid for supper. No salt passed around. Mind games constantly in play. Plates of food fly in all directions.

Friday 8/4/72—Punitive breakfast (s-o-s). More property issued. Everyone has received some except this writer. An exchange of prisoners (10) between I & H units. good supper. Well prepared. We received order of merchandise we bought from store. An exchange of prisoners (10) between H and I unites. Visits re-instated, limited to one hour.

Aug 5/72—first chance for a shave at ten minutes shower, tin or aluminum mirror on wall of bathroom. Lock up razor.

Aug 7/72—they take away Miranda's breakfast because he was asleep!

8/8/72— exchange of short, t-shirt, pants, towel—cold morning, no blankets, some guys get sick with cold. Some guys complain they can't write because they don't have address (family, friends, lawyers) and can't remember them. Later this day they pass blankets. One a piece.

8/10/72—They pass some yellow papers with sentencing—indefinite sentences—They started serving food in regular trays and regular spoon. Also regular cups. Also exchange of bedclothes. They gave one extra, so now we have two sheets. Some of us still don't has pillows, and those with pillows don't get pillow case. For the first time they leave one of us be orderly for a little while.

8/11/72—Exchange of clothing in the morning. They took Miranda's breakfast again. Miranda's wife and sister have come from Puerto Rico to visit with him. They gave them only one hour. Early in the afternoon. Small envelopes are given. Commissary—some property.

8/12/72—Miranda get another hour visit (from 9 to 10AM)

8/13/72—"   " (" ")

8/15/72—Miranda and others get cuestionare (cuestionario) from Dellums. Send their replies that same night. That night, a couple of mouses running around become a big topic of conversation and excitement.

8/16/72—The heat wave keep on. Maybe over a hundred degrees in here—Nails keep growing longer and longer.—So is hair.

August 17, 1972—Thursday. On this day a fire erupted in H unit, a segregation unit. The smoke was so thick that no one was able to see the ceiling. The men were forced to place their heads in the toilet bowls of their cells and flush the toilets in an attempt to breathe fresh air. When the officials became aware of this, water and electricity was turned off. The ventilation system which usually pulls fresh air from a recreation area into H unit, was at this time, reversed so the smoke was forced back into the unit. The officers made no attempt to put out the fire. Medical treatment was not given to anyone. After the fire, approximately 40 guards entered H unit equipped with helmets and clubs and removed all personal possessions including clothing, legal papers, medications, glasses and mattresses from everyone. The materials gathered were thrown against a wall in the recreation area and left there. The inmates were forced to strip and suffer from smoke inhalation.

#2—We claim for a fan for the heat, there is none, heat is suffocating us. They also keep lights in corridor burning. Late at night a convict downstairs get a heart attack. He's taken to hospital. Before that another guy, Patterson—have had an epileptic fit. This heat is hell.

August 18, 1972—Friday. Assistant Warden Fenton, armed with an axe handle, Captain Buzzard, armed with a sawed off baseball bat on a leather strap and about 20 correctional officers with riot sticks and wearing gas masks, entered H Unit of Segregation on the eve of this day. The inmates were forced to remove their clothing and were then handcuffed. The officers then came marching by each cell with a gas fogger on wheels, and tear gassed each one through out areas A, B, C, D, of H unit. After the smoke cleared, all cells were again stripped of all personal possessions. Again, medical treatment was not given. Having water and electricity turned off again the inmates had no way of clearing themselves from the teargas. The men remained naked for three days. Guards refused to remove garbage for one week. Showers were allowed five days later, this being the first change to wash off the tear gas. On this same day Attorney Arnold M. Jochums was denied entrance to the prison, with the "reason" being insufficient guards on duty and late notice was supposedly given.

"I" unit #2—went to a shower. Take a look. There is no fan. We ordered at store same type of pen they allow at "H" unit. Were denied. We kept writing with little bit pencils. At 10 PM there is again noise claiming for a fan.

8/19/72—"I" unit #2—They passed around some papers with charges to a couple of guys charging them for the noise, etc.

8/20/72—"I" unit #2—We heard some kind of additional trouble happened at "H" unit. Downstairs (at "I" unit) the double a cell.

August 21, 1972—Monday. Again of this date Attorney Arnold M. Jochums sought entrance to the prison and was denied.

August 22, 1972—Tuesday. Arnie got to see Dillard Morrison on this day, being the first chance to find out anything about the incident. Dillard looked bad. He was covered with mosquito bites from having no screen windows. He let Arnie know what was happening. Following this day, Arnie was able to see more inmates each day and more letters started coming in around August 30, 1972.

"I" unit #2—Raining. A guard became insolent with the orderly. Dr. Schwarz walked by. Couple of hacks go around telling guys to take papers from ventilators. That they don't want nothing there. Also to take anything from the bars, including medication. Day before the 21st, they don't want to give roll of toilet paper, but only a few sheets. They take Martinez away to "H" unit in shorts and handcuffed. Also Leon. The trouble sprung up by provocations about the paper in the ventilator and medicine Martinez kept in the bars, so as not to put them on the floor. Papers are thrown out in the corridor. Things get noisy. Orderly refuses to clean.

8/23/72—Guard ask one by one if anyone want to sweep corridor. Nobody volunteer. In the morning. At night a convict do clean corridor. They took another convict away to "H" unit, handcuffed (Big D,

Dave's pardner). They bring gallo and Donald from "H" Unit (We heard it's been seven days since last they took a shower and how they took the mattresses away at H unit. Also about the teargassing and beating there.

8/24/72—Miranda gets the hay fever. It also seems like if ventilators been closed. No air at all coming from them.

8/25/82—They pass pocketbooks. Orderly out to clean. Guards do not want to let convicts have hot water, nor do they want to takes papers or cigaretes to the downstairs tier. So orderly then refuse to mop. Heard how they beat D. McKinney, a brother, in his cell in population because he refuse to come out of the cell. And how guards threw him head first inside a laundry basket. Heard how they beat Seth, Rob and Al.

8/27/72—Dave received an acknowledgement of receipt from Dellums. Compa Raúl received a cuestionaire from American Civil Liberties

8/28/72—They brought Jimmy from the other side—handcuffed

8/29/72—Alberto calls home, his mother was sick, she is well now.

8/30/72—Alberto y Beto llevados a carta por success en segregación. [*Alberto y Beto talked to court for events here in segregation.*] Lawyer from Carbondale came to see tapon—9:50 to 10:50 AM

8/31/72—They start taking us one by one to walk and take a shower for half an hour en corridos in front of the calabozos. Freeman caseworker—comes by—exchange bedclothes—they don't want to give sheets to Jimmy, though he don't has any—another provocation—confusion about showers—there is a protest—I tried to explain to hacks and all they did is ask me if I want or not a shower.

September

9/1/72—They handcuffed beto and took him to "H" unit.

9/2/72—Miranda lost his breakfast again.

9/3/72—We get letters from Dellum (written the 28th of August) acknowledging receiving more cuestionairs

9/4/72—Goldberger's letter opened. Case counselor Hammond's reply "we had a new man"

9/5/72—Miranda takes a subscription for the Marion newspaper. During recreation and shower they did not give clothes exchange to the guys, but in the night they give to the rest. Some more noise because of it. An incident happened between jimmy and a guard. We were talking about the german cops killing the jews and the arabs in Munich and the hack thought (i guess) that we were talking about him and stood in front of Jimmy's cell and ask him if he thought that Jimmy was a tough guy. Another charge for him.

9/7/72—Jimmy got a cuestionnaire. He filled it and sent it out. They brought Haskell Johnson in a wheel chair. They charge Jimmy with eight counts, guess it comes because he filled out cuestionaire.

9/8/72—Haskell has not been able to get up from bed to eat.

9/9/72—They took Parker's breakfast away, hacks made him wake up ask for his milk, they did not give it to him. Two lawyers came to see tapon—2–3 PM (Jochum and Michael). I heard a convict say that in H unit hacks took personal properties and threw them in garbage can.

9/10/72—I heard Lewis also was beaten. Bug out and is in the hospital. I heard Victor Bono was put in isolation because he tried to send a letter to the press about the events in Marion. Miranda wrote to his lawyers. Freddie got a visit. Miranda lost his breakfast again. I heard Brown made parole and they took it away. Freddie said they are putting phones in the visiting room (in the restricted room). Freddie was threatened by the hacks if he don't fix his moustache and goat for the visit.

9/11/72—Sour milk, Jerry blew his top. They took him to H unit. Jimmy got upset because of it.

September 11, 1972—Monday. A class action lawsuit was filed on this day, Adams et al. vs. Carlson et al. on behalf of all men held in segregation status at the U.S. Penitentiary at Marion, Illinois. The suit alleges that men were placed in segregation units in violation of their constitutional rights to what they are charged with, to face their accusers, to call witnesses and to have the assistance of an attorney. The suit seeks an injunction to prevent further assaults on the men by the correctional officers and to compel the institution to return the men's clothing, including legal papers and correspondence and maintain a semblance of humanity. Monetary damages in the amount of $50,000 for each plaintiff is being asked to repay them for physical and mental damage suffered as a result of their confinement and inhuman treatment. This case was brought to Judge Foreman and States Attorney Frederick Hess in East St. Louis. The judge continued everything until the first week in October when someone representing the prison should be present.

9/12/72—We finally got a barber (Ruiz)

9/13/72—at 3:00 AM they took the watch away from the wall. More charges to Jimmy, they bum rap him for agitating about Jerry.

9/14/72—Doctor comes around. Check Haskell. Said he can't move him from segregation. Some hack put a string on his light because he can't get up to handle it. We got letter (copy) of brief Victor Bono sent to court. Lawyer Jochum came to see Tapon 2-3 PM. We heard on radio about our case in court (5 PM).

9/15/72—They gave me a big pencil (I should say to Miranda). We got bic pen finally. Freddie got a visit from Jochum and his ruca.

9/16/72—Jimmy got a visit. hacks told him that Freddie, Albert, Taps thought they got something going. They told his brother they were doing him a favor by letting him see Jimmy for one hour. He comes from far away. They took lawyer's address away from Jimmy. They left medication for Haskell in the bar, he can't get up to pick it up, an hacks don't give it to him. Freddie got a visit from wife (or was supposed to). Brown is taken to court in Georgia.

9/17/71—We signed papers stating Haskell drank water from the toilet for eight days.

9/18/72—They took Jimmy downstairs to ask him if he wanted a guard to defend him. I read on Idaho paper where Badillo ask better treatment for federal prisoners or worse Atticas could happen. He proposed legislation to such effect. Haskell got a letter from his sister back. His cell stink real bad. He have not been able to shower or clean his cell. Heat is back. Gallo called loudly for his medication. asked to move to cell 7. Nothing done. cell 18 is where he live, is too hot and lack of any air. Gallo want to help Haskell take a shower. Denied.

September 20, 1972—Wednesday. We received official notice that Adams et al. vs. Carlson et al. will be heard on Tuesday October 3 at 1:30 PM by Judge Foreman in Benton, Illinois. Miranda asked for a change of cell. Nothing doing.

September 21, 1972—Thursday. We sent affidavits to describe belongings taken away from the inmates and one on necessary legal materials taken. These were sent to 47 inmates now in segregation, some accompanied by newspaper articles. Haskell finally was able to take a shower. He is getting better.

9/22/72—Miranda lost his breakfast again. Lawyer came to see tapon.

9/23/72—We heard about troubles at Atlanta penitentiary. At 3:03 PM They take Freddie chained to the boxcars because he protested that they don't let him see his wife. It was the 2nd straight time they stopped the visit. Buzzard took him away, plus the goon squad.

9/24/72—Jimmy spent hours trying to fish a box of cereals. He asked hack to give it to him. Denied.

9/26/72—Lawyer talked to gallo. read in K.C. paper about trial inside of Leavenworth. Saw Haskell shuffling his feet with a walking stick and holding the wall, coming from showers.

9/27/72—We got affidavits about personal property from Jochums

9/28/72—Dave got sick. Later they took him to H unit in chains, or handcuffed. Day before Pete got letter from legislator. Lawyer from Chicago came to see Tapon. Counselor says that tomorrow chief probation hack will send case workers to notarize affidavits. They take Frenchie to hospital in stretcher. He come back later.

9/29/72—hacks make noise in doors. Repairing one door. Case worker Freeman come to notarize affidavits. Lawyer Chicago come to see Albert and Miranda. Librarian Dee says that we are not allowed to make subscriptions from here. se llevaron Haskell. (*They took Haskell back to population).

October

October 3, 1972—Tuesday—Our hearing was set to be heard today at 1:30. We arrived at the courthouse in Benton, Illinois. The U.S. Attorneys were present along with the Assistant Warden, Charles Fenton. 18 prisoners—our witnesses were delivered in state cars wearing handcuffs. The two sides met in chambers with Judge Foreman for about three hours. The outcome was that because the prison officials were not served with a copy of the complaint, the hearing would be postponed. The judge said he would set a date in the near future.

October 14, 1972—The men on "D" range of "H" unit in protest of receiving small quantities of food and it being cold, protested this by not turning in their trays or spoons after meals. This continued through the following day.

October 15, 1972—In response to the protest, guards refused to give showers to men on "D" range. Also, these men were served sack lunches at breakfast. At noon meal a guard came in and said if utensils were returned, hot food would be served. Again, sack lunches were served at lunch and supper, even though the men returned their trays and spoons. At 10:47 P.M. the riot squad, about 30 men, in full riot gear dress along with Assistant Warden Fenton, armed with pick handle, and Fry entered "D" range to conduct a shakedown of cells and strip search. The procedure was for each man to be stripped, handcuffed to cell door, removed from inside of cell, all belongings removed from cell and men returned to cell with no clothes on. Three of the 18 men on "D" range refused to be handcuffed, but agreed to being stripped and would come out of cell peacefully. The first man was Raúl Estrada. Because of his refusal to the handcuffs, he was maced by Lt. White, the cell doors were opened and about four guards rushed him and beat him. About 10 guards carried him to the boxcar, a closed front cell on B range. A second man, Daniel Sappington also refused the handcuffs, but agreed to the strip and would come out peacefully. He was also maced and when the cell door was opened he was rushed by about four guards and beat. The third man to receive the same treatment was Eddie Adams. After the Lt. maced him, four guards rushed Eddie and literally "beat the shit out of him." He has suffered many bruises, abrasions, and two black eyes. After these beatings, Raúl Estrada was placed in a box-car, which is a cell completely closed on all four sides.

October 16, 1972—Monday—At around 10:45 P.M. the riot squad again with Fenton and Fry, all dressed in full riot gear and armed came back to "D" range in hope of stirring the prisoners to resist. On this day, they were unsuccessful. But again, they went through another shakedown of all 18 prisoners housed on "D" range. This time there was a cameraman present who taped the whole deal. It's funny that he wasn't present on Oct. 15, the previous night when there was beatings. After this strip search, Eddie Adams was taken to a box-car, located in the same area where Raúl Estrada was sent. While trying to survive in this cage, Eddie suffered from ten black-outs during a two week lock-up. He was told by doctors "it's all in your head." On this day one of the lawyers representing the inmates in the suit filed against the prison, was denied to see Eddie Adams or any other prisoner.

October 17, 1972—Tuesday—Today the lawyer was allowed to visit some of the prisoners. To his surprise, he was escorted to a small visiting room where he was told all his future visits would take place. The style of the visits consists of two sides, one for the lawyer, one for the prisoner. The two sides are separated by a full glass partition and communication is done via monitored telephones. This act is in complete violation of attorney-client privileges. Our two lawyers representing the prisoners are the only lawyers in the country forced to visit clients via monitored telephones and this is the only federal prison in the country to have this whole set-up. After requesting to see Eddie Adams, the attorney was bewildered at seeing Eddie being dragged down the hall by two guards. he was in such bad shape, he had no control over his body. His left eye was completely closed and his right eye half closed, vision and stability were poor, but strength and togetherness were strong.

October 18, 1972—Wednesday—Upon returning to the prison to visit Eddie Adams, the attorney saw the guards escort Eddie, into this visiting room, in a wheel chair. And up to now, Eddie still uses the wheel chair. Also on this day, the attorney visited the other two prisoners who were beaten. Danny Sappington, one of these men had cuts on his wrists and the rest of his body. He received no medical attention. Raúl Estrada, during the visit, could not sit down at all. He said he had much pain in his side where an unremovable bullet is located. He was very unstable at the time and was afraid of falling over.

October 24, 1972—Tuesday—Because, to this date, the court set no date for a hearing on the preliminary injunction filed on October 3 and because of the beatings and harassment going on between these two dates, a visit by the People's Law Office in Carbondale and Chicago was made to the judge in E. St. Louis to get something done right away. The two motions were heard on this date. The first was that the judge rule the attorney-client visits via telephone and glass partition improper and for the prison to return the right of regular visitation to the attorneys and clients. The second was that the judge allow an outside physician to enter the prison in order to give medical help to Eddie Adams. Both motions were denied.

October 27, 1972—Friday—Another day was spent in court arguing the government's motion to dismiss the suit. This motion was denied.

The judge has the motion to dismiss the suit as a class action and to dismiss asking for monetary damages of $50,000 for each of the 150 prisoners under advisement. The date was set on our preliminary injunction hearing for Nov. 2 and 3, 1972.

November

November 2, 1972—Thursday—Today was our "day in court", We called nine witnesses. the first to testify was Vern Thogmartin, 36, of Kansas City, MO. He testified to events which occurred in the segregation unit, since the lock up on July 23. There were tear-gassing and beating incidents which he testified to. He talked about how the prison violated the rights of each of the men to a hearing on their charges, not being able to call witnesses, not knowing who their accusers were, cross-examined and not having a lawyer present. The second man to testify was Dillard Morrison, 51, from New York. He described how he was put in segregation, the beatings, and teargassing which followed and how, after all property was taken from, the need and refusal of obtaining his medicine. Dillard has a highblood pressure problem and it is necessary for him to take medication for it. He went four days without medicine. Dillard has been on this medicine since 1967, the third to testify was Eddie Adams, 32, of Chicago. Eddie testified, from a wheel chair, about the beating he received on October 13 and lack of medical care after the beating. He also described the Aug. 18 incidents of tear-gassing and beatings. Eddie recalled being approached by a guard and inmate, being asked to negotiate on the work-stoppage of July 17. He told the guard he had no influence on the men and wouldn't want to get involved in a situation where he would end up in segregation. After much thought Eddie decided to negotiate getting no results except being placed in segregation. Lanier Ramer, fourth to give testimony, said that while doing his regular job of transporting job from inside C unit to the outside part, he saw clear plastic bags full of personal belongings and other personal possessions which were brought from segregation units and thrown on garbage trucks, then taken away. Larry Snead, the fifth witness, showed evidence of a set of legal papers he found in a trash can in the education department. Also, the papers belonged to a friend of his, who Larry was working with on a case. The sixth witness, Albert

Mares, testified that at his hearing on the charges for him being placed in segregation, he was told by Assistant Warden Fenton that the slip of paper stating his charges was lost and he would have to remain in segregation until the board found them. Albert was also to testify on a letter he received from his lawyer requesting legal materials necessary to take his case. Because Albert didn't have the letter, he was requested to return to court the following day with the needed letter as evidence. The seventh witness for the plaintiffs was Rafael Cancel Miranda, a Puerto Rican nationalist. He testified to being denied visits. His wife comes from Puerto Rico and is able to visit him only once every 18 months. Her last visit in October was restricted to one hour. Kenneth Rogers, a Jew, was last to give testimony on this day. Kenneth was a student at the local junior college and university. He's acquired 56 hours of credit since January of this year. Since his confinement in segregation, his studies have been denied him and hasn't been able to practice his religion under this restricted placement in segregation. His materials needed for worship have been denied him and the food he is served does not meet the dietary restrictions of his religion.

November 3, 1972—Friday—Today ended testimony for the plaintiffs with Albert Mares returning to give his letter from a lawyer to the court as evidence.

The remainder of the day was given to defendants (prison officials) to give their side of the story.

The first witness called for the defendents was Dr. Hubbard, a prison hospital doctor. His testimony dealt with Eddie Adams conditions and the fact was established that x-rays taken of Eddie never left the prison—which is a rule—until many days after they were taken. He also testified to the many bruises and abrasions on Eddie's body. The third witness was Dr. Schwarz, a prison hospital doctor. He testified that after the Aug. 19 tear gassing, water for the men was turned off. This meant the men had no way of treating themselves from the tear-gas. He also talked about Eddie Adams bad condition and how he found it necessary to admit Eddie to the hospital. But there was some delay in this. He said Eddie was brought to the hospital after the Oct. 15 beating handcuffed on a stretcher. He admitted that it was impossible for Eddie to inflict these injuries on himself. Assistant Warden Fenton was the last to testify. He said that policy statements from the federal bureau policy were not followed. Also he tried to talk on the new Marion policies, but the attorney for the plaintiffs objected due to the fact it has no bearing on this case dealing with July 17—not—on past procedures.

The judge closed the hearing by giving the attorneys ten days to file their answers to the hearing. He will make a ruling on the preliminary injunction within ten days following the filing of the answer.

Both days, all the witnesses for the plaintiffs were brought and held in handcuffs and leg irons.

Call to Action • July 17, 1972

THE CONVICTS OF THIS INSTITUTION OF MARION PRISON HAVE IN THE PAST EXPERIENCED MANY DIFFICULTIES WHICH WERE RESOLVED BY A COLLECTIVE EFFORT. AND THIS COLLECTIVISM IS BEING CALLED UPON FOR STILL ANOTHER SERIOUS PROBLEM CONFRONTING US TODAY THAT MUST BE RESOLVED BY WHATEVER MEANS NECESSARY.

ON OR ABOUT JULY 15, 1972, IN THE EVENING OF THIS DAY IN QUESTION, AN OFFICER OF THE CUSTODIAL STAFF DELIBERATELY PROVOKED AN INMATE BY HIS AGGRESSIVENESS, WHICH RESULTED IN A STRUGGLE BETWEEN BOTH OF THE MEN INVOLVED. WHEREUPON THE INMATE JESSE LOPEZ WAS SUBDUED BY OTHER OFFICERS AND PLACED ON OR IN SEGREGATION. HOWEVER, IT IS IMPORTANT TO STRESS THAT BY DELIVERATION THE OFFICER WAS ARMED, HENCE PREPARED TO COMMIT ASSAULT ON ANY INMATE BY POSSESSING A CONCEALED WEAPON WHICH IS AGAINST ADMINISTRATION RULES.

IT IS OFTEN NECESSARY TO REMIND EACH OTHER THAT WE'RE ALL PRISONERS AND AS SUCH, WE SHOULD BE OLBIGATED TO INSURE EACH OTHERS HEALTH WELFARE AND LIFE, IN THIS INSTITUTION. AND IN ADDITION THIS COULD HAVE BEEN YOU OR ME THAT WAS ATTACKED. SO IT IS IMPORTANT THAT ALL OF US REALIZE THAT WE SHOULD VOICE A UNANIMOUS PROTEST AGAINST SUCH BRUTAL AND ARBITRARY TREATMENT, BROUGHT UPON US PRISONERS BY THE WARDEN AND HIS STAFF: NOW BEFORE IT IS TOO LATE!!

THEREFORE, TO DEAL WITH OUR IMMEDIATE PROBLEM, WE: THE CONCERNED PRISONERS ASK EVERY PRISONER TO COOPERATE IN A GENERAL WORK STOPPAGE, IF JESSE LOPEZ IS NOT RELEASED BY 12:00 O'CLOCK TODAY (7-17-72), AND IF ASSURANCE OF THE PROSECUTION OF THE OFFICER IN QUESTION (HILLARD), IS NOT FORTHCOMING.

WE ASK ALL CONCERNED PRISONERS NOT TO LET THEMSELVES FORGET THOSE PRISONERS WHO WILL BE LOCKED UP AS A RESULT OF THEIR PARTICIPATION IN THIS PEACEFUL DEMONSTRATION OF PROTEST!!!!

We Must Fight the Enemy[3]

First, it must be determined who "We" are. Second, it must be understood who the "Enemy" is. Third, we must unite to "Fight" the enemy in all effective ways.

>
> Those who uphold NINE VALUES,
> 1. Unity
> 2. Freedom
> 3. Justice
> 4. Equality
> 5. Opportunity
> 6. Knowledge
> 7. Happiness
> 8. Dignity
> 9. Peace

for ALL men, and are concerned with action that will reduce the enemy's power to function in any old way—are WE. It must be understood, kept in mind, that trying to shape and organize the people around our assumptions is wrong. Each individual has his understanding, his ideas, his way, his degree of commitment, and his values; and these are his truths for however long they last. Day after day, week after week, year after year, we deal out negative judgments about the people; not recognizing, or forgetting, that individual persons are involving themselves in important issues. Even if the involvement is not in concrete action it is involvement with an idea, and ideas are based on values.

Proceeding, then, from the fact that there is more than one understanding, more than one idea, more than one way of doing, more than one degree of commitment, more than one interpretation of values—the challenge becomes ONE of bringing the many "I's" together into a single "WE." What is meant by Social Responsibility? When the individual is responsible to and for the society, when the society is responsible to and for the individual; to be held accountable and capable—is Social Responsibility.

Marion is a society. The conditions that prevail in the larger society are to be found here on a lesser scale. Experience has proved to us that attacking those conditions individually are rarely successful, but united action has been, and can be, successful. If men are really concerned about conditions and unity it would seem strategically correct to determine the conditions in this Marion society around which the majority of its population is willing to unite. There are so many, so a list of priority is in order. A plan of action would include a time limit for implementing the deeds of the people, and a step by step escalation of methods to be used in forcing the demands of the people. This would have the effect of limiting to an insignificant few those who can find no issue or method they are willing to support. The policies of this government, and recent actions it has taken against civil and human rights should make the most optimistic and least interested persons suspicious of its intentions.

In the event that the King Alfred Plan become a reality (and there is overwhelming evidence that the government has prepared well for the "National Emergency" that will initiate it) unity is the only possible hope that prisoners will have of staying alive and out of the clutches of those who are waiting at Vacaville, Atascadero, and Butner. It is fast closing to a point where real or imagined differences, antagonisms, interests, will no longer be something to live by but the reason for getting killed because of—by authorized, mindless, robots . . . deadly agents of the real enemy.

In POWER and BROTHERHOOD, P.P.L.F. [Political Prisoners Liberation Front]

Notes

1. Though Ramer's account, "The Day Has Come" (a photocopy of which Salinas possesses in his private papers) suggests that approximately 50,000 copies of this report had been distributed a year later, I have not been able to locate a copy for reference and/or inclusion here.

2. A "pozo" is a well, or hole.

3. Circa August 1972, authored by Vern Thogmartin.

Texas Department of Corrections
HUNTSVILLE, TEXAS

To Whom It May Concern:

The undersigned, Director of the Texas Department of Corrections, certifies that _____

_____ SALINAS, Roy. _____

Reg. No. __165336__ was convicted of a felony to-wit: _____

_____ Poss Of Marihuana (1) _____by the District Courts of

_____ Travis _____County, and sentenced on

the __26th__ day of __November__, A.D., 19_61_, to _15_ years confinement in the Penitentiary.

Received at Huntsville, Texas _____2-9-62_____

Released on Reprieve of Sentence_____ Proclamation No._____

Released on Conditional Pardon_____ Proclamation No._____

Released on Parole_____ 5-4-65 _____ Proclamation No. __65-1450__

Discharge from _____ Parole _____

Date of discharge _____ 6-29-74 _____

Remarks __5-19-67 Proc 67-1098 Revoke Parole__

__11-21-72 Proc 72-4969 Reinstate Parole__ and set aside revocation.

Witness my hand and seal of office this the __3rd__ day of __July__, 19_74_.

_____ W. J. ESTELLE, JR. _____ Director

By _____ Chief
Bureau of Records and Identification

BILLY R. WARE

RO-3

_____, Member
TEXAS BOARD OF PARDONS AND PAROLES

Facsimile of Salinas' arrest and parole record from Texas Department of Corrections (1974)

Post-Prison Interviews

The final section of *raúlrsalinas and the Jail Machine* includes two post-prison interviews with Salinas conducted twenty years apart. The first interview, "Resisting Mindfuck," from the Seattle-based anarchist newspaper the *Sunfighter*, demonstrates Salinas's continued commitment to prisoners' rights struggles. By exposing in grim detail the brutal brainwashing techniques prison authorities practiced against prisoners to fragment their solidarity with one another, Salinas also makes clear that these group manipulation techniques were merely the first front of an effort to exercise social control of groups outside prison. Occurring simultaneously with the government's insidious COINTELPRO initiative designed to undermine the anti-war and Civil Rights movements, the manipulation of prisoners reveals not only the threat these prisoners represented to the social order inside prison, but also the ends to which authorities were willing to go to quell challenges outside of prison.

As Salinas explains, the ability of a critical mass of prisoners to see through this pacification program—an ability based on their political insight, resolve, and experience—was unanticipated. Having been targeted for transfer to Marion with other "difficult" prisoners from around the country, many prison intellectuals were cognizant of their solidarity across race and class lines; consequently, the anti-prison, multiracial *espirit de corps* of some members of this group only further intensified. The *Sunfighter* interview provides insight into how some prisoners maintained their sanity and their humanity through resistance, and it shows how the prison authorities broke laws in their desperate effort to break the human spirit.

The second interview, conducted on the occasion of Salinas's visit to Stanford University to finalize the acquisition of his personal archives, closes the book by offering readers a portrait of a writer who is reflecting on his life as a journey of transformation. We gain insight into his childhood and the roles that his family, culture, barrio, school, and the police played in shaping his sense of self. Defining himself as "post-pachucho and pre-bato loco," Salinas outlines how at a very young age it became necessary for him to develop a resistant identity in order to maintain his personal integrity. His vernacular aesthetics, in language and through the expressive symbology of graffiti and tattoos, emerged from a negative dialectic with school and police authorities who denounced his "difference" with the mainstream by attempting to force conformity upon him. But this negative dialectic shaped a positive mode of expression as he found a means of affirming his identity *through* resisting the social mandates that sought to control his behavior and forms of expression.

By connecting the evolution of his resistant identity in prison to an identity inextricably linked to his political development, we see that Salinas's sense of purpose, his world vision, and his artistic sensibility have become more finely honed over the years. Through a profound and deliberate spiritual and intellectual growth sparked by fellow prisoners who became his teachers, this new way of looking at and living in the world transformed his aesthetic sensibility into a poetics of resistance that is intended to both "critique and inspire." As he muses on his literary influences, the development of Chicana/o literature, and his place within this canon, we can also see how Salinas has evolved into a quintessential poet of the Americas with his stylistic, multilingual innovations and cross-cultural, pan-American perspective.

In addition to the motifs of the journey, ongoing transformation, and resistance, this interview also presents the writer's efforts to resolve contradictions at multiple levels, within himself and with society—both personal and political. In doing so, we capture a picture of Salinas in his own words in a way that enables those who do not know him to gain insight from his life that can teach us about our own individual and collective journeys.

Resisting Mindfuck

from *Sunfighter* (1974)

I WAS IN LEAVENWORTH in '72 when we had like 3 sit down strikes.†
We were in the hole at Leavenworth and other people were in the hole
throughout the country for different strikes. There was a lot of unrest,
the shit was coming down, you know. After the Attica and the San
Quentin tragedies, prisoners were saying who knew when they're
going to shoot us down, and if we're going to die, we might as well be
making a stand. This is what was going down around the country, the
mood of the prisons, you know, very much inspired by Brother George
Jackson and some of the other prison fighters. We defined ourselves as
political prisoners. We were political prisoners because we had started
a process of political awareness and because now we're standing up
and saying we're not just common criminals, man. OK, so we were
convicted by a racist court, by the ruling class machinery, but now
we're developing into something else, and we had more respect for
ourselves than just being criminals. And, like, if the shit is wrong in
the hospital, we're going to let you know, and if the laws for parole
are ridiculous, we're going to talk about it, write, petition, and do
whatever we have to, stand up and fight or get killed . . .

So they decided to ship us out of there to Springfield MO. and
Marion, Ill. That was the most beautiful show of solidarity, when they
took two chain buses out, 64 prisoners. When we left the first group at
Springfield, there were people who were strong hard convicts,
weightlifters, young dudes that were fighting in chains—and we were
embracing one another and crying. Shit, I saw it and I felt it and everybody was saying "Well, wherever we go, wherever we go, we're
already in it, we're in an Army." Yeah, and it just jelled right there that

we're just not ordinary criminals—they're carrying us out of the joint because we were becoming effective, we were making some noise and people were listening. "OK, take care man," you know, black, white, Chicano, Indian, everybody, man, and shit, them pigs couldn't deal with it . . .

Now Marion was built to replace Alcatraz, you know, so it's a super secure joint. It holds about 600 prisoners. This place was going to be the dumping ground, the last stop for anybody who articulated their grievances or who saw something wrong within the prison and dared to struggle against it.

So what developed out of this is that we arrived at Marion and at the same time people arrived from McNeil Island, [Lanier] Red Ramer, Mike Cassidy, who were very active in the prison struggle, black brothers like Charles Warren out of Atlanta, GA., and Akinsiju from New Orleans, Chicano brothers like Alberto Mares, Eddie Sanchez, came together here at Marion and everybody went to the hole.

But this hole was weird, man—individual cells, your light is on all night, they bring books to read, sheets, they even brought us malts. When they let us out, they took us before the disciplinary committee and they said, "Well, like here you don't have to go around . . . dissenting, because here you can let your hair grow a little longer, you can wear a mustache, your shirttail out, you can go eat at whatever hour on Sunday, you can get up late, there's a golf course, and there's a very good group to get into, in fact we suggest you get into that group, and that was the Escalapian [Askelepeion] Society, which was also called Groder's Guerillas, after the shrink who invented it.

So they let us out into population and, shit man, all this talent was out on the grounds. Right away we started moving, checking things out. And some of the people who were already there start telling us "Hey man, this place is all right," and all along the corridor there are speakers, they pick up your rap wherever you're at in the joint, and they've got closed circuit TV cameras all around. And they tell us about Groder's Guerillas, "and you know so-and-so, who was very active over at Leavenworth, he's joined them now." Well what are they doing man? "Shit, they have preferred housing, and they have access to all the equipment, and they're the only people who receive groups from outside . . . it's good here, we got an inmate advisory committee, and they give you books here man, you can sign up, you can order science fiction, westerns, or some hot spicy novels, you know." And we said, "Hey man, how about the *Prison Diary of Ho Chi Minh*, or how about Che," you know, and they say "I don't know, but they give you anything you want . . . "

So we began to do some research on what the Groder's Guerillas were all about, and one of our best researchers was Red Ramer, and he started documenting things and asking questions, and getting next to people, and that's how we were about to come up with the report that Dr. Edgar Schein had made back in the 60s. Dr. Edgar Schein, he's an associate professor of psychology at Massachusetts Institute of Technology, and he presented a paper in 1962 to staff members and senior administrators of the U.S. Bureau of Prisons, and the name of the paper he delivered was "Man Against Man, Brainwashing." His quotes to them at that time were: Take this back to your prisons and just think of what you can do. In terms of experimentation," he says, "for instance, all the Black Muslims . . ."

We had been protesting not being able to get political education material—so we formed a little group, we formed around the student union—everybody was taking college courses, getting carbon paper, hustling for legal work, and all that. So they showed a stag film— that's how loose they were getting. Playboy was in, Danish nude books were in, cock stories, in order to deviate the prisoners from the political material, you know. So they showed a stag film and of course most of the prisoners went for it, and we were kind of disturbed, so the second time they showed a stag film we really protested, and we started talking to the brothers and educating them, so they started coming down on us.

But what kicked the whole thing off in terms of getting back in the hole . . . we had been at Marion for 90 days . . .

[Jesse Lopez, now one of the Leavenworth Brothers, was thrown in the hole after a run-in with a guard. In a show of solidarity, the prisoners locked down the joint for one week. 150 resisted, even when the rest of the prison went back to work, because their grievances concerning the conditions of segregation and the hole weren't being met. They also wanted Jesse Lopez out of the hole, and the guard fired. All 150 were put into another unit that had been specially stripped to create another hole. Ed.]

So, at that point is when they started in on their psychic oppression. That is what we called it, psychic genocide and psychic oppression. And it was in keeping with what this dude Edgar Schein had said. Like he had said "segregation of all natural leaders," for one. "Use of cooperative prisoner as leaders in all sanctioned groups," so you know, those people that were Groders' would infiltrate all the other groups, and they would sort of like stand up. We were in the hole now, and they would kind of pick up the banner, counter to what we were doing, you know, for the Man. "Repression of group activities not in line with brainwashing objectives," OK, they did that. "Spying on the prisoners, reporting back private material, exploitation of opportunists and informers," you know, they were going through our mail, they were withholding shit that was coming in . . .

In some places it's more of a systematic thing. Like in Springfield, MO. they had the START program, Special Treatment And Rehabilitative Training. Like the way they started doing it with Eddie Sanchez and others is that they put them in the hole and they chained them, completely nude. So then the following day they give them a pair of shorts, and then the next day they give them a pencil, but no paper, and each day you progress, and if your behavior is not in keeping with what *they* want it to be, then you start back from nothing. The reward and punishment trip is what START was about.

Now in Groder's they were using things like psychodrama, aversive therapy, a conglomeration of Eric Berne's Transactional Analysis, part of the process of the Synanon House, dressing-down sessions where they just give you the third degree. People think it's like a self-help or improvement program, this is how they come in. Now if they had a certain behavior, like if they were snitches, they were going to go to that group because they needed help, you know, the pressure was too much, if they were homosexuals who considered homosexuality a problem to them, or a hang up, well they were put in there and given the third degree. Like somebody would just humiliate you, call you a snitch and a rat and a punk and a dick-licker, shit like that, and then they had primal attack therapy, and the primal scream, they'd hit pillows, and yell "I'm a snitch" or "I don't want to be a punk," shit like that, you know. They start playing on their weaknesses or their faults, and then they give them what they consider a new image of themselves, but what it's doing is domesticating them. Schein says, "convincing the prisoner they could trust no one, treating those who are willing to collaborate in far more lenient ways than those who are not."

Now, brothers and sisters in the joint are all into changing, because they know they're not happy where they're at, and a lot of them go into the Man's therapy because they figure there's no other alternative, you know, "I'll go into this program because the Man says I'm fucked up because I'm in the joint," but a lot of people don't realize that there's change and there's change . . .

Political change is really not forced or induced—once you get started, you are your own impetus, your own motivator, and you seek out those people who are into changing things. The only reward is that you're doing some work for the people, and that you're trying to bring about some change for human beings in cages all over the world, and so you're not going to be rewarded or punished, that's the difference. There's no coercion to gain a political awareness, there's an invitation and an introduction, but definitely not any coercion or jive or bullshit. You don't have to bullshit a person to help them develop politically, man, in fact, you have to be more truthful, and there's not the deviousness there is or the ill-intent to change people, which is what they want to do. They want to say "we're going to change you and make you another person." Well not everybody wants to be. Like I wanted to deal with the causes for me going to prison, but I wanted to deal with them, you know, in the prisoners' way, not in the Man's way, because I've always been against the Man regardless of why I went to prison.

And like, 3, 4 years ago, at Marion, at first it was going to be called the National Detention and Behavior Modification Research Center, and they had contacted governors throughout the country to send their "unmanageable" state prisoners, plus all the political activists in the federal system, but it was aimed also at that time at getting all the Angela Davises, the Dan Berrigans, the people who hadn't been to prison but were political activists, and we said, like, they're not going to stop there, because BF Skinner is saying, "We've go to take it to the schools." And we were saying, hey, they're going to do behavior modification on welfare recipients, they're going to change their behavior so that women don't have kids, you know, that's insane . . . Ok, the SLA, I know they exposed a lot of bad shit that needed exposing, though I didn't understand all their moves, but one thing that was never mentioned too much was that the black dude they offed in Oakland was instituting an identification, mug-shot, intelligence bureau for school kids. They were going to save the black community from black people, and they were going to do it at the expense of the youth, by implementing these programs in the schools . . . So it is being used. That's what the prisoners were saying at this point. It will eventually lead to modifying the behavior of political activists throughout the country, it's a calculated move across the country. The prisoners were just saying that it was coming down on them first for obvious reasons . . .

So here were 150 prisoners that Groder had been waiting to have in captivity to deal with. The first day we were all held incommunicado, not allowed to write, denied writing materials, tobacco, personal hygiene and cleaning supplies, and these items were normally always issued upon being put in the hole. The next day we were allowed to receive mail and newspapers, but not to write anything out. Schein says "preventing prisoner contact with anyone non-sympathetic to the method of treatment and regiment of the captive populace." We could see the other prisoners going to work, and we started harassing, so they came in, and first they wrote out tickets on everyone who'd been banging, and then they gassed us. On the third day the disciplinary committee started calling everyone to read the charges against them. The charges ranged from instigating and agitating to inflammatory remarks and congregating in groups, and some were charged with being leaders, you know, leader of the black prisoners, or leaders of the chicanos, or leaders of the white radicals, and then a blanket charge was filed on everybody for rattling the bars and banging the bunks when we'd seen the guys going to work. So they stopped the newspapers on the third day. They suspended visits, another right that is rarely tampered with even when you're in segregation. The fourth day the medical assistants, MTA's [Medical Technician Assistants], made their rounds, no treatment, just very bad, you know verbal treatment. They sprayed the windows across the corridors so we wouldn't see the guys going to work. A prisoner learned that his mother suffered a stroke when she learned about all of this, and he asked for the customary phone call and was denied. Then, at the shower time, this prisoner goes out, sits down and refuses to budge, so a five man goon squad comes in and starts to take him out, and we all start shouting not to beat him up. They were "building a group conviction among the prisoners that they'd been completely abandoned by and isolated from their social order". In other words, they'd tell us that outside in population dudes didn't give a shit about us, and that wasn't true, there were dudes writing all this shit, man, sending it out to all these people.

By this time, the prisoners, since we're all making noise and everybody's incommunicado, "What's going to happen," first days, you know, it's hectic, people started breaking down emotionally, their nerves, you wouldn't sleep because everybody wanted to know what was happening at all hours of the day or night. Schein says, "Implementing treatment policies the effect of which is to disorganize all group standards among the prisoners; placing prisoners into new and ambiguous situations for which the standards are kept deliberately unclear, then putting pressure on them to conform to what is desired in order to win favor and a reprieve from the pressure." So the MTA's came around, always with real shitty attitudes, and started bringing around tranquilizing drugs, librium and valium, and they would dispense them freely to anyone who said they couldn't stand it, nerves and after a while brothers would start breaking down and demanding that librium and shit, and MTA's would come and rush more librium and valium. But most of us weren't going for it.

We saw how that shit rendered you helpless, and let them dominate over you. Inside, the brothers were discussing the drugs, and how, they were opening attorney-client mail. Some the dudes were aggressive dudes, maybe waiting for a letter from home, and they'd become violent, want to kick the dude's ass. Well these are the dudes they'd shoot with thorazine to subdue them and for 3 days we couldn't talk to them, and in that 3 day period psychiatrists would come and start talking to them, "you're not going to make it here, man . . . you're doing a life sentence, you're too violent . . . you're not going to make it here, but the START program in Springfield is not what you may think it is, but you're eligible and you can make it there, but we're not going to put you on it unless you ask us to . . . and, you know . . . you won't get another chance to get out of the hole." They were playing on dudes while they were under that shit. So a lot of us decided we couldn't get violent over, anything, we don't want to get sick, we don't want to take drugs, so we were being careful, and we were trying to convince the other brothers to create that awareness.

Ok, so they took all our personal belongings, all our legal material, all our books, so this is what we filed in court. We went to the hole in July of '72 and I left in November of '72, but the rest of the brothers didn't get out till September of '73. So those 150 dudes spent a year and a half in the hole, and some of them are still there now.

† Published in *Sunfighter,* 1974 (pp. 4–6). The *Sunfighter* was a Seattle-based anarchist newspaper. This interview was excerpted from a longer discussion with Salinas by *Sunfighter* staff.

Una Plática con Raúl Salinas

An Interview by Ben Olguín and
Louis Mendoza

Stanford University, May 5, 1994

BEN: Raúl Salinas is a poet, publisher, and a well-regarded activist.
We are particularly excited to have Raúl with us today. He
brings us a powerful message of struggle and transformation.
Raúl is one of the contemporary permutations of the organic
intellectual who has worked in and written about a variety of
struggles, from the barrio, to the prison, to the university, to
the jungle in Chiapas. He brings a message of transformation
that accompanies this struggle. Transformation has been crucial in his struggle for social justice. Transformation that he
himself embodies, in the sense that he has evolved from, to use
his words, "an individual in the grips of criminal mentality,"
to a renowned and respected activist for human rights causes
throughout the world.

LOUIS: Like many of our lives Raúl, your life has been shaped by
social institutions, from your family, to correctional institutions, the institutions of higher education, and various governmental institutions. These institutions have had a tremendous
impact on your life, and mark the many contradictions as well
as transformations which have made you who you are. For
instance, you have gone from being in one of the most brutal
federal penitentiaries in 1972 to now in 1994 sitting on the
City Charter Review Committee for the City of Austin.

BEN: Maybe you could begin with your youth, your pachuco experience, how you defined yourself as a pachuco, and explain how that led to various other transformations into a pinto and a prison activist.

RAÚL: Well I think that in talking about transformation . . . we would have to begin with family, which is something that's very seldom mentioned in terms of myself as a writer. I do have a family and I think that the initial transformation of myself as part of a family out into the world almost without a family has to be taken into account. I have some very strong familial roots even though they were ruptured and severed for many years as a result of my long incarceration. But the strong family base with the matriarchal system under my maternal grandmother, who had a family of all daughters, therefore the family had a strong sense of the woman who provides and maintains a family. Also, I have to credit the initial source for my love of literature and for me being a writer to my mother. Also, my grandmother, who died at 96 years of age, wrote in 1917 or 1920 a corrido after my grandfather was jailed for shooting a man at a house baptism in west Texas. While he was in jail my grandmother wrote a corrido, which I am trying now to piece together with the help of my aunts. But my mother is still an influence today, we compete in going to the library. She is very active and reads. So those are my beginnings as a writer if I am going to look back and see what my influences were. The first influences were from my mother and grandmother. That love of literature I carried with me to the streets. As a youth, like many youths around this country, I fell victim to the social conditioning of the streets and all that that entails, including the devastation as a result of the drugs. I became involved as a youth in all that negative aspect of our social order. So it was a rebellion of sorts, as well as a defiance that very early on led me to the streets as a young little vandal. Maybe now for the record I should state that I considered myself as a pachuco within the culture. However, historically I fall between being post-pachuco and pre-bato loco. But those are terms applied in academia, in the field of social work. People referred to us as los pachuquillos, but we were not the zoot suitors. That was my uncles, my relatives. In fact in the fifties, there was an element of Chicanos throughout the country who referred to ourselves as "hipsters." We were already influenced by the urban American life. And so I entered in public schools with that understanding of knowledge and love of literature and an understanding of knowledge as something addicting. I entered school knowing how to read. At nine, I was reading in Spanish because my mother read and continues to read in Spanish. So my mother prepared me. In school I was considered a smart kid, but also a little brat. That was one of the earlier contradictions in my life that I could never be put down in the educational system as being a dumb kid because I excelled; yet, I was a troublemaker. I dealt with that contradiction throughout my school years until I was kicked out.

BEN: Let's pick up on that point right there, on that vernacular literary family tradition. On those first attempts to express yourself through this rebellious youth, through your pachuquismos, your defiances, and many other forms of writing, through your preliterary writing, if you permit me to use that term, such as the tattoos.

RAÚL: Oh yes. The symbols of, well as I say in a poem, the symbols of our youth, the art form of our youth, they're the earliest expressions. I think that I even connected them to the playing blocks. The ABC blocks which is how my mother taught me to read. Later in my rebellion, the placas (which are not something new) the graffiti, was our assertion of existence. We are somebody, we are a people, I am alive. Tapon. Con Safos. That was the earliest expression and it combines the rebellion with the need to express oneself. Later on, yes, tattoos, which I believe my first tattoo was at the age of twelve. From there on during my junior high and high school years I wrote things pertaining to my studies. I studied American lit in high school like everybody else. I then looked at American lit, the schoolhouse poets as they were known then, Longfellow, Whitman, Emerson. We had to read them. T. S. Eliot and all those other languages that they had. "The Wasteland," for example, bilingualism. Later we were being looked upon as different or foreign because we had bilingual constructions in our writing.

BEN: Bilingual and also multimedia. I just flipped to your poem, the poem you're best known for, "Un trip through the mind jail" and I see how you so effectively blend in graphic arts. You have the same placas that you have here in the text, you have here on your hand.

RAÚL: I think it's one of the earliest, at least in modern times of Chicano writings, it's one of the first poems that utilizes graffiti as a stanza. That's a stanza inasmuch as I understand the construction of the poem.

LOUIS: Raúl, you've spoken about how when you were young, you used these different forms of artistic and linguistic expression and sometimes they took the forms of the tattoos on your body as a youngster. Did these things have a sort of dynamic effect on your identity in terms of your relationship to institutions that is through your instructors or other authority figures? Did they mark you in different kinds of ways and shape your life?

RAÚL: Well, yes. I think that the fact that I was doing this was an affront to the educational system. For example, the first tattoos, we were putting them on in the school grounds, during school hours. Their response was to look at me as a weird kind of person, and they usually saw you, if you're a "troublemaker" according to the stereotype, as a little deficient, or dumb, or not too bright. They had to deal with the fact that I was intelligent and still defying that sort of institutional kind of boxing in of sorts.

LOUIS: I am curious why, even at a young age, do you think that the authority figures get so freaked out when you take control of your own body to mark yourself. You're not harming anyone else, right? What principle do you suppose is being violated when you do that?

RAÚL: Well, it's threatening. It's threatening because you are taking command of your own destiny so to speak. This is my body. It rankles their whole mindset. The mindset is important. This is my way of dealing with it for myself. That mindset gets boggled. It shakes the status quo, so to speak. There is no formula to deal with this kind of guy, or this kind of person. So we label them, we Special Ed them or we do whatever and compartmentalize them until we push them out.

BEN: I am particularly fascinated by your challenge to structures of authority, the school system, etc., and at the same time it's not just a challenge and fighting against something because you are also defining your own subjectivity. It is really interesting to me to see how it's not just a matter of you saying that I'm Tapon, but you're also putting La Loma on here, and you're locating yourself in your own barrio. Could you talk a little more about that?

RAÚL: Well, it's part of, I think, the conscious or subconscious, if you will, assertion of existence. I think land, which we have been so dispossessed of historically as a people, is the first thing one needs to identify with, and a barrio, good, bad, or indifferent, the internal colony that it may be, like reservations of native peoples, it's home and so you make the best and you adapt. But how can I challenge an institution as Tapon? Well as Tapon from La Loma, I'm not alone then. High school, white high school, across town, rich high school. This is my homeland. I come from the barrio of La Loma and that centers me somewhat. There are people there, there is culture, there is food, there is music, that has nurtured me and I come from that. As Corky once said, you know, I return to the circle of life, which is my own people. Go back to plan A, you know, our roots. I think that for me it's something that I could use to stand up to the world, or whoever I was challenging as a young man. Whatever I saw was containing me as a person with not only identity, a person individually, but coming from some space, having a base to challenge the world. And La Loma at that time was the base.

LOUIS: What about hostile forces that infiltrated that home space? Can you talk about that in terms of how you were often at odds with different sectors, whether it's authority figures, or institutions?

BEN: As a pachuco for example, what was your response when that collective home space that you defined, that collective polity, that comunidad was violated by, for example, a police car patrolling? Or a certain business that didn't want to serve Mexicans or what have you?

LOUIS: Were the police hostile when you were a youth?

RAÚL: Oh definitely, definitely. Well now in my adult life, the social critic that I have become, I see that that harassment has always been there. Because we were different, because we were challenging the norms of society. You're targeted. You are the wayward youth. You are the vandal. You are the troublemaker. And so your area is patrolled more because there is less political clout. There is less voting power and all those things that go with colonias and barrios. And so those forces that supposedly protect society saw us as threats to that which they protect and so there was harassment. That is initially how I came to be. So you fight back in the only way that you can. How do you fight the police as a teenager? Anything from trashing to vandalizing, to criminal mischief, to breaking windows, to flattening cop cars tires, to whatever just to get back because every time they bust you, you get your little butt whipped and slapped around. Whether if it's for suspicion, and as young kids, I think that especially then, it was certainly a bit more brutal than it is today. I guess in good old common horse sense you can't just beat up somebody for a long time, or lock them up, or kick them around and expect them to respond in any positive way. I think the law of survival forces you to react and that is what we did, reacted rather than respond. It resulted in a lot of jails and the life of imprisonment.

BEN: We're touching on something that I really want to explore, but before we get into that I want explore this whole vernacular mode of resistance a little bit more. We are talking about breaking windows, flattening tires, etc., as ways to kind of protect the homespace, defend oneself as an individual . . .

RAÚL: And to ease the anger because you get angry every time they come patrolling your neighborhood. It doesn't seem like they patrol anybody else's neighborhood. The stereotype is there and that is what they have to go by.

BEN: And they also had your mode of resistance, in terms of placazos, every time you put a tattoo on to challenge them and at times to define yourself, that is also a signal to the chota just like the Raiders' jacket is today to the police officers.

RAÚL: Definitely, once you have your tattoos, that's the whole thing that we did with our crosses. My cousin got his cross, so yeah there were consequences. I got my first crucita at the age of twelve. I guess I was in seventh grade.

BEN: So in a sense, as Mexicans from La Loma, a low income neighborhood, dark skinned, indigenous features, you're already marked, but you're marking yourself further. Can you talk a little bit of how your own actions of marking yourself more led to further harassment? I remember once you told me that the cops would take inventory once they stopped you. Is that right?

RAÚL: Yes, oh yeah. I mean it's part of your rap sheet. Identifying characteristics, marks and scars, right? They have the stuff and they catalogue what you've got. Right forearm a panther or dragon or whatever you have. They begin the dossier. For us it started as children really. I was declared a juvenile delinquent at the age of thirteen by the county or the state courts of Texas in Austin. From that point on 'til 1972 until I came out of prison a grown man, thirty-eight years old, I believe. That is how long the standoff between me as an individual and societal forces lasted.

BEN: Was there a particular instance when your tattoos wound up being a deciding factor in your exclusion from your home space, your removal from your home space to prison, a confinement? Or was it just more of a ordinary day-to-day cataloguing of your placazos in defining you as a criminal, or criminal element, or somebody they didn't want as part of their society?

RAÚL: I don't know how much it had to do with the tattoos themselves. The more tattoos I had, the more I kept getting busted. The more they had a catalogue of my tattoos. I don't think any one tattoo . . . it's just the idea, how dare you? You know that kind of attitude. For me anyway, the more they felt it was uncool, the more that I felt that it was cool. And I'm not saying that is the sole purpose of reason for me putting on tattoos, but that is one of the elements that certainly was part of the whole process.

LOUIS: It became something to identify you with your compas out in the street, that you each maybe had your own placa, your own circle?

RAÚL: Right, on the one hand that is what I am saying. It's several elements within that process rather than one, it was an act of defiance to the cops. Yeah, I got them, man. I know you don't like them. But that was to the cops, that was one element of the things. I don't see it as the only one. For the camaradas yeah, I got them. Again for the record, La Loma is the neighborhood, that's my barrio that I identify with. We didn't live in the barrio of La Loma, we lived right outside the barrio boundaries. We were kind of in between two barrios, but the fact that my mother worked, single-parent, and then later married, during the war she worked. I stayed with my aunt who lived in the heart of La Loma. So my daily hanging out with the bro's was in La Loma. So my identifying barrio is La Loma. In terms of turf and gangas: There was la calle seis but I was from La Loma. So it's just a technicality that I didn't live and grow up in the barrio of La Loma, my relatives were there and that's my ganga.

BEN: I am really interested in how your tattoos operate in other manners in other situations, specifically for example in prison. How did the significance of some of the tattoos change? For example, the Virgen that you have on your chest and the Cristo that you have on your back. Can you talk a little bit about that?

RAÚL: I think we can look at the history of tattoo art or tattoos as an art form and you have all the gamut of opinions from they're all exhibitionists, this or that. Well it's religious iconography, and all these terms, mutilations, exhibitionism, that to me are terms that people with tattoos and people that do tattoos don't use. I understand some of them, but yes my background. My family is Catholic. I wasn't a devout Catholic. I went through the religion because that was my family religion. I don't consider myself a religious person. Today I practice the Native American way and I have a sense of my spirituality. I don't have a religion. So I am sure that the Virgen de Guadalupe, which I have on my chest and the Cristo *ecce homo* which they call the crucified Christ, certainly . . . I understand the religious nature of them as icons. On the other hand, more so for my self, and for prisoners who use these symbols, they are more cultural than religious, I think. They have become cultural symbols, even the huelga symbol. Even the strike that is going on right now. It's like the symbol is their protection, but it's another kind of protection, its somewhat like my turtle spirit protection is to me now. So it was more of a cultural image than a religious icon. But that's me, some other bro's might think that as long as I am in prison, I'll be protected or something. But in prison . . . that's an assertion. If it blows the mindset of society outside, then it blows the mind umpteen thousand times more in the mindset of prison guards and prisons because there you are supposed to be confined, robbed of your freedom and mobility, with no contact with anything that identifies you as a human being. First you're reduced to a number and you can't wear clothes other than prison clothes. You can't have any other things than prison things. Some of those things are changing . . . and then to have a tattoo on your chest, or on your back, or on your arm, or on your leg, that you didn't have last month, tattooing is illegal, is considered contraband in prison. "How dare you go and mark yourself and get away with it" it says to the guards who like to pretend they are all knowing with pistols and rifles and gun towers and bars! "How dare you get away with it?" "Well, that's interesting," we say. "We'll get away with it some more." So tattooing, which is an illegal contraband activity, becomes the ultimate slap in the face of the prison.

BEN: How did you guys get away with it? How did you divide the labor? How did you protect yourself from getting caught . . . and how did you protect yourself against retribution for this so-called "self-mutilation"?

RAÚL: Well, yes and that is how they look at it, self-mutilation. They know what's best for us so they're supposed to protect us from self-mutilation and here we are self-mutilating ourselves and mutilating others, right? Which shatters their whole myth of who has got control of this prison. Or of this individual or this human body and there is a very common clichéd phrase "you can lock up my body but you can't jail my mind," well in this case we were saying, "you can lock up my body but you don't determine what is done to it, I do." They can't deal with that. How you get away with it, is you have to have someone stand in point. Your jigger man. That person makes sure that the guard, as he makes his rounds through the cell blocks and through all the tiers of cell blocks, they know when he comes around. Someone is watching while you're tattooing. So that becomes your partner. Then when he's doing work, if he's an artist, then you be the watch man for him. Those are some of the ways that we did it and got away with it.

LOUIS: Given that conformity to the institution's laws, control was so important, so paramount, whoever defied that sort of urge was forced to conform. How did resisting conformity play itself out in constructing your cultural identity in prison? To what extent was that linked to further consciousness-raising on your part about who you were in society?

RAÚL: Oh yes, the more I learned about myself and when I discovered . . . when the writer in me began to emerge, I had other tools and ways of expressing those things, so that I could present it in a different way. But also the fact that I was reading more and learning more and gaining the confidence that I had a history. That I came from somewhere, that there was something to who I was because there was a rich culture and the more I learned about the culture, the more I became interested in the history, and the more I read the history of Chicanos and Mexicanos, including the war of 1846 and 1848 with the signing of the Treaty of Guadalupe. The more I learned about the conquest and then it wasn't just about Mexicanos and Chicanos and then I began to see the political arrogance of domination and conquest. I began to develop ways to express that through my writing. Also, as a result of making connections with people from other places who also have fought as a people or as nations who have gone through this political domination and conquest and seeing in it an affinity and solidarity with other struggling forces that enabled me to break out of that "criminal mentality" and I began to seriously study political thought. The times were right, the sixties were the years when I was in prison. Though I am of the fifties generation, I consider myself a late bloomer because I was imprisoned during the sixties at the height of the anti-war movement, at the height of the Cuban Revolution, Viet Nam, the student movements, the black movement, all of these forces were plaguing society. There was a lot of unrest by the Anglo youth of the society that enabled the rest of us . . . I attribute a lot even to the anti-war and the hippie movement, which enabled at least laws to relax, to expose things on a higher level. I began to define myself within a political space and that was very strengthening.

Again you mentioned a word that I think that I have lived, chewed, eaten, tasted, spit out, vomited, and that is transformation. Just thinking of the word right now I get a little emotional because transformation as I know it is very painful. And I think the one poem that I try to describe what is happening to me is called "enorme transformación" and it's all in Spanish. In it I'm saying like what the hell is happening to me man, something is going on inside my head. Whew! It's painful man. When you guys say transformation, to me it's like I went through a meat grinder and came out something else and when I think about it's very hard to deal with. So, yeah, it was a transformation. I think it's also in the letters that make up my introduction [to *Un Trip Through the Mind Jail*], which says, and it's a letter to one of my colleagues and it says that I can feel it happening and I can see it. Let me check the passage out to clarify.

BEN: I just want to thank you for sharing this because when you are talking about your transformation that really is a part of my own transformation. And I think it's a transformation that occurs whenever people hear you read as well.

RAÚL: I was writing I guess to Joseph Sommers, a man who was very instrumental in helping me with that transformation. And I say something like this: "un proceso de transformación mental see it occurring, feel it surging within, it's at once amazing extremely difficult to grasp, painful and frightening!"

LOUIS: One of the catalysts for transformation that you mentioned had to do with studying and reading. I was wondering if you could talk a little bit about the process, the relationship between your change and the reading you did in the cages. How did that influence your writing?

RAÚL: Well, as I said, I happened to be in prison during the sixties. I arrived at Leavenworth Federal Penitentiary in 1967. Again, Vietnam, Cuba, I happened to come to a penitentiary where some of the most brilliant minds that I've ever met came together. The Puerto Rican independence fighters who had tried to address the question of colonization in Puerto Rico and had fired into the ceiling of the U.S. Congress in 1954 were there. As was their compañero who had been in the assault attempt of Harry Truman at Blair House in 1950. Here was a linguist in command of seven languages, a man, Don Oscar Collazo, who taught me acentuación in Spanish, where the accents go. He would give classes in Spanish to Chicanos. But las frases or the sentences were all from Pedro Albizu Campos for example. We knew Zapata. Then after the Cuban Revolution, we knew about Che Guevara and we knew about Ho Chi Minh because these are things that are coming into the prison. Smuggled, I might add. But then here we know about Pedro Albizu Campos, a Puerto Rican patriot. We begin to interact with all of the brothers from the Black Liberation Army who had been in Atlanta, Georgia, in Attica, in Terre Haute, Indiana, who came there and began to engage us in Swahili. They were learning their languages. So we were in the hole. By then we're active and my teacher is a Chicano from Rio Grande Valley, from McAllen. I don't know, you guys are asking me stuff that . . . I mean I'm glad but it's hard . . . because I'm reliving it. Ramón Chacón from del Valle Rio Grande placed in my hand the first copy of *Wretched of the Earth* by Frantz Fanon, which I absorbed and grabbed. And by this time these books were our salvation. These books were what we needed because it wasn't about tattoos anymore. Tattoos, I had them on. I had something else to say and it couldn't be said with tattoos anymore. Somehow we had exhausted that one. I am using those terms just to communicate, but then it's our teaching. Then it's like, yeah I'm reading Amilcar Cabral and I know about national culture and liberation, and yes I'm trying to learn about my culture and politics and art and the aesthetics of art. And my defiance became an art. Not just mine but I am speaking for a generation of people that were with me, my teachers. And it's beautiful thinking right now that a Chicano from El Valle, from the orange picking area of Texas, was a brother that was bringing us these writings that were so new and so refreshing to us that we were absorbed in it. So this gave us more ammunition, it showed us how to respond more than react. How to develop and articulate our grievances. How to stand up and begin to develop discipline. They're not going to look at me as a gangster. They're not going to look at me as a criminal. Why? Because I am not doing criminal things. I'm clean. I'm respectful to other people. I'm studying. I'm taking care of myself. I'm doing physical exercise. I want to be in good shape, of good mind because this is the enemy and I have to be in top shape.

LOUIS: I think most people know you primarily through your poetry, some of which was written in prison and some documents your life outside, your political involvement. But you also wrote a lot of different kinds of writing while in prison. Some of it was personal, journals, diaries, and letters. I know that you wrote journalism and that you were involved in writing legal briefs. You, of course, always wrote poetry, but can you talk about some of the other experiences and practices you brought in from the street into the prison whether it's different influences, literary or musical, that continued to shape who you were in prison?

RAÚL: Well, I think that the streets for the youth that I was and my contemporaries at the time was attracting for one. We became, so to speak, "children of the night." We couldn't find that satisfaction or happiness within the daylight, where we were beginning to consider society the enemy. So the streets were a refuge of sorts. I mean we found refuge, really, in the streets. The things that were on the streets that led to the prison were the negative aspects of street life. But again as a player and a lover still today of music, the lights, the sounds of people on the streets certainly gave me that affinity with other people marginalized such as we consider ourselves to be and we lived in a community that was both Chicano and African American. We were in a black community and a brown community that was mixed and so the music of that particular community certainly became a part of us. To this very day, as both of you know, I am a lover of jazz. Jazz is a music that I love and respect. I knew individuals and I followed it and became a student of jazz history. It just seemed natural to me when I became a writer in prison and began to express my hurts and my pains and trying to determine who I was and the transformation that needed to come about. Jazz music was also one of the things that saved me in prison, that kept me sane. As a writer I wrote in the newspaper, "The Echo" at the Texas Penitentiary at Huntsville. For a year and a half I wrote 14 columns under the banner of "Quartered Notes" and I used my street name Roy, Roy Salinas. And there are 13, 14 articles in which I by that time having read so much of jazz history and jazz literature, I began to be influenced by some of the jazz critics. One to this day, he is no longer with us out of San Francisco, Ralph J. Gleason, who very much influenced me when I think of myself as a jazz columnist, which I was for over a year. So I dealt with jazz, the jazz period of the 40's, 50's and 60's, from the bebop period. Then the jazz music itself began to manifest itself in prison as another element of resistance. I guess resistance. Resistance is a term that I have lived with for a long time. Music became another form of resistance. I said it somewhere, "Here I was a Mexican Indian in one of the most racist prisons in the country writing about African American music." To me that certainly was a form of defiance and a form of resistance. So I began to write jazz articles. Then as I developed my writing, my poetry I began to write jazz poetry. I then took the next logical step of development and transformation in that I actually picked up a horn. Like so many people who were influenced by the jazz greats of that period, I also came to recognize and love the musical genius of Charlie "Bird" Parker.

LOUIS: You have several references to jazz musicians in your work—

RAÚL: Oh yes, because they are very important in my transformation. So I naturally picked up the alto saxophone because Bird was the alto saxophonist supreme. To this day he is one of the greatest musicians in this world that ever lived, bar none, any type of music. He understood the classics and pop music as well. So jazz is also another very real part of who I am, something I have incorporated, a culture that I have embraced out of love and respect and solidarity. These things also help me to survive. So yes, my life as well as my writings are full of the jazz references that I so much loved.

BEN: Jazz brings up a very interesting point in regards to Chicano culture because here we have a Chicano deploying jazz inside prison as part of his repertoire, his means of resisting and at the same time identifying oneself as part of a collectivity. The thing that fascinates me is to see how you are drawing from African American culture, drawing from your own culture, and merging something new, a new collectivity. You are crossing borders inside prison, a paradigmatic border itself.

RAÚL: Yes, and that had to do with the poem I mentioned that almost choked me up emotionally, I began to realize that it is not only I who suffers. I was turned on to so much suffering that people have undergone in this world that it wasn't enough to be a Chicano suffering. If African Americans, black people were suffering it wasn't enough if white people who were prisoners were suffering, I didn't know at the time, we didn't know, I'm beginning to realize I wasn't the only individual there, uniquely transforming. This was a movement, and people, I didn't know that I was adopting this jazz thing as a tool of defiance and resistance. I was doing it because here was a people marginalized on the streets who had a music like I did, who had a culture, like I did. And once imprisoned, there is no other choice. My brother's in the next cell with me, and he happens to be black, and I am brown, and next to us our brother is white, and you can't afford anymore to make those distinctions. At least not in my prison world. There are other prison worlds of exploitation of man by man. But in my prison, and I call it mine because they had me, and eventually I think I had them. There was a lot of realness of people wanting to change into something else, to become a force, a positive energy that would transform things. I like that word transform because that's what it was all about. We were daring to transform things and the first thing we had to transform was ourselves. And we used Amilcar Cabral, and Malcolm X, and Dizzy Gillespie, and Charlie Parker. But we didn't know we were arming ourselves with these tools and weapons of resistance that were going to enable us eventually to resist. Because if we had stayed thinking about how we were going to get another shot of heroin in this prison, and how am I going to mess over this youngster who is weaker than I am, we couldn't have changed. We were going to eventually eat each other up and our political development would have been stifled.

LOUIS: So making these cross-cultural connections enabled your political development and marked a progression for you. Can you identify some examples of how this manifested itself in your poetry and where this cross-cultural connection led to unification?

RAÚL: Yeah. The fact that I was writing about jazz journalistically and that I later incorporated jazz music into my writings. But also those teachers that were enabling us to take this larger and more dangerous stance brought about this heightened political awareness. This did not go unnoticed without reaction on the part of the prison. The more we developed and joined hands across color lines, the more we became a threat. In the 60s because of this intense political awakening across the prisons of amerika, the repression became so intensified that this gave rise to what is called the Prison Rebellion years. We had Attica, one of the most devastating battles, Santa Fe, New Mexico, San Quentin . . . the Soledad Brothers. San Quentin prison . . . the murder of one of our most beautiful teachers. I was not in prison with him. It was his writings from one cage to another that inspired so many criminals transforming from a criminal mindset that he was responsible for. So poetically, this is a long way to answer your question, I have a poem that I wrote about this. I think it's important to know the context. My poem to George Jackson, my brother, my teacher, "News from San Quentin."

LOUIS: Tell us about that poem.

RAÚL: Leavenworth is like Grand Central Station with chain buses (because you go in chains). You are transferred from different federal prisons and Leavenworth is like Grand Central Station where you go to Terre Haute, Indiana, Oklahoma and the day that George Jackson was murdered they locked us up. And they brought in a reform school bus of youngsters. They came in and they're jiving in the holding tank. They don't care, they're loud. How the hell are we going to get some news and we are praying and we couldn't get no news. These youngsters were talking about soul music. And the title that I chose was "News from San Quentin," but there was no news. And so that's how I said see you later to my brother and teacher until we could be together again plotting conspiracies.

BEN: And I'm struck particularly by that last line "Strange things beginning to occur." I'm thinking in terms of Chicano culture. Here you are paying homage to this great warrior from within the walls, you're also defining and contributing to the development of Chicano(a) culture. Can you talk a little about how you see Chicano culture in relation to all the other cultural influences that shape your life?

RAÚL: Well, I think, as I said earlier, the realization that oppression is not unique to any one people. And the realization that when you're down, the question is, how are you going to survive together as human individuals regardless of tattoos or no tattoos, frizzy hair or short hair. There was an urgent necessity for survival, especially during the prison rebellion years, to stand together, and I think that see that, having understood and after gaining the confidence of knowing who I am is how I see battling what Richard Rodriguez says is inevitable in this country and that is assimilation. I'm not afraid to go taste other cultures, world cultures . . . as Mexicano and as an Indio. I'm not afraid to lose that. That's what I'm taking to them in return. That's what I'm offering them. It's a cultural exchange. That is what strengthens and enriches the movement against oppressive forces.

LOUIS: Speaking of poetry in service of politics, I think one of your major contributions is someone who comes of age and finds wholeness and beauty in this vision of unity. But you also went beyond that and included critique in your poetry. You are not afraid of being critical about what's going on in the barrios, the violence going on. I'm thinking, for instance, about "Trip thru the Mind Jail," where you write about the fights over petty things. To me, these things are really important for criticism. They talk honestly about where we are, to assess a situation. Do you see yourself doing that constantly when you're writing poetry?

RAÚL: I feel, then, again, I have to defend my art against those schools of criticism, who present otherwise that somehow politicizing art results in sloganeering, pamphleteering, rhetorical rantings and I reject that theory, that school of thought because of the struggle and difficulty in trying to craft my art. I'm trying, first of all, have it be art not rhetoric or sloganeering. And I have to be careful because I am a performance oral poet within the oral tradition and some people don't understand that and may think it is just rhetoric. Then, I have to find those elements of world literature, the imagery, the metaphors, the simile, the innuendos, the irony, because I know those things from literature and I will continue to use my art to expose corruption, to expose unjust situations. But I'm also going to try to use my art as idealistically and romantically as we embraced the early Chicano movement and Aztlán concepts. I do not want to for the sake of our children (black, blue, brown, yellow, white, whatever) to romanticize my having been a junkie. The pachuco was not something to glorify. I don't want our youth to be pachucos as we tell our youngsters and I quote José Montoya "we don't want you to change your khakis and your bandanas. We just want you to change your attitude towards life." That's what I'm saying, pachucos were not these glorious Hollywood versions of our people and we were not just abstract noble warriors. I criticize the young black brothers who were there when we were crying for George Jackson. Chicanos cried for George Jackson, Anglo brothers cried for George Jackson and yet I'm criticizing these young brothers who dream of one more Cadillac and afro-do and jivists and I'm saying, we lost a brother, a revolutionary brother and you youngsters . . . I have to continue teaching those youngsters and future ones so I can't make it romantic. I can't glorify those things that were devastating to my life and other lives and so, yes, I'm going to critique. I will never use my art, haven't to this point, to trash for the sake of trashing, but I will use my art to critique even our own, even myself.

BEN: To critique and to inspire. I think the oral tradition that you're working is beautiful art. It speaks to the imperatives of the historical moment. Here is your poetry, written in prison in the 60's and 70's, is still speaking in 1994 in Stanford University where four Chicanas are on a hunger strike fighting for justice for Chicano/a Studies.

RAÚL: It speaks to us today I think, because some things haven't changed in 25 years and that has spurred me to continue at the age of 60 to speak out against those same things.

LOUIS: Let's go back to that oral tradition that Ben spoke of. There are several oral traditions that you invoke in your poetry. There is Mexicano, Chicano, but there's also Native American as well as a newer tradition invented by the Beats, invoking thoughts and image and words in their work. Can you talk about those influences? I know they are very different, but nevertheless an important part of your work that people haven't looked at is the Native American tradition and the Beat influence.

RAÚL: Well, I think they are different, but they are not, at least, as I bring them into a center, the Beat influence and my work in my life. I am of a generación del 50, but late bloomer from the 60's. The Beat literary movement in this country and I'm not speaking of the "beat-nik" *Time Life* magazine image, the Beat literary movement in this country is a very balanced movement and I am also somewhat part of that movement. I lived in this society. I grew up here in the 50's. I knew the music. I knew the literature of the schools, but the Beats were "beat." They were marginalized. They were the white Negroes to quote Norman Mailer's essay, which defines that hipster, the Anglo hipster that I was living, the brown hipsters that we were. Then, the Beat is another marginal figure that was not wanted because he/she wore dark glasses and sat around and played bongos, the Hollywood image. So, they are no good like blacks and junkies and Mexicans. There is another marginalized figure. So, it is not coincidental or fragmented. They are very real parts of who I am. They took the jazz music because they were also outcasts. They took the jazz music because it is beautiful music that was also cast out; one of the truest American art forms yet, relegated, like our conjunto music for so many years until it got trendy, to the cantinas. Jazz is the same way. The roadhouses, the juke-joints, that's where I kind of cut my eye-teeth. That's part of that so then, the Beat was American literature that somehow didn't fit with Edgar Allan Poe or Ralph Waldo Emerson or T. S. Eliot. These are my kind of folks. Ted Jones, Jack Micheline before Kerouac and Ginsberg and Gregory Corso and Herbert Huncke. These are real people to me. It is not some book that I read. These are people I walked the streets with. From Greenwich Village later years to North Beach, where I also came to meet with Lawrence Ferlinghetti. I am an American poet and I think that the young literary critics of today, two generations later, are asking some important serious critical questions, that the critics two generations ago blew it, lost it. Pigeon holers: prison poet, Chicano poet 60's, that means I will not develop beyond the 80's or 70's or 90's. I am not writing like I was then, but there is Chiapas like there was Vietnam. There are the sisters sitting out there just like people were in Seattle at the University of Washington during Wounded Knee. So, I have the influence. I went to the American schools. I understand literature. I am an American, continentally speaking. So, yes I am a poet. I write of universal themes, but I have chosen the way to go as a poet, committed, a committed writer, an engaged committed writer. But I write of love. I write of rivers, of children, birth and mango trees and mimosa trees. I am a poet. I write of everything. I write surrealistic. I write funny poetry. I write crazy poetry and so it's within that tradition. The Native American tradition, because of my political work, because again, embracing our brothers inside Leavenworth and Marion and learning more about who they were and how they were our cousins and our Indian roots and how our oral tradition and how their chants relate. When I left prison and went to Washington state, where I had never been, and the Indian people were fighting the government . . . just to fish, to fish for their salmon on the river. They had to defend their nets at gun point and they called us to assist and I had to go. As a result, I get embraced by this culture and nurtured and strengthened by the spirituality of the ceremonies so that just to catch a fish and take it to the tribal people as a first ceremonial feast couldn't help but affect me and influence me and the more I was adopted and embraced and taken care of. Because I was in exile and could not return to my home, these became my people and so now people can say that "I want to be Indian or whatever." They don't know, again, the pain of that transformation. You have read "On Becoming" and it is a response. It is not easy for me to go teach wearing one braid let alone two braids and have people say "ya viste ese Chicano es Indian." I have buried Indian people. I have been at the birth of Indian people and I have walked across this land and I have been jailed because of supporting the Indian people's rights. They are my relatives. They taught me that. They took care of me when I could not be home in Texas. I have a collection of my experiences with the American Indian Movement, with the Leonard Peltier Defense Committee, with the Association of Survival of American Indians and with the International Indian Treaty Council. I write chants and I use refrain and the drone element to bring chanting as a way of channeling energy and bring us together and to get our minds focused on one thing that we need to do; to free a brother, to try to move in the right direction, to save the people's homeland in Big Mountain or the right to fish. My poetry certainly had to be influenced. I have to speak about injustices. I have learned the songs, like last night the Northern Plain songs, I knew a couple of them that the drummers and singers were doing. I have to incorporate that into my work. They are our cousins; they are oral tradition, we are oral tradition.

BEN: We are Americans and your poetry is American and as you said in the Pan American sense. It fascinates me to see these intersections with the Beats and Native Americans and African Americans.

RAÚL: I'm rich. I don't consider myself unique that I have all these things. I consider myself rich. This is what someone gave me. I am not inventing. This is not technical stuff for classes or to have a good little chapbook. This is all I have learned. This is what people have given me. I am giving it back.

BEN: You are giving it back in many ways by participating in the evolution of contemporary Chicano culture and literature. What I wanted to ask you was to take a little step back and start thinking about those early periods when Chicano literature was coming into fruition through the Floricanto Festivals, the Canto al Pueblo, the intersections with the prominent writers and activists, who sometimes were one and the same.

RAÚL: Yes, that's a very beautiful part of my life. When I was released from Marion Prison in 1972, I went to Seattle. Because I was under federal and state parole, I could not return to Austin, so because of some beautiful people like Tomas Ybarra-Frausto, Antonia Castañeda and Joseph Sommers, I was enrolled at the University of Washington. I went there as a student for two semesters. They were using all my work and the third semester I was teaching as an instructor. The First Festival Floricanto organized at the University of Southern California in November of 1973 was the first encuentro of Chicano/Latino writers. "Trip through the Mind Jail" already had a life of its own and so I was invited. I came there to read. Again, by this time, I had already read Montoya because Luís Valdez of Teatro Campesino was writing to me in Leavenworth and he said, "I need to connect you with a brother whose writing is so similar to yours" and he turned me on to José Montoya and I had read Ricardo [Sánchez] so, by the time I got there, here I am in the midst of these beautiful writers and so that gave rise to Festival Sexto Sol at Stanford, Festival Sol de Santa Clara at the University of Santa Clara and across the country Canto al Pueblo and for a period of time, it was very beautiful. Those early years are what some critics have called the Chicano Renaissance, of course mostly men. Teresa Acosta is an important Tejas writer who has not been really looked at. Again, critics have blown it. Young literary critics I think are paying attention. Teresa Acosta, important Tejas writer like Angela de Hoyos; both are important Texas writers because of their grassroots. They are not anybody up here. They continue to write and contribute to literature from their space, which is not out in the bright light world. But very few sisters, important sisters, received recognition, and I need to mention them. The first, at that time, lesbian writers Veronica Cunningham from San Diego, Lynn Romero, who was working with Juan Felipe Herrera and Alurista, but very few. It wasn't until the next wave in the mid 70's that some women began to emerge and start to make a little dent in the mindsets and attitudes of those days. And once out, we had to deal with our own contradictions of how we saw and treated women. Not that we are totally free today of those mindsets of how we look at women, especially in Mexican culture. Again I don't like to think that it's machista because they are not from the U.S., I think that the U.S., or the sexism in this country is perpetuated from the same system that does the profiteering and the exploiting. But certainly we have to stand up and the sisters when you begin to break it up, were slapping us into awareness and reality. We have had to change our positions and attitudes, . . . we have to move out of the way because they were also as militant as the men were in wanting to assert their existence and identity, and rightfully so. Like I said it's been a learning process, and we still have a long way to go, we are all impacted by the sickness of sexism, and racism as well. But in terms of women, the double standards, so even the first wave of women were writing somewhat under the shadow of men. Not that they didn't have their own writing; they do and that is why they eventually broke through that. In the 80's it was not a question of not being "allowed to," not that they were asking us permission back then, but the assertions that they were making and their defining, not by *our* standards, but by *their* standards and that has given rise today to now the cross-cultural, now gender questions. They are important in any world.

LOUIS: I see some trends, if I can point this out quickly. On the one hand, one of the ways they broke out is through the feminist presses. It just got so that Chicanos had to develop their own presses. So I wanted to talk about the publishing industry and some of the trends that are going on, but also I think there is another interesting observation because it was true to me too that the women, more so than the men, in the Chicano Movement made those cross-cultural alliances in some of the early anthologies of the women's writing, such as *This Bridge Called My Back* or *Compañeras*, are doing the same thing. In their work they've collaborated with African American and Asian women. You don't see too many anthologies in which men are forming many cross-cultural alliances and to me that's interesting. Do you agree?

RAÚL: Again, it depends on what part of the country you are in. I happen to have been very fortunate to be in some right places at the right time, both good and bad. I feel proud of the fact that I am in one of very early anthologies that dealt with the term "third world people." Which now they use people of color as a term that we feel good with. It's really kind of an underground classic because not too many people outside of the Bay Area or Califas or people that were really into literature know about it, and that's the anthology *Time to Greez!* that was edited by Janice Mirikitani, a fantastic Asian sister from the Bay Area, Roberto Vargas, Alejandro Murguía, my first publisher with Editorial Pocho Che. So there haven't been that many but there are on the east coast with the Nuyoricans and African Americans, but not like the women of color, Cherríe Moraga, people like Gloria Anzaldúa who have taken that and they are doing it. But of course today we are all comrades, these sisters, and they struggle with us and we still stumble, they stumble because they have taken it on themselves and we stumble still trying to support them and be right by them. We don't always succeed, there are still contradictions . . . there are things we have got to work out. But I think the future is positive.

LOUIS: One of the elements of your poetry that nobody has talked about is the erotica. Chicanas have been willing to talk about the body in ways that no one else did prior to, say the 80's. And you have a lot of erotica in your poetry that I think is really interesting.

RAÚL: Yes, as a poet I have dealt with everything. I think we were talking about it in the context of the emergence of the women writers, the Chicana-Latina women writers and how they have developed and published these anthologies with other writers of color dealing in a large part with sexuality. Erotica in literature is another genre or area of literature and I certainly have dealt with that myself. As a lover of life and the human form and the woman counterpart, and having beautiful experiences, I have written erotica. I have not published much and this again is my kind of explanation, when writing from the streets I can write about those experiences, about the junkies and the sisters selling their bodies, again not in the form of exploitation, nor in a glorified or sensationalized sense but just the realness of those experiences. The harshness. I call them in some poems the sisters of the equal sufrimientos. It seems to me with this new consciousness—wanting to be more sensitive in these modern and enlightened times in this changing world, it seems a little bit more difficult, at least for me, for men to try and express erotica today because we are trying to be more sensitive to those things that have gone on before, the way we treated and looked at women. But I think it's come into being more. And I think it's very valid, just like the whole gay and lesbian question has been brought up and it's a helluva education that we've received in the past ten years as a country, as a people that heterosexuals ourselves have to also have our erotica that is not seen as exploitative. I mean the love making that I do with my lady is beautiful and intense love making, and if I describe it with the elements and the universe, and with the planets and stuff, and the beauty of a breath, I will be doing so out of that love and respect for the human body and the respect for the sexual act itself, which I consider as beautiful, spiritual, and sacred. The question is how to write my erotica because I want to be sensitive because I have been a man in society, and have seen women in all the other ways men have seen them. I don't want to do it the old way; I want to be the new man. So then I have to be careful, but I don't want to censor myself or have my sisters think I am writing to cheapen them as a piece of chattel or property that objectifies them. They are experiences that come from love and I do hope that when I publish my erotica, I am trying to now find the best way . . . Ray Gonzalez, who is a very important editor and anthologist has done some important anthologies, has a new anthology of erotica for Latino men which will be one of the first where we are saying we are going to deal with the question of erotica rather than deal with this man and esta ruca, y nalga, y whatever, but seriously looking at the beauty of an erotic poem. I consider myself a poet and I hope someday I'll be considered a great poet. I want to write great erotic poetry too. I don't want it to be trash. I don't want to trash my sisters.

I don't want to use erotica to sell in a porn shop. I want erotica to be about love. But it's touchy. Because all of the devastation that we have inflicted on each other as men and women, it's still difficult to write that, but I want to write that as purely and honestly as I can.

BEN: Aside from the product itself, erotic poetry brings another issue into light and that is the consumption of these products, this cultural work. Consumption comes to mind because the bodies in the erotica, as I said produce the poem, the literary product. I want to see what you have to say about where Chicano Literature has gone in terms of its evolution and its production and consumption specifically in terms of the institutionalization of authors, which comes, of course, with the exclusion of certain types of authors. For example, we'll have Gary Soto who is in every anthology under the sun, someone who is not nearly as an expert craftsmen as you are. And then we have Raúl Salinas who continues to be, at least up to this point, excluded from the mainstream.

RAÚL: First of all I think Gary Soto, who I know is of another generation, and so I think some of the stumbling that we did, some of the pioneering, so to speak, . . . made it possible. I don't think Madison Avenue is going to rally around Chicanos who are writing bilingually, who are attacking every system from the church to the academy to the courts, is going to be a wooed and courted by establishment publishers. On the other hand because we kicked enough, the doors in academia and elsewhere the next generation had it not quite so difficult. There were some things that changed also in the characteristics that became an identifying characteristic throughout in the early years, one of these is the use of bilingual modes. In the late 70's and into the early 80's the next generation, either being more astute and wanting to publish and seeing bilingualism wasn't as marketable because they were able to get into the campuses which we were busting the doors down to do. And I say we because I am part of generation that went all over to try to do what the sisters are still trying to do here, is make these institutions accountable and receptive. And the fact that they were writing in English and certainly are influenced, as we were by the American literary world, it became somewhat more palatable for Madison Avenue to packet and market Chicanos. And that's cool, Gary right on. He sees the world a little bit differently than I do, and he is in academia. So he has a different or better way than I to express those things, at least in his prose work. Me, without academic training or formal education, I don't quite agree or don't subscribe to his way of writing. We didn't begin to write with our goal to reach Random House or Norton or Time Warner, with all due respect. Still, as a commodity, and having studied politics or political thought and seeing surplus value and commodities and what's in the market place and what's the trend, we can make or break. I still have questions. I still have contradictions, I mean I'm in the process of selling my archives. I am a sixty-year-old man, hopefully I will live to be as old as my grandmother, she is ninety-six, but if I don't, I haven't made a nickel off of anybody. I don't care to make a nickel off of anybody. I think my work right now is being given the respect by students, graduate and undergraduate students and a new wave of literary critics who have not had my work made available to them because of the omission on the part of some academics, and that is sad. There is a generation that is crying today for work which is out of print; they did not share in its assessment the first time around and they want it and some people have not made it available. I think that my work being somewhere in an institution of this society, which are institutions that sometimes kick us out. Yes, I think that I will consider having my work there, accessible to students who are coming to me, saying they are literally hungry to get my work. So that is the contradiction that I have to live with, the fact that some of our young brothers and sisters are being published by mainstream America, American publishers. This still leaves me with the question: so now your book will be in every airport in the country, what about my sister, brother, most of my gente, and I am privileged now, I am one of the privileged and understand that they are not going to these airports, and the books are $25 and $35 each. I am glad that my contemporaries and the younger ones that came after who are all my friends, most everybody in letters, Chicano-

Latino letters in this country somehow have touched my life or I have touched them, they are all my friends, they are my relatives. And I embrace them and I love them and I want success for all of them. I hurt and I pain for some of them because I somehow have a different understanding of the system and the brutality of it that I know they will get eventually sucked up and they'll be writing for an editor in New York who is dictating and demanding the changes without any sensitivity at all to the culture, to the trends, to anything. And so we are still caught up in their definition of good writing. But being the ideal dreamer that I am, I still have hopes that someday it'll be better.

LOUIS: It all speaks to the continuing contradictory relationship you have with institutions and with the culture industry.

RAÚL: And I understand them as contradictions and I try to live within them and not allow them to be antagonistic contradictions.

BEN: You can look at them as contradictions that allow for synthesis.

RAÚL: Right. It's like assimilation and living in American society. Our people traveled on foot, our people traveled in ancient times by horse, I have to get here because the students have invited me to be here and more importantly because students are challenging the institution. So I'm going to avail myself to a 747 jet. I can't ride old paint across the desert to get here. I'm going to avail myself to technology. I have resisted becoming high-tech, but I understand the importance of the computer world. I have brothers like yourselves who I give material to and they in turn make that transformation for me into the high-tech world. And I'll make that transformation myself eventually. Again, as much on my own terms as possible.

BEN: I think you continue to transcend worlds.

RAÚL: As Montoya says, "on our terms, ese."

BEN: That's a humorous comment, but it's profound because you have transgressed once more into a new institution. Unlike prison which tried to keep you in, this institution, universities like Stanford, have tried to keep you out, but you said, "no man, these walls don't exist for me. In my terms, I'm going in. I'm going to transform your institution."

RAÚL: Yes, but I wasn't outside their doors asking them to let me in either. I'm coming here on my own terms. . . . I talk about this in one of the early poems I wrote in Seattle when I first got to campus. It's called "A'nque la Jaula Sea (on Campus) No Deja de Ser Prisión." What I said in there is that even though the cage is gilded, or made of gold, it's still a prison. You know, Gertrude Stein's "A rose is a rose is a rose." A prison is a prison is a prison, right? When I went to Seattle and went to the university for the first time, I was equating prison and the university in these first free-world poems. I'm saying, here's another prison. Back then I was already looking at it. I'm thinking, "Will I be devoured by this beast?" In prison I had a number, but so does my school I.D. card, which you need for everything on campus. I used to blow the students' minds because I was asserting that the university was a prison of sorts. I described my dorm room in an aged mid-Victorian home as "mi celda solitaria." In many of these early post-prison poems I'm making connections between academia and prison life.

BEN: At the same time you're transforming this one, the fact that your archives will be deposited at Stanford . . .

RAÚL: I don't know about transforming this one (laughter). I'll try.

BEN: You're helping to facilitate the transformation of many people. Take your reading last night for example. It spoke directly to our struggle here, to the Chicana/Chicano students on strike. They were clearly inspired by the wisdom you carry as a veterano.

RAÚL: And I was inspired by them. One of the youngsters came up to me and asked: "You've been at it a long time, haven't you?" And I said, "Yes, I have." He then asked, "What keeps you going?" And I told him, "You do, and this institution that treats students like that, that keeps me going." He just looked at me and said, "Wow, man."

But I don't think I'm anybody. On the one hand, you say I'm important because I've done these things. On the other hand,

I still consider myself a cucaracho, a homeboy. That's the other thing, if Random House is going to publish me and it's going to cause me to look down my nose at you, I don't want it. That's a prison, too. It is for me, anyway. I'm not saying that that's true for my sisters and brothers who've published with them, but that's how I feel about it.

BEN: It's very evident where you stand in relation to the bigger picture. It's something that will last forever. It's your legacy.

LOUIS: Thanks for sharing your life with us.

RAÚL: Thank you both for believing in me.

■ ■ ■

In honor of those who did not survive the "prison rebellion" years, and in solidarity with those prison fighters who continue to struggle, I commit the remainder of my life to exposing the inhumanity of the jail machine.

A luta continua.

raúlr x salinas
c/s

Photo by Mary K. Bruton, MKB Photography

Bibliography

Archival and Manuscript Sources

Raúl Salinas Papers, M0744, Department of Special Collections, Stanford University Libraries, Stanford, Calif.

NEWSPAPER ARTICLES

The Echo, Hunstville State Prison, Texas Department of Corrections
    "Quartered Notes." February 1964. Box 26, Folder 15.
    "Quartered Notes." March, 1964. Box 26, Folder 15.
    "Quartered Notes." April 1964. Box 26, Folder 15.
    "Quartered Notes." June 1964. Box 26, Folder 15.
    "Quartered Notes." July 1964. Box 26, Folder 15.
    "Quartered Notes." September 1964. Box 26, Folder 15.
Aztlán de Leavenworth, Kansas, United States Federal Penitentiary
Aztlán's Statement of Philosophy (Numero 1, Año 1, 5/5/70) Box 7, Fólder 1.
    "Nueva Estrella en el Horizonte" (Numero 1, Año 1, 5/5/70) Box 7, Fólder 1.
    "Music for the Masses" (Numero 1, Año 2, 2/21/72) Box 7, Fólder 2.
    "Note from the Editor" (Numero 1, Año 2, 2/21/72) Box 7, Fólder 2.
    "Repaso" (Numero 1, Año 2, 2/21/72) Box 7, Fólder 2.
New Era, Leavenworth, Kansas, United States Federal Penitentiary
    "New Era, Now Era: Note from the Editor" (Fall 1970, 4–5) Box 5, Folder 18.
    "Sometimes, Champs Turn Up in the Strangest Places" (Fall 1970, 42–45) Box 5, Folder 18.

"An Essay on Semantics in the Joint" (Spring 1971, 25) Box 5, Folder 18.

Entrelíneas, Penn Valley Community College, Kansas City, Missouri
"Portrait of an Artist" (Vol. 1, no. 5–6, pp. 3–5) Box 1, Fólder 13.

Sunfighter
"Resisting Mindfuck: An Interview with Raúl Salinas" from (1974) Box 7, Folder 14

Letters

Carolyn Salinas to Raúl Salinas (2/24/68) Box 4, Folder 33.

Carolyn Salinas to Raúl Salinas (10/25/70) Box 4, Folder 33.

Maria Elda Cisneros de Mendoza to Raúl Salinas (12/29/1970) Box 5, Folder 46.

Tish Sommers to Raúl Salinas (12/29/1970) Box 5, Folder 46.

Joseph Sommers to Raúl Salinas (12/29/1970) Box 5, Folder 46.

Tomás Ybarra-Frausto to Raúl Salinas (12/29/1970) Box 5, Folder 46.

Raúl Salinas to Maria Elda Cisneros (circa early 1971) Box 5, Folder 46.

Raúl Salinas to Joseph Sommers (circa early 1971) Box 5, Folder 46.

Raúl Salinas to Tish Sommers (circa early 1971) Box 5, Folder 46.

Raúl Salinas to Tomás Ybarra Frausto (circa early 1971) Box 5, Folder 46.

Glauco Cambon to Raúl Salinas (1/6/1971) Box 4, Folder 15.

Frances Hill to Raúl Salinas (2/2/1971) Box 4, Folder 33.

Raúl Salinas to Glauco Cambon (4/29/1971) Box 4, Folder 15.

Glauco Cambon to Raúl Salinas (5/4/1971) Box 4, Folder 15.

Glauco Cambon to Raúl Salinas (6/17/1971) Box 4, Folder 15.

Jaimy Gordon Aztlán de Leavenworth (6/17/1971) Box 4, Folder 40.

Raúl Salinas to José Angel Aguirre (6/21/71) Box 3, Folder 2.

Raúl Salinas to Jaimy Gordon (6/21/1971) Box 4, Folder 40.

Raúl Salinas to Glauco Cambon (circa July 1971) Box 4, Folder 15.

Raúl Salinas to EL CHICANO c/o Aztec Productions (9/9/71) Box 3, Folder 2.

Raúl Salinas to Glauco Cambon (10/28/1971) Box 4, Folder 15.

Glauco Cambon to Raúl Salinas (11/3/1971) Box 4, Folder 15.

Raúl Salinas to Joseph Sommers (11/4/71) Box 5, Folder 46.

Raúl Salinas to Antonia Castañeda Shular (11/17/1971) Box 4, Folder 19.

Glauco Cambon to Raúl Salinas (11/19/1971) Box 4, Folder 15.

Raúl Salinas to Américo Paredes (circa early December 1971) Box 5, Folder 23.

Américo Paredes to Raúl Salinas (December 6, 1971) Box 5, Folder 23.

José Limón to Raúl Salinas (December 7, 1971) Box 4, Folder 54.

Raúl Salinas to Mario Cantú Jr. (circa early January 1972) Box 4, Folder 58.

Antonia Castañeda Shular to Raúl Salinas (1/26/1972) Box 4, Folder 19.

Raúl Salinas to Antonia Castañeda Shular (2/23/1972) Box 4, Folder 19.

Raúl Salinas to Stephen Torgoff (circa late February 1972) Box 3, Folder 1.

Raúl Salinas to Dorothy Harth (3/2/1972) Box 4, Folder 46.

Antonia Castañeda Shular to Raúl Salinas (3/2/1972) Box 4, Folder 19.

Raúl Salinas to Antonia Castañeda Shular (3/3/1972) Box 4, Folder 19.

Joseph Sommers to Board of Pardons and Paroles (4/4/1972) Box 5, Folder 46 .

J. Berger and George Young to Joseph Sommers (4/7/1972) Box 5, Folder 46.

Armando Mendoza to Raúl Salinas (4/13/1972) Box 5, Folder 7.

Jaimy Gordon to Raúl Salinas (5/8/1972) Box 4, Folder 40.

Wesley Noble Graham to Raúl Salinas (6/8/1972) Box 4, Folder 41.

Raúl Salinas to Jaimy Gordon (6/13/1972) Box 4, Folder 40.

Raúl Salinas to Charles W. Hoehne (6/25/1972) Box 4, Folder 48.

Raúl Salinas and Lanier Ramer to Allen Ressler (6/25/1972) Box 5 Folder 31.

Raúl Salinas to Wes Graham (6/26/1972) Box 4, Folder 41.

Jaimy Gordon to Raúl Salinas (7/6/1973) Box 4, Folder 40.

Raúl Salinas to Alan Ressler (7/6/1972) Box 5, Folder 3.

Alan Ressler to Raul Salinas (7/12/1972) Box 5, Folder 31.

Raúl Salinas to Joseph Sommers (7/24/1972) Box 5, Folder 46.

Segregation Committee to Raúl Salinas (7/28/1972) Box 6, Folder 27.

Raúl Salinas to Dorothy Harth (8/7/1972) Box 4, Folder 46.

Raúl Salinas to Dorothy Harth (8/12/1972) Box 4, Folder 46.

Antonia Castañeda Shular to Raúl Salinas (9/13/1972, Stanford) Box 4, Folder 19.

Raúl Salinas to Board of Parole, George Young (9/15/1972) Box 6, Folder 27.

Raúl Salinas to Mario G. Obledo (9/29/1972) Box 4, Folder 41.

José Angel Gutiérrez to Raúl Salinas (9/29/1972) Box 4, Folder 44.

Raúl Salinas to José Angel Gutiérrez (10/1/1972) Box 4, Folder 40.

Raúl Salinas to Antonia Castañeda Shular (10/8/1972) Box 4, Folder 19.

Antonia Castañeda Shular to Raúl Salinas (circa mid-October 1972) Box 4, Folder 19.

José Angel Gutiérrez to Raúl Salinas (10/26/1972) Box 4, Folder 40.

Raúl Salinas to Antonia Castañeda Shular (10/23/1972) Box 4, Folder 19.

Jaimy Gordon to Raúl Salinas (10/31/1972) Box 4, Folder 40.

Antonia Castañeda Shular to Raúl Salinas (11/2/1972) Box 4, Folder 19.

Raúl Salinas to Antonia Castañeda Shular (11/14/1972) Box 4, Folder 19.

Raúl Salinas to Alberto Gudino (11/21/1972) Box 4, Folder 22.

José Angel Gutiérrez to Raúl Salinas (12/29/1972) Box 4, Folder 40.

Raúl Salinas to Rubén Estrella (2/1/1973) Box 4, Folder 32.

Raúl Salinas to Antonia Castañeda (1/3/1974) Box 4, Folder 19.

OTHER DOCUMENTS

"On the History of CORA and *Aztlán*." Unpublished paper. Box 8, Folder 7.

"The Marion Strike Journals." Box 1, Folder 14.

"Call to Action." Box 1, Fólder 14.

"We Must Fight the Enemy." Box 1, Fólder 14.

INTERVIEWS

"Una Plática con Raúl Salinas." Interview by Ben Olguín and Louis
Mendoza (1994). Transcript of videotape in Salinas Papers,
M0744, Department of Special Collections, Stanford University
Libraries.

PHOTOS

Salinas at Festival de Flor Y Canto at USC, Box 13, Folder 25.
Box 13, Folders 9 and 10.
Salinas and large group of friends in prison yard, Leavenworth, Box
15, Folder 6.
Salinas and group around table with paper, 1970, Box 15, Folder 10.
Salinas at desk, Box 15, Folder 10.
Box 15, Folder 19.
Box 15, Folder 8.
Salinas with friends in cell at Leavenworth, 1970, Box 15, Folder 8.

FACSIMILES

Salinas certification for Army, Box 6, Folder 4.
Salinas' "Certificate of Mandatory Release" from Marion Federal
Penitentiary, 1972.
Salinas' arrest and parole record from Texas Department of Correc-
tions, 1974.

Texas State Library; The Center for American History, University of Texas at Austin

The Echo. "Quartered Notes." January 1964 (microfiche).
The Echo. "Quartered Notes." November 1964 (microfiche).
The Echo. "Quartered Notes." December 1964 (microfiche).
The Echo. "So Much Mystery, So Much Misunderstanding." Thanks-
giving Day, 1964. (microfiche).

Raúl Salinas Personal Collection

Letters

Carolyn Salinas to Raúl Salinas (7/9/68).
Raúl Salinas to Eleanor Salinas (2/15/1972).
Beto Gudino to Raúl Salinas (circa late February 1972).
Raúl Salinas to Mario Cantu Jr. (2/29/1972).
Pun Plamandon to Raúl Salinas (3/3/1972).
Raúl Salinas to Kell Robertson (3/6/1972).
Raúl Salinas to Robert Chandler (6/26/1972).
Raúl Salinas to Walter Quintero, Committee for Prisoner Humanity & Justice (6/28/1972).
Raúl Salinas to Armando Mendoza (9/5/1972).
Raúl Salinas to José Angel Gutiérrez (9/9/1972).
Raúl Salinas to Richard Tanner (9/10/1972).
Raúl Salinas to Don Edwards (9/12/1972).
Michael Deutsch to Raúl Salinas (9/15/1972).
Raúl Salinas to Nita González (9/20/1972).
Raúl Salinas to Pathfinder Press (9/22/1972).
Raúl Salinas to Arlene Dewberry (9/24/1972).
Hermelinda De La Cerda to Raúl Salinas (circa late October 1972).
Raúl Salinas to Frances Hill (10/28/1972).
Raúl Salinas to Janet Barbour (11/6/1972).
Raúl Salinas to Ron V. Dellums (11/13/1972).
Jay Lewis to Raúl Salinas (circa late November 1972).
Tony J. Craven to Raúl Salinas (1/26/1973).
Raúl Salinas to Dan, Ana, and friends (circa fall 1973).

Secondary Sources

Abbott, Jack. *In the Belly of the Beast: Letters from Prison*. New York: Vintage, 1991.

Blunk, Tim, and Raymond Luc Levasseur, eds. *Hauling up the Morning: Writing and Art by Political Prisoners of the United States*. Trenton, N.J.: Red Sea Press, 1990.

"Facts on Prisons and Prisoners." Online Publication. The Sentencing

Project. *http://www.sentencingproject.org/pdfs/1035.pdf* (visited 12/12/04).

Franklin, H. Bruce. *Prison Literature in America: The Victim as Criminal and Artist*. Westport, Conn.: Lawrence Hill, 1978.

"From Alcatraz to Marion to Florence—Control Unit Prisons in the United States." Pamphlet, undated. In the Salinas Collection, housed at Stanford University Special Collections.

Griffin, Eddie. "Breaking Men's Minds: Behavior Control and Human Experimentation at the Federal Prison in Marion, Illinois." St. Louis: National Committee to Support the Marion Brothers and the National Alliance Against Racist and Political Repression. Pamphlet, 1978. In the Salinas Collection, housed at Stanford University Special Collections.

Gugelberger, Georg, ed. *The Real Thing: Testimonial Discourses and Latin America*. Durham, N.C.: Duke University Press, 1996.

Mendoza, Louis. "Afterword: Barrio Aesthetics, Displacement, and Memory." *East of the Freeway: Reflections de mi Pueblo*, by Raúl Salinas (pp. 103–109). Ed. Louis Mendoza. Austin: Red Salmon Press, 1995.

———. "Preface: Some Reflections on Twenty Years of *Un Trip Through the Mind Jail y Otras Excursions*," by Raúl Salinas (pp. 1–5). Houston: Arte Público, 1999.

———. "The Re-education of a Xicanindio: Raúl Salinas and the Poetics of Pinto Transformation." *MELUS* 28, no. 1 (Spring 2003; Special Issue: *Literature and the Idea of Social Justice, ed.* Garuav Desai, Supriya Nair, and Felipe Smith): 39–60.

Mann, Corame Richey. *Unequal Justice: A Question of Color*. Bloomington: Indiana University Press, 1993.

Matthieson, Peter. *In the Spirit of Crazy Horse*. New York: Penguin, 1992.

Olguín, Ben V. "Tattoos, Abjection, and the Political Unconscious: Toward a Semiotics of the Pinto Visual Vernacular." *Cultural Critique* 37, no. 3 (1997): 159–213.

raúlrsalinas. "Crash Landing." In *Un Trip through the Mind Jail y Otras Excursions*. Houston: Arte Público Press, 1999.

———. *Beyond the BEATen Path*. Austin: Red Salmon Arts. (2002)

———. *East of the Freeway: Reflections de mi pueblo*. Austin: Red Salmon Press, 1995.

————. *Los Many Mundos of raúlrsalinas: un poetic jazz viaje con friends*. San Diego: Calaca Press, 2000.

————. *Red Arc: A Call for Liberación con Salsa y Cool*. San Antonio: Wings Press, 2005.

————. *Un Trip through the Mind Jail y Otras Excursions*. Houston: Arte Público Press, 1999.

Shakur, Assata. Preface to *Hauling up the Morning: Writing and Art by Political Prisoners of the United States,* ed. Tim Blunk and Raymond Luc Levasseur. Trenton, N.J.: Red Sea Press, 1990.

"Stop the Deaths: Close the Marion Control Unit, Free the Political Prisoners." St. Louis: National Committee to Support the Marion Brothers. Booklet, 1978. In the Salinas Collection, housed at Stanford University Special Collections.

Ybarra-Frausto, Tomás. "Introduction to the First Edition." *Un Trip through the Mind Jail y Otras Excursions* (pp. 7–14). Houston: Arte Público Press, 1999.